AGROFORESTRY FOR BIODIVERSITY AND ECOSYSTEM SERVICES – SCIENCE AND PRACTICE

Edited by **Martin Leckson Kaonga**

INTECHOPEN.COM

Agroforestry for Biodiversity and Ecosystem Services – Science and Practice
Edited by Martin Leckson Kaonga

CBS, Edition 2016

Published by InTech

Janeza Trdine 9, 51000 Rijeka, Croatia

Publishing Process Manager Oliver Kurelic

Technical Editor Teodora Smiljanic

Cover Designer InTech Design Team

Additional hard copies can be obtained from orders@intechopen.com

Agroforestry for Biodiversity and Ecosystem Services – Science and Practice,
Edited by Martin Leckson Kaonga
p. cm.
ISBN 978-953-51-0493-3

INTECH

open science | open minds

Contents

Preface

As rates of deforestation and land degradation, and losses of biodiversity and ecosystem services, continue to rise globally, the international community is faced with the challenge of finding land use interventions that can mitigate or reduce the impact of these environmental issues. Agroforestry, the integration of trees in farming systems, has the potential for providing rural livelihoods and habitats for species outside formally protected lands, connecting nature reserves, and alleviating resource-use pressure on conservation areas. In the last three decades, there has been a growing interest in agroforestry because of its biodiversity and ecosystem services it delivers. Therefore, trees are increasingly being planted as part of farming systems. A recent global assessment of tree cover found that 48% of the world's agricultural land had at least 10% of tree cover. However, widespread adoption of agroforestry is still tampered by a myriad of factors including *inter alia* the design features of candidate agroforestry innovations, perceived needs, institutional constraints, the availability and distribution of factors of production, and perception of risks. Understanding the science, and factors that facilitate the adoption, of agroforestry and how they impact the implementation of agroforestry is vitally important.

This book consists of eight chapters, which are broadly divided into two themes. The first five chapters examine design features and management practices of selected agroforestry practices, and their effects on ecosystem functions and productivity. In the first Chapter, Rodríguez-Estéz et al. provide a synthesis of existing knowledge on the ecology of the dehesa, a Mediterranean agrosilvopastoral system, and how the Iberian pig production system enhances biodiversity and ecosystem services. The synthesis includes empirical data from on-going studies of the dehesa and grazing behavior and performance of Iberian pigs finished on acorns. The authors conclude that farmers conserve, prune and reforest oaks to maintain fruit production to feed and fatten Iberian pigs during the *montanera* or pannage, which result in conservation of biodiversity and associated ecosystem services.

In Chapter Two, Kaonga and Bayliss-Smith describe a conceptual model that summarises current knowledge on ecological processes, drivers, and stressors responsible for carbon cycling, and further demonstrate how the model could be used to estimate major carbon pools and fluxes in tropical improved fallows using data from eastern Zambia. Chapter Three reports original findings of a study on the effect of environmental drivers on diversity of parasitoid wasp communities in two cacao agroforestry systems in the Bahia state of Brazil. Speber et al. evaluated parasitoid wasps of Hymenoptera of parasitica series and Chrystoidea super family in the *cabruca* cacao agroforestry system (cacao planted under a thinned natural forest canopy) and in a *derruba total* (cacao planted under a canopy of trees introduced after clear felling of natural forest). The authors conclude that tree species richness is of uttermost importance in structuring Hymenoptera communities in tropical agroforestry systems, and that seasonality alters this relationship, acting on particular Hymenoptera taxa.

Efhami Sisi et al., in Chapter Four, review the effect of management practices on anatomical, physiological and morphological characteristics of trees in agroforestry systems. They specifically assess the impact of initial spacing between trees and tree-crop inter-planting on tree growth and wood properties in a tree-alfalfa intercropping system in a temperate region. In Chapter five, Chesney reviews the science of shoot pruning of the woody component in agroforestry systems and the impact of this management practice on the functional equilibrium between the shoots and roots of the woody component. These first five chapters collectively suggest that the design and management practices of an agroforestry system determine ecosystem functions, and biodiversity that undergirds the ecosystem services provided.

The second cluster of chapters focuses on factors that facilitate the adoption or non-adoption of agroforestry systems. The authors of the last three chapters argue that increasing the scale of adoption and the impact of agroforestry innovations requires actions that are based on an understanding of the dynamics of adoption and the critical factors that determine whether farmers accept, do not accept, or partially accept, innovations. Place et al., in chapter Six, review factors underpinning recently adopted agroforestry systems and policy-related constraints to widespread adoption of agroforestry. They specifically identify policy issues for facilitating adoption of desirable agroforestry practices and gradual diminution of undesirable policies. In Chapter Seven, Msuya et al. use the Tanzanian agroforestry development context to explore how existing national policy and institutional setups facilitate or constrain development of agroforestry policies and suggest the available options for developing agroforestry policy. In the last chapter, Degrande et al. present original results of a five-year study undertaken by the World Agroforestry Centre in Cameroun to evaluate relay organizations and rural resource centers as a model for participatory domestication of trees.

This book is a collection of field studies and literature review by experienced researchers. It covers different disciplines within agroforestry and provides a balanced description of subject matter, drawing examples from a variety of regions and agroforestry systems.

Martin Leckson Kaonga
A Rocha International, Sheraton House, Castle Park, Cambridge, UK

1

Consumption of Acorns by Finishing Iberian Pigs and Their Function in the Conservation of the Dehesa Agroecosystem

Vicente Rodríguez-Estévez*, Manuel Sánchez-Rodríguez, Cristina Arce, Antón R. García, José M. Perea and A. Gustavo Gómez-Castro
Departamento de Producción Animal, Facultad de Veterinaria, University of Cordoba Spain

1. Introduction

The dehesa is an ancient agrosilvopastoral system created by farmers to raise livestock, mainly on private lands. This system is highly appreciated by society and enjoys legal protection of the authorities because it is rich in biodiversity, a home to critically endangered species (Iberian lynx, imperial eagle and black vulture); a significant carbon sink; ethnologically and anthropologically valuable (culture and traditions); and is known for its scenic value. The dehesa also underpins rural development and is valuable for, inter alia, ecotourism and rural tourism; hunting and shooting; fire prevention; wood and charcoal; and for fodder (grass and acorns). However, most of these values do not produce any benefit to farmers and they do not receive any kind of support from these contributions.

The dehesa is both a resilient and a fragile system; its resilience derives from the perseverance of its operators, and its fragility is its susceptibility to unfavourable economic factors that influence its profitability (Siebold, 2009).

Livestock grazing is an integral management component of a dehesa and undergirds the conservation function of the system. The livestock component, including cattle, accounts for the largest fraction of revenue from the dehesa. However, the Iberian pig is the most appreciated and highly priced livestock, because of its outstanding quality of cured products when finished on acorns in the dehesa.

Although farmers do not receive any support from society for the contribution of the dehesa to welfare of society and the environment, they still conserve, prune and reforest oaks to maintain fruit production to feed and fatten Iberian pigs during the *montanera* or pannage. The ability of the Iberian pig breed to feed on acorns is a key feature in maintaining the dehesa. Despite the pivotal role that the dehesa plays in biodiversity conservation and human welfare in the Iberian Peninsula, quantitative and qualitative information about the ecology and productivity of this Mediterranean agrosilvopastoral system is scarce. In the absence of documented evidence of the biological value and ecosystem services of the system, biodiversity and human livelihoods are threatened.

* Corresponding Author

This chapter synthesizes existing knowledge on (i) historical and ecological perspectives of the dehesa, and the factors affecting acorn production and composition; (ii) acorn as a feed for Iberian pig production and nutritional value of acorns and their effect as a fattening diet in the dehesa; and (iii) how the relationship between the Iberian pig and the dehesa contributes to maintenance of biodiversity in the dehesa and its profitability. This work is based on an extensive literature review of publications and the authors' on-going studies in the dehesa and the grazing behaviour and performance of the Iberian pig.

2. The dehesa

2.1 The origin, definition, and evolution of dehesa

Oak woodlands and savanna are an extensive forest type in Mediterranean climate regions of the world; known as hardwood rangelands in California, "dehesa" in Spain, and "montado" in Portugal (Standiford et al., 2003). Specifically the term "dehesa", with its many definitions, refers to an agroecosystem. The first definition focuses on the word´s etymology: "deffesa", a Latin word for defence, referring to an early system of grazing land reserved for cattle use (for the breeding, grazing and rest), a fenced plot of land protected from cultivation and complete deforestation. According to Coromines (1980), there is evidence of the use of the word "dehesa" since the Middle Age (924); previously, the visigothic laws used the term "pratum defensum" with the same meaning.

The Spanish Society for the Study of Pastures (S.E.E.P.) defines "dehesas" as surfaces with trees that are more or less dispersed and a well developed herbaceous stratum, the stratum of shrubs having been eliminated to a great extent; these have an agricultural (ploughed land in long term rotations) and stockbreeding origin; and their main use is for extensive or semi-extensive grazing, using grasses, browse pastures and fruits of trees (Ferrer et al., 1997). This is a landscape like savanna; however, dehesa is an agroecosystem mainly associated with trees of the genus *Quercus*. Costa et al. (2006) indicate that the evergreen oak (*Q. ilex rotundifolia*) is the priority specie in the 70.1% of the dehesa surface.

Palynological analysis of Neolitic sites evidenced the existence of this agroecosystem since 6000 years ago (López Sáez et al., 2007), when the Mediterranean forest was cleared to have grasslands while conserving the *Quercus* trees; mainly evergreen oak (*Q. ilex rotundifolia*) and cork oak (*Q. suber*). Besides, the distribution of evergreen oak (*Q. ilex*) forests have been severely impacted by human transformation in the Iberian Peninsula, and at the same time there has been a selection of trees looking for higher production of fruit, and bigger and sweeter acorns (Blanco et al., 1997). The historical expansion of the dehesa is linked with the Castilian Christian reconquest of the Iberian Peninsula from the Arabian and the subsequent repopulation and redistribution of land; and with the establishment of the long distance transhumance, where the dehesa area was the wintering pasture (from November to May).

Nowadays, the most widely accepted definition for dehesa is that of an agrosilvopastoral system developed on poor or non-agricultural land and aimed at extensive livestock raising (Olea and San Miguel-Ayanz, 2006). The characteristics of traditional dehesa uses in the Iberian Peninsula (southwestern Spain and southern Portugal) are (adapted from Carruthers, 1993):

- Natural reforestation and selection of trees for fruit production

- Regular pruning and diverse use of the tree layer (firewood, charcoal, fodder and acorns for human consumption and grazing animals)
- Mixed livestock of cattle, sheep, pigs, goats, etc. (mainly sheep from autumn to spring and finishing pigs during autumn and winter)
- Use of hardy and autochthonous breeds
- Low stocking densities (0.5–1 suckling ewe equivalent per ha)
- Shepherding and regular livestock movements (transhumance and trasterminance)
- Control of pasture productivity through directing livestock manure to selected places by nocturnal penning (called "majadeo" or "redileo")
- Extensive tillage in change with 3–20 years of fallow
- Numerous marginal uses (bee-keeping, hunting, edible wild plant and mushroom collecting, etc.)
- Employment of numerous specialized workers
- No use of externally produced fodder and energy

The traditional dehesa adopted a strategy of efficiency and diversification of structural components to take advantage of every natural resource (multiple, scarce and unevenly distributed in time and space) of its environment with a minimum input of energy and materials (Olea and San Miguel-Ayanz, 2006). Silviculture is not aimed at timber production but at increasing the crown cover per tree and at producing acorns (Olea and San Miguel-Ayanz, 2006), although there is no definitive evidence of successive better acorn masts after pruning (Rodríguez-Estévez et al., 2007a). On the other hand, in recent years, pruned biomass of browse and firewood have low value, and this wood´s only worth is to pay the woodcutters; however the pruning of adult trees is good to maintain the health of the trees and the forest mass when ill branches are cut. For the farming component, the major goal of land cultivation is preventing the shrub invasion of grasslands and supplying fodder and grain for livestock, harvesting being a secondary goal (Olea and San Miguel-Ayanz, 2006). Hence the current use and valuable production of the dehesa is mainly livestock breeding. Rodríguez-Estévez et al. (2007b) point out that cattle participate in the dehesa creation and are indispensable to its maintenance, while silviculture and agriculture are very secondary once a dehesa is kept in equilibrium with grazing. Due to that diversification and efficiency, the dehesa was also a very versatile system and was able to successfully satisfy human requirements and that has been the secret of its survival (Olea and San Miguel-Ayanz, 2006). However, from the last quarter of the twentieth century, its economy is totally dependent on livestock production and its associated subsidies.

Today, the dehesa is the most unique and representative agroecosystem of the Iberian Peninsula, currently consisting of more than four million hectares in the southwest (Fig. 1) (Olea and San Miguel-Ayanz, 2006), extending over Extremadura (1.25 million hectares), western Andalusia (0.7 million hectares), the south of Castilla-Leon and the west of Castilla la Mancha in Spain, as well as the Alentejo (0.8 million hectares) and the north of the Algarve in Portugal, where it is called "montado".

Most dehesas are divided into large estates (>100 ha) and are held in private ownership. Hence their conservation depends on good farming practices. The term dehesa has become internationalized and is being used in different languages. Furthermore, nowadays it is considered as an example of a stable and well managed agroecosystem from an ecological point of view (Van Wieren, 1995). The dehesa has evolved over centuries into a sustainable agrosilvopastoral systems with conservation and human livelihood functions.

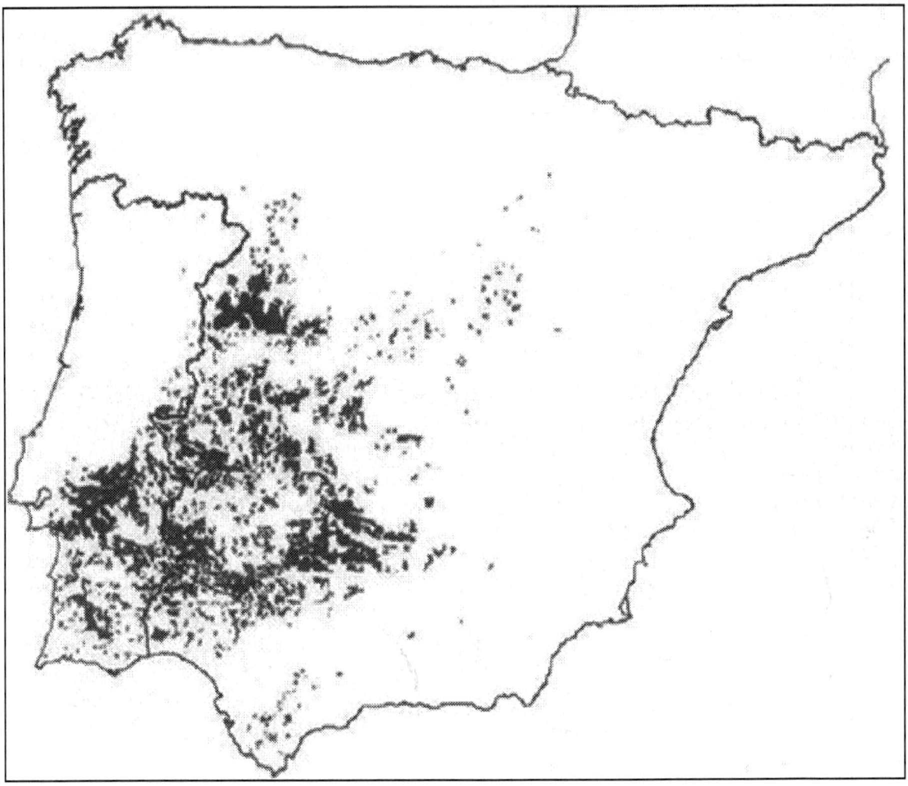

Fig. 1. Geographical distribution of the dehesa in the Iberian Peninsula.

2.2 The dehesa as a cleared forest

According to Rodríguez-Estévez (2011), the reason for conservation of the evergreen oak was its role as panacea or cultural tree due to its numerous uses: fuel (wood, coal and cinder), construction (beams and fencing), crafts, folk medicine, tanning, human food (acorns) and animal feed (acorns and tree fodder) and animal protection (shade and shelter). Besides, there are other values such as microclimate regulation and pumping of nutrients from the ground. All of them were possible reasons for conservation of *Quercus* trees when clearing the Mediterranean forest in the past centuries.

A dehesa should have a minimum number of trees, although the SEEP definition does not provide this specification (Ferrer et al., 2001). Different regulations have tried to establish this minimum from the 15th century (Vázquez et al., 2001) to now; for example: 10 trees per hectare (MAPA, 2007) and a surface of canopy projection between 5% and 75% (Presidencia,

2010). Viera Natividae (1950) proposes an ideal tree cover of 2/3 of the land for *Quercus suber,* while Montoya (1989) indicates a maximum of 1/3 for *Q. ilex.* These proportions match up with the number of good producer trees that are naturally present in the *Quercus* mass of the Mediterranean forest, and with the usual densities of the good pannage dehesas (Montoya and Mesón, 2004). Montero et al. (1998) show that the highest production of grass and acorns in the dehesas of *Quercus ilex* and *Q. suber* is reached when the tree density equivalent canopy cover of 30-50% is achieved.

Fig. 2. Aerial view of an area of dehesa (Summer 2011, Fuente Obejuna, Córdoba, Spain); at the bottom of the image is the Natural Park "Sierra de Hornachuelos", included in the Biosphere Reserve "Dehesas de Sierra Morena".

Traditionally, the ideal denseness for dehesa is 45 adult trees/ha (Rupérez Cuéllar, 1957). Several studies have estimated the number of adult trees for dehesas of *Q. Ilex* to be in the range of 20-50 trees/ha (Cañellas et al., 2007; Escribano and Pulido, 1998; Espejo Gutiérrez de Tena et al., 2006; Gea-Izquierdo et al., 2006; Vázquez et al., 1999) (Fig. 2). However, Plieninger et al. (2003) found a lower density in cultivated dehesas (18.9 trees/ha) than in grazed areas (38.6 trees/ha) and those invaded by brushy ones (38.6 trees/ha). The same authors also gave a mean of 16.6 trees/ha for aged or diminished dehesas.

The decline in numbers of *Quercus* spp. (referred to as the "seca" syndrome) is due to fungi and several defoliators, which is serious for *Q. ilex* and *Q. suber,* causing an important problem of mortality (Fig. 3). In some areas, average annual mortality ranges from 1.5 to 3% (Montoya and Mesón, 2004). This is considered to be the main problem of the dehesa, due to currently low or no natural regeneration (Olea and San Miguel-Ayanz, 2006). Intensification of land use through the current increase in livestock stocking rates for profit maximization has led to over-exploitation of forage, leading to suppression of oak regeneration under these circumstances.

The European Union Common Agricultural Policy subsidy for extensive livestock production compensated farmers for negative livestock value. However, authorities make a serious mistake when they consider 170 kg of nitrogen per hectare and year as the maximum limit of excretion for extensive exploitation, as it is established by the European Nitrates Directive (Council of the European Communities, 1991). Pulido García (2002) reported that the average stocking rate increased by 84% between 1986 and 2000 in the Extremadura region. The average stocking rate of 0.46 LU/ha is much lower than the maximum stocking rate of 1.4 LU/ha established by the EU threshold of extensification (Council of the European Communities, 1999). However, Olea and San Miguel-Ayanz (2006) suggest that the sustainable stocking rate of the dehesa is 0.2 - 0.4 LU/ha.

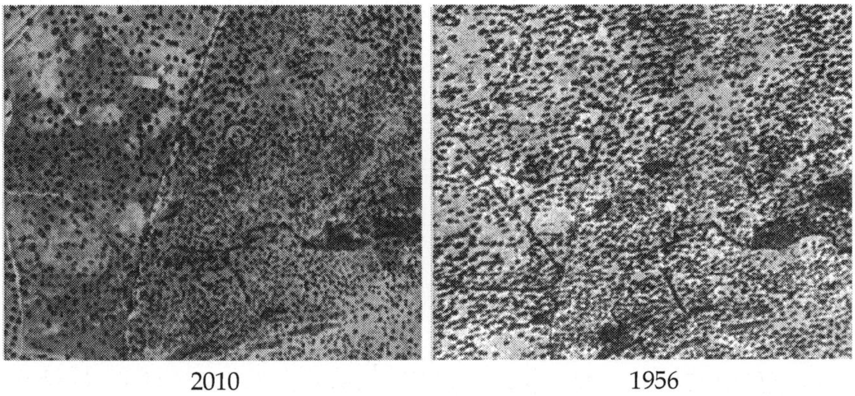

Fig. 3. Aerial view of an area of dehesa (Cañada del Gamo, Fuente Obejuna, Córdoba, Spain).

2.3 The ecological values of the dehesa

The typical environment of the dehesa is marked by two fundamental features: the Mediterranean character of the climate (dry summers and somewhat cold winters) and the low fertility of the soil (particularly P and Ca), making arable farming unsustainable and unprofitable (Olea and San Miguel-Ayanz, 2006). Within this difficult environment, the dehesa has arisen as the only possible form of rational, productive and sustainable land usage. The dehesa is a highly productive ecosystem and has been qualified as "natural habitat" to be preserved, within the European Union Habitats Directive, because of its high biodiversity (Council of the European Communities, 1992). This directive considers it as a "natural habitat type of community interest" included in the "natural and semi-natural grassland formations", where it is called "sclerophyllous grazed forests (dehesas) with *Quercus suber* and/or *Q. ilex*"; besides, it advises the designation of special areas for dehesa conservation (Fig. 4).

The dehesa harbours wildlife that is typical of the Mediterranean forests, but it is also enriched with representatives from other habitats, including steppes and agricultural environments. Dehesas are widely recognised as being of exceptional conservation value

(Baldock et al., 1993; Telleria and Santos, 1995; Díaz et al., 1997; Rodríguez-Estévez et al., 2010a). Thirty percent of the vascular plant species of the Iberian Peninsula are found in the dehesas (Pineda and Montalvo 1995). Marañón (1985) discovered 135 species on a 0.1 ha plot in a dehesa in Andalusia and considered the dehesa one of the vegetation types with the highest diversity in the world at this scale, having the highest one between the Mediterranean ecosystems (Fig. 5). Dehesas are the habitat of several species which are rare or globally threatened including black vultures (*Aegipius monachus*), Spanish imperial eagles (*Aquila adalberti*) and Iberian lynx (*Lynx pardina*); besides 6 to 7 million woodpigeons (*Columba palumbus*), 60000 to 70000 common cranes (*Grus grus*), both of them with diets based on acorns, and a large number of passerines depend on the dehesas as their winter habitat (Tellería, 1988).

Cork tree (*Quercus suber*) at the bottom and wild olive tree (*Olea europaea sylvestris*) on the right of the image.

Evergreen oaks (*Quercus ilex rotundifolia*)

Fig. 4. Iberian growers foraging in a dehesa during spring in dehesa San Francisco (Fundación Monte Mediterráneo, Santa Olalla del Cala, Huelva, Spain) organic farm in the Natural Park "Sierra de Aracena y Picos de Aroche", included in the Biosphere Reserve "Dehesas de Sierra Morena".

Although the dehesa productivity is low when compared with modern intensive agricultural production systems, its model inspires agri-environmental policies to maintain and promote farming practices compatible with nature conservation and biodiversity (Rodríguez-Estévez et al., 2010a). In this sense, Gonzalez and San Miguel (2004) indicate that the meadow is a paradigm of balance and interdependence between production and nature conservation, where its high environmental values are a result of its extensive management, balanced and efficient, which can be considered a powerful conservation tool.

Fig. 5. Pregnant Iberian sows grazing in a dehesa during spring (Turcañada S.L., Casa Grande, Fuente Obejuna, Córdoba, Spain).

3. Acorn production in the dehesa

The productivity of acorns (the most important food resource for autumn and winter) is 10 times higher in a managed dehesa compared to a dense *Quercus ilex* forest (Pulido 1999). It is estimated that *Q. ilex* does not give an optimal yield of acorns until it is 20-25 years old. Rodríguez-Estévez et al. (2007a) estimated a mean acorn yield of 300 to 700 kg/ha; with yields of 8-14 kg/tree for *Q. ilex*, 5-10 kg/tree for *Q. suber* and 1-11 kg/tree for *Q. faginea* (Table 1). Acorn yields are extremely variable, both between and within years and individual trees. Rodríguez-Estévez et al. (2007a) also assessed the effect of density of adult trees (optimum estimated in 20-50 trees/ha), masting phenomenon (with cycles of 2-5.5 years and asynchrony between trees), individual characteristics of trees (genetic potential, age, canopy surface, etc.), tree mass handling (with favourable effect of tilling, moderate pruning and sustainable grazing), meteorological conditions (mainly drought and meteorology during flowering) and sanitary status (*Lymantria, Tortrix, Curculio, Cydia, Balaninus* and *Brenneria*) on acorn production. They concluded that tree density was the factor with greatest effect on the acorn production per hectare and tree in any dehesa.

Quercus spp.	kg acorn/tree	g acorn/m² canopy	References
Q. faginea	1 to 11	-	Medina Blanco, 1956
Q. canariensis	0.8 to 3.7	11.6 a 48	Martín Vicente et al., 1998
Q. suber	4.5 to 11	-	Medina Blanco, 1956
Q. suber	5 to 10	-	Montoya, 1988
Q. suber	0.6 to 16.9	19.5 a 171.1	Martín Vicente et al., 1998
Q. ilex	16.74	-	Medina Blanco, 1956
Q. ilex	4.4 to 20	-	Rupérez Cuéllar, 1957
Q. ilex	7 to 8	-	López et al., 1984
Q. ilex	10 to 15	-	Montoya, 1989
Q. ilex	14.8	-	Cabeza de Vaca et al., 1992
Q. ilex	10 to 14	-	Espárrago et al., 1992
Q. ilex	12 to 14	-	Espárrago et al., 1993
Q. ilex	14.8	-	Benito et al., 1997
Q. ilex	7.1 to 25.3	115.8 a 285.8	Martín Vicente et al., 1998
Q. ilex	18	-	Porras Tejeiro, 1998
Q. ilex	4.3 to 11.9	-	Vázquez et al., 1999
Q. ilex	14.1 to 5.2	-	Vázquez et al.,2000b
Q. ilex	4.5 to 8.4	-	Vázquez et al., 2002
Q. ilex	5.7 a 13.2	-	García et al., 2003
Q. ilex	12 a 65	-	López-Carrasco et al., 2005
Q. ilex	15-21	100	Gea-Izquierdo et al., 2006
Q. ilex	10.3 a 45.6	-	Moreno Marcos et al., 2007
Q. ilex	9.7	-	Hernández Díaz-Ambrona et al., 2007
Q. ilex	-	59.6 a 278	Lossaint and Rapp, 1971
Q. ilex	-	14	Verdú et al., 1980
Q. ilex	-	189.4	Gómez Gutierrez et al., 1981
Q. ilex	-	120.4	Escudero et al., 1985
Q. ilex	-	75.2	Leonardi et al., 1992
Q. ilex	-	25.9	Bellot et al., 1992
Q. ilex	-	1.0 a 237.4	Cañellas et al., 2007
Q. pyrenaica	-	48.6	Escudero et al., 1985

Table 1. Acorn production of *Quercus* spp in dehesas and Mediterranean forests (Resource: Rodríguez-Estévez et al., 2007a).

There is a high intraspecific variability in acorn traits and they account for 62% of the variance of the biomass of acorns (Leiva and Fernández-Ales, 1998). Besides, in most areas, there has been an historical selection favouring trees with larger acorns. Acorn weight, size and shape present a lot of variability between species, individuals and areas. From a sample of 2000 acorns from 100 evergreen oaks (20 acorns per tree) of a traditional dehesa, the average weight of an acorn was 5.7±0.2 g, with averages of 4.4±0.2 g and 2.5±0.1 g of kernel fresh and dry matter (DM), respectively (Rodríguez-Estévez et al., 2009a) (Fig. 6).

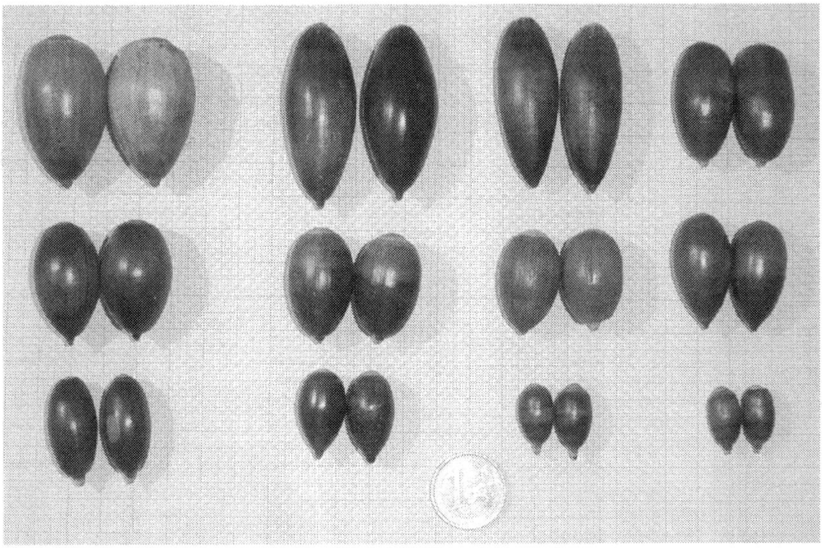

Fig. 6. Acorns of evergreen oaks (*Quercus ilex rotundifolia*) found under 12 different close trees in a dehesa (the coin is an Euro).

Chemical contents of acorn kernel	Nutritive value (g $100g^{-1}$ DM) (mean±S.E)	
	Grass	**Acorns**(1)
Dry matter (DM)	24.05±1.52	58.05±1.28
Ash*	8.74±0.79	1.94±0.03
Crude protein*	15.73±0.73	4.71±0.21
Crude fibre*	21.28±0.78	2.83±0.09
Crude fat*	5.24±0.41	10.22±0.49
NFE*	64.83±4.56	65.46±0.62
Metabolic energy (MJ/kg DM)(2)	10.27	17.6

Table 2. Nutrient composition *(g/100 g DM) of acorn kernel and grass in the dehesa and Mediterranean forest; (Rodríguez-Estévez et al., 2009a). (1) Acorn kernel makes on average 77% of the whole fruit. (2) From García-Valverde et al. (2007).

Acorn kernel composition (Table 2) is variable and is influenced by its own maturation process and external agents (humidity, parasites, etc.) (Rodríguez-Estévez et al., 2008, 2009b). In contrast, shell and cotyledon proportions show higher homogeneity. Shell composition has a very high level of tannins and lignin, which affects its digestibility. Kernel has a very high level of glucids (80% of DM) and lipids (5-10% of DM), with oleic acid content upper 60%; however, protein level is very low (4-6% of DM) (Rodríguez-Estévez et al., 2008). Many wild and domestic species eat acorns; however, in the dehesa, acorns are used to feed fattening Iberian pigs because this breed is the single one capable of peeling them and because it raises the highest commercial value. On the other hand, the autumn production of grass has been estimated at 200–500 kg DM per hectare of dehesa (Medina Blanco, 1956; Escribano and Pulido, 1998).

4. The Iberian pig

The term Iberian pig refers to a racial group of native pigs from the Iberian Peninsula, which originated from *Sus mediterraneus* in ancient times (Aparicio, 1960; Dieguez, 1992). It is characterized by its rusticity and adaption to Mediterranean weather and environmental conditions, and fat producing ability with a high intramuscular fat content (Aparicio, 1960). A great amount of genetic heterogeneity exists, with black, red, blond and spotted varieties (Aparicio, 1960), the black and the red being the most abundant, and with or without hair. The popular name "pata negra" comes from their very narrow and short extremities, with pigmented hooves of uniform black colour. At the end of the finishing phase (140-160 kg) called "montanera" (meaning pannage) they can reach 60% carcass fat, 15 cm backfat thickness and 10-13% intramuscular fat content (López-Bote, 1998).

4.1 The traditional husbandry and breeding system of Iberian pig

The traditional husbandry and breeding system of Iberian pigs was described 2000 years ago by Columela, the Hispano-Roman writer. The Iberian pig has been raised for centuries to produce meat for dry-cured products (hams, shoulders and loins are the most valued). This carries on being the main objective of the production system. Besides, nowadays the quality of the meat products is emphasized; mainly due to its very specific properties and healthy mono-unsaturated fats with a high content of oleic acid (around 55%) from acorn diet and a very low concentration of linoleic and palmitic acids (around 8 and 20% respectively) (Flores et al., 1988). Currently, the Iberian pig production is restructuring, after a great increase of census during the last decade when it reached nearly half million of reproductive sows.

Consequently, there is a new market for fresh meat from intensive farming imitating the acorn diet fatty acid profile, exploiting the image of traditional products and consumers lack of information and trying to avoid official control based on the fatty acid profile (López-Vidal et al., 2008; Arce et al., 2009).

The whole traditional productive cycle of the Iberian pigs was organized to get them physiologically capable of foraging acorns during their finishing phase (montanera). An important aspect of their traditional handling is a long period of growing (or pre-fattening) and feed rationing, with diet based on natural resources (according to the availability of each dehesa land): spring grasses, stubble in summer, agriculture by-products, etc.; in order to take advantage of the pig compensatory growth (Rodríguez-Estévez et al., 2011).

Traditionally, farrowing occurred twice throughout the year, usually piglets born in December-January and June-July (one flock of sows with two batches per year), and the animals were weaned when over 1.5-2 months of age. The range of ages at the initial time of their montanera was therefore very wide (from 21-22 to 15-16 respectively), slaughtering the oldest pigs at almost 2 years old.

Nowadays, the batch for montanera finishing is usually the youngest one and it is pure Iberian breed; while piglets born in December-January are Duroc-Jersey crossbred intensively and fed with formulated compound feed. On the other hand, the montanera finishing system has its own legal regulation (MAPA, 2007), and it does not allow to begin finishing at an age lower than 10 months and limits the beginning weight from 80.5 to 115 kg; besides, it establishes that pigs should gain a minimum of 46 kg (4 *arrobas*; 1 *arroba* is a Spanish measure equivalent to 11.5 kg) grazing natural resources (mainly acorns and grass) during a minimum of 2 months.

Fig. 7. Iberian growers foraging the remains of acorns in a dehesa at the end of winter, which will be slaughtered after their second *montanera*, around 10 months later (dehesa Navahonda Baja, Natural Park "Sierra Norte de Sevilla", included in the Biosphere Reserve "Dehesas de Sierra Morena").

Pigs are slaughtered at high liveweights (14-16 *arrobas*, equivalent to 161-184 kg) because quality characteristics of the cured products require an extremely high carcass fat content and meat with high intramuscular fat content.

4.2 Acorn consumption by the Iberian pig

The legal requirements of Iberian pig meat and cured products (MAPA, 2007) does not allow offering pigs any supplementary feed, salt or mineral supplements during montanera;

hence, pigs are entirely dependent on natural resources during this finishing period, of at least 2 months. Studies, based on direct and continuous *in situ* observations of ingestive bites taken by continuously monitored pigs (during 10 uninterrupted hours per day of observation), show that the Iberian pig montanera diet is based on acorns and grass with 56.5 and 43.3% of grazing bites respectively; while only other nine resources (berries, bushes, roots, carrion, straw, etc.) were consumed at a frequency ≥0.01% (Rodríguez-Estévez et al., 2009a). This means a daily intake of 1251 to 1469 acorns or 7.13 to 8.37 kg of whole acorn and 2 to 2.7 kg of grass, during 6.1 to 7.1 foraging hours (Fig. 8).

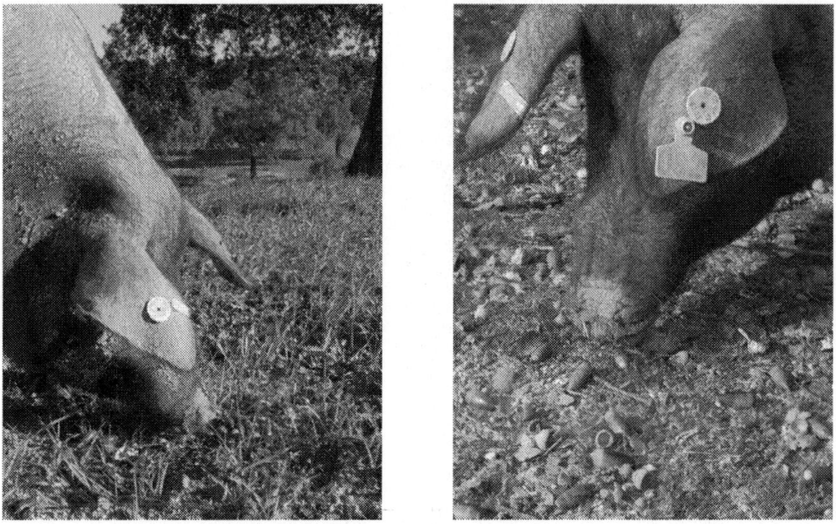

Fig. 8. Iberian fatteners foraging acorns in a dehesa during montanera (from November to February) under the control and inspection of the Denomination of Origin "Los Pedroches" (Turcañada S.L., dehesa Casa Alta, Fuente Obejuna, Córdoba, Spain).

Iberian pigs peel acorns and split their shells due to the high content of tannins in shells; notably, this is the unique breed and domestic animal known to have this skill. However, during peeling there is an amount of kernel wasted per acorn (18.9±1.2 percent) and it presents a high degree of variation influenced by differences in the morphology and size of the acorns (Rodríguez-Estévez et al., 2009c). As a result of this, a positive correlation has been observed between the weight of the waste kernel and the weight of the whole acorn, as well as the diameter (Rodríguez-Estévez et al., 2009b). This could explain why the Iberian pigs deliberately select certain oak trees (eating at least 40 acorns per visit), while avoiding others (eating less than 10 acorns per visit) in spite of large numbers of acorns under their canopies (Rodríguez-Estévez et al., 2009c). Differences observed between the sought out and rejected acorns at the start and end of the montanera season are too large to be only a matter of chance, suggesting that Iberian pigs must form associations between variables when choosing to eat or reject the acorns from a specific tree. Pigs tend to select heavier acorns at the start of the montanera season, while at the end their selection is based more on the composition of the acorns. So, Rodríguez-Estévez et al. (2009c) observed that acorns with mean weights of 5.73±0.37, 6.93±0.28 g were rejected and sought after, respectively, at the montanera start (November), and those weighing 3.18±0.2 and 3.44±0.11 g were rejected and sought out, respectively, at the end (February).

Fig. 9. Iberian fatteners foraging acorns in a dehesa in winter, close to their slaughtering (dehesa Navahonda Baja, Natural Park "Sierra Norte de Sevilla", included in the Biosphere Reserve "Dehesas de Sierra Morena").

The foraging and grouping behaviour of these pigs entails a balance between competition for resources and space (under tree canopies to eat acorns) and cooperation to look for the best patches (oak masts) with the heaviest and healthiest acorns. This behaviour has been termed as "Chase Optimal Foraging" (Rodríguez-Estévez et al., 2010b). Pigs walk a daily distance of 3.9±0.18 km to visit 96±3.7 trees in order to get a mean intake of 56.4±2.34 MJ of metabolic energy (ME) provided by grass and acorns (Table 3) (Rodríguez-Estévez et al., 2010c). With that intake the average daily weight gain of Iberian pigs has been found to be 0.79±0.03 kg during montanera fattening period. So, the corresponding food conversion rate, expressed in terms of whole acorns required to achieve the reported growth rate, taking into account the contribution of grass, is 10.5±0.75 (Rodríguez-Estévez et al., 2010c).

	Wet basis (kg)	Dry matter (kg)	Metabolic energy (MJ)
Acorn kernel	4.9±0.22	2.9±0.13	51.3±2.32
Grass	2.7±0.23	0.5±0.04	5.1±0.43
Total	7.6±0.31	3.4±0.14	56.4±2.34
Percent from kernel	66.9±2.19	85.1±1.32	90.4±0.93
Percent from grass	33.1±2.19	14.9±1.32	9.6±0.93

Table 3. Daily ingestion of acorn kernels and grass by fattening Iberian pigs grazing in the dehesa over the montanera season, mean±S.E. (N=60) (Rodríguez-Estévez et al., 2010c).

5. The Iberian pig and the dehesa conservation

In a past, there were similar pig fattening systems to the Iberian pig one in other European countries (Fig. 10). For example, in Great Britain, the Common of Mast was the right to turn out pigs during a season known as pannage, and it has survived in the New Forest; but finishing only 500-600 pigs per year. However, in other countries, the pig presence and its grazing and rooting habits became considered dangerous to the forests. Hence, the Iberian one is the only pig breed known which contributes to conservation of an ecosystem, considered a sustained production and a model for organic farming (freedom, welfare, and grazing diet without any chemical supplement). A very low stocking rate and a well conserved dehesa are necessary conditions to finish Iberian pigs grazing acorns and grass. These are the reasons because its contribution to conserve natural areas and to rural development is recognized by the Spanish authorities (MAPA, 2001 and 2007).

Fig. 10. Calendar page for November of "Les Trés Riches Heures du Duc de Berry" (France, 1410-1416).

Besides legal trends and consumer demands related to animal welfare, alimentary security, environmental protection, etc. have generated an interest in outdoor swine production systems (Edwards, 2005). Furthermore, the montanera finishing system is of a great interest due to the differentiating characteristics that it provides to the carcasses and the products derived from them (e.g. healthy fatty acid profile). As a consequence, the meat of Iberian pigs is in great demand; and pigs, fattened under the traditional system, have been sold at prices up to 160% higher than conventionally raised animals, and dry cured hams sold between 350 and 500% higher in a recent past (FAO, 2007). Indeed, the main constraint for further increasing the output of these products is not lack of demand, but the limited range of the breed's traditional habitat. Besides, when fattening pigs in the dehesa, acorns are the most limiting resource during the montanera, because unlike grass, their supply is not continually renewed during the montanera season (Rodríguez-Estévez et al., 2010c).

To protect the system (the very effective couple Iberian pig and dehesa) and consumers from fraud, the Spanish authorities established the minimum standards to market Iberian pork and cured products (MAPA, 2001 and 2007). However, these standards have not been enough and have contributed to consumer confusion, while having favoured intensive production and marketing of cross breed Iberian pigs (Rodríguez-Estévez et al., 2009d).

According to the legal requirements of the current quality standard for the Iberian pig (MAPA, 2007), they need to be able to reach the slaughter weight (≥161 kg) only with natural resources consumed during grazing. To know the high food conversion rate of finishing Iberian pigs in the dehesa (10.5±0.75 kg of whole acorns to gain 1 kg, besides the contribution of grass) is the key for establishing their stocking rate in the montanera season (Rodríguez-Estévez et al., 2010c). Bearing in mind that an adult evergreen oak (*Q. ilex rotundifolia*) produces an average of 11 kg of acorns (Rodríguez-Estévez et al., 2007a), it could be assumed that a grazing Iberian pig requires the total annual production of acorns of an adult evergreen oak to obtain 1 kg weight gain (Rodríguez-Estévez et al., 2010c). So, stocking rate could be estimated dividing the number of adult oaks of a dehesa by the expected weight gain; a minimum of 46 kg according to quality standards (MAPA, 2007). Furthermore, having in mind the fact that Iberian pigs selectively feed on acorns with preferred traits (Rodríguez-Estévez et al., 2009c), the previous quotient should be considered a minimum to guarantie finishing only based on acorns and grass.

Quality standards demand a stocking rate <2 pigs/ha of dehesa, considering a minimum density of 10 trees/ha (MAPA, 2007). However, an average figure of 35 adult evergreen oaks/ha of dehesa has been reported (see Rodríguez-Estévez et al., 2007a). Accordingly, the stocking rate should be <1 pig/ha of dehesa so that the minimum standard of 46 kg weight gain, based only on natural grazing, can be achieved under sustainable conditions (Rodríguez-Estévez et al., 2010c).

Pigs should be as old as possible and adapted to grazing to make the best use of natural resources (mainly the limited acorn mast) while foraging during the montanera. The mean average daily gain for those pigs is 0.76±0.01 kg/day, and it is very much influenced by the age (Rodríguez-Estévez et al., 2011), due to a compensatory growth. To raise these pigs (older than a year and adapted) the best system is the traditional extensive one, based on a grazing diet. Hence, to produce profitable Iberian pigs finished on acorns is necessary to have well conserved dehesa lands (in terms of a high adult tree density and good pasture) to graze before and during the montanera season; all this implies expenses for: clearing brushes (mainly *Cistus* sp.), pruning, reforestation and fencing (to contain wild boars from the forests and, sometimes, to keep cattle out of wooded lots) (Fig. 11).

Fig. 11. Iberian growers grazing in a reforested dehesa at the end of spring (Natural Park "Sierra Norte de Sevilla", included in the Biosphere Reserve "Dehesas de Sierra Morena"). The perimeter fence and a firebreak are in the first line of the picture.

6. The protection of the traditional Iberian pig production

It is necessary a very clear and strict differentiation of Iberian pig production systems, without the current euphemistic official quality denominations (MAPA, 2007); for example, the two conditions to label a product as from "cerdo de campo", meaning "country pig", are >0.066 ha and ≥100 m between feeder and drinking trough, which is ridiculous. According to MARM (2010), 81.5% of slaughtered pigs in 2009 were reared in intensive farms, very far from the image that consumers have of Iberian pigs.

The establishment of more stringent standards, the requirement for more accurate controls to avoid frauds (for example: infrared spectroscopy; Arce et al., 2009) and a greater consumer information are keys to protect the traditional Iberian pig farms, because to maintain the montanera finishing system it is essential to conserve the dehesa agroecosystem and its profitability. In this sense, it has been proposed to establish stocking rates on the base of adult oaks density (a mean of 46 trees/pig), very easily calculated with the use of geographic information system (GIS) (Rodríguez-Estévez et al., 2010c).

Besides, the extra cost of an Iberian pig finished on acorns is estimated in more than 175 €/pig (1.1 €/kg live weight) to pay growing feed, labour (swineherd), pannage and financial cost. In other words, while the pork market does not pay this extra cost it will not be worth the traditional finishing system; because, currently it is more profitable to fatten pigs on feed using the good image of the Iberian breed (associated to the tradition and the dehesa) to sell these.

7. Conclusions

The dehesa is both a resilient and a fragile system created by farmers to raise livestock. This system is highly appreciated by society and its potential future support is mainly based on its ecological values. The continued supply of public values from private woodlands depends on their economic value and the opportunity costs of competing land uses. The last decade, its profitability has depended on its acorn production as a feed for fattening Iberian pigs. As pigs need a very high amount of acorns for finishing these require very well conserved dehesas (with optimal density of adult oaks).

The couple Iberian pig and dehesa has proved to be very effective; so much the Iberian pig is called the dehesa jewel, but the first needs this agroecosystem to reach its highest quality properties (organoleptic and nutritional ones); and the second needs a clear commercial differentiation for Iberian pork and cured products in order to receive a high price to maintain and conserve the dehesa. Hence, the Spanish authorities should be responsible for protecting this traditional system from fraud and unfair competition. In this way, farmers economy could be enough to conserve this unique ecosystem and its values for the whole society.

8. References

Aparicio, G. (1960). Zootecnia especial. Etnología compendiada. Imprenta Moderna, Córdoba, Spain.

Arce, L., Domínguez-Vidal, A., Rodríguez-Estévez, V., López-Vidal, S., Ayora-Cañada, M.J., Valcárcel, M. (2009). Feasibility study on the use of infrared spectroscopy for the direct authentication of Iberian pig fattening diet. *Analytica Chimica Acta*, Vol.636, pp. 183–189, ISSN: 0003-2670.

Baldock, D., Beaufoy, G., Bennet, G., Clark, J., (eds). (1993). Nature conservation and new directions in the EC common agricultural policy. *Institute for European Environmental Policy*, HPC, Arnhem.

Blanco, E., Casado, M.A., Costa, M., Escribano, R., García, M., Génova, M., Gómez , A., Gómez, F., Moreno, J.C., Morla, C., Regato, P., Sainz, H. (1997). Los bosques ibéricos. *Editorial Planeta*, ISBN: 84-08-01924-4, Barcelona, Spain.

Cañellas, I., Roig, S., Poblaciones, M.J., Gea-Izquierdo, G., Olea, L. (2007). An approach to acorn production in Iberian dehesas. *Agroforestry Systems*, Vol.70, pp. 3-9, ISSN: 0167-4366.

Carruthers, S.P. (1993). The dehesas of Spain - exemplars or anachronisms? *Agroforestry Forum*, Vol. 4, pp. 43–52.

Coromines, J. (1980). Diccionario crítico etimológico castellano e hispano. *Ed. Credos*, ISBN: 978-84-249-1362-5, Spain.

Costa, J.C., Martín, A., Fernández, R., Estirado, M. (2006). Dehesas de Andalucía: caracterización ambiental. *Consejería de Medio Ambiente de la Junta de Andalucía*, ISBN: 84-96329-81-X, Sevilla, Spain.

Council of the European Communities. (1991). Council Directive 91/676/EEC of 12 December 1991 concerning the protection of waters against pollution caused by nitrates from agricultural sources. *Official Journal of the European Communities* L 375, pp. 1-8.

Council of the European Communities. (1992). Council Directive 92/43/EEC of 21 May 1992 on the conservation of natural habitats and of wild fauna and flora. *Official Journal of the European Communities* L 206, pp. 7-50.

Council of the European Communities. (1999). Council Regulation (EC) N° 1257/1999 of 17 May 1999 on support for rural development from the European Agricultural Guidance and Guarantee Fund (EAGGF) and amending and repealing certain Regulations. *Official Journal of the European Communities* L 160, pp. 80-102.

Díaz, M., Campos, P., Pulido, F.J. (1997). The Spanish dehesas: a diversity in land-use and wildlife. In: The common agricultural policy and its implications for bird conservation. Pain, D.J., Pienkowski, M.W., eds. *Academic Press,* ISBN: 9780125442800, London, UK.

Dieguez, E. (1992). Historia, evolución y situación actual del cerdo Ibérico. In: El cerdo Ibérico, la naturaleza, la dehesa. *Ministerio de Agricultura, Pesca y Alimentación,* pp. 9-35, ISBN: 84-7479-948-1, Madrid, Spain.

Escribano, M., Pulido, F. (1998). La dehesa en Extremadura. Estructura económica y recursos naturales. Colección Monografías. *SGT-Servicio de Investigación y Desarrollo Tecnológico. Junta de Extremadura,* Mérida, Spain.

Espejo Gutierrez de Tena, A.M., Martínez Bueso, M., del Pozo Barrón, J.L., Espejo Díaz, M. (2006). Avance de los resultados del inventario forestal en las fincas piloto con arbolado del proyecto Interreg-IIA Montado-Dehesa SP4.E13. In: Espejo, M., Martín Bellido, M., Matos, C., Mesías Díaz, F.J. (eds). Gestión ambiental y económica de del ecosistema dehesa en la Península Ibérica: ponencias y comunicaciones presentadas en las Jornadas Técnicas celebradas en el Centro de Investigación Agraria Finca La Orden, Guadajira (Badajoz), 9-11 noviembre 2005. *Consejería de Infraestructuras y Desarrollo Tecnológico. Junta de Extremadura,* Mérida, Spain.

Ferrer, C., San Miguel, A., Ocaña, M. (1997). Propuesta para un nomenclátor definitivo de pastos en España. *Pastos,* Vol.17, No.2, pp. 125-161, ISSN: 0210-1270.

Flores, J., C. Birón, C. Izquierdo, L., Nieto, P. (1988). Characterization of green hams from Iberian pigs by fast analysis of subcutaneous fat. *Meat Science,* Vol.23, pp. 253-262, ISSN: 0309-1740.

García-Valverde, R., Nieto, R., Lachica, M., Aguilera, J.F. (2007). Effects of herbage ingestion on the digestion site and nitrogen balance in heavy Iberian pigs fed on an acorn-based diet. *Livestock Science,* Vol.112, pp. 63-77, ISSN: 1871-1413.

Gea-Izquierdo, G., Cañellas, I., Montero, G. (2006). Acorn production in Spanish holm oak woodlands. *Investigación Agraria: Sistemas y Recursos Forestales,* Vol.15, pp. 339-354, ISSN: 1131-7965.

González, L.M., San Miguel, A. (2004). Manual de buenas prácticas de gestión en fincas de monte mediterráneo de la red Natura 2000. *Ministerio de Medio Ambiente,* Madrid, Spain.

López Sáez, J.A., López García, P., López Merino, L., Cerrillo Cuenca, E., González Cordero, A., Prada Gallardo, A. (2007). Origen prehistórico de la dehesa en Extremadura: Una perspectiva paleoambiental. *Revista de Estudios Extremeños,* Vol. 63, No.1, pp. 493-510, ISSN: 0210-2854.

López-Bote, C.J. (1998). Sustained utilization of the Iberian pig breed. *Meat Science,* Vol.49, No. Suppl. I, pp. 17-27, ISSN: 0309-1740.

López-Vidal, S., Rodríguez-Estévez, V., Lago, S., Arce, L., Valcárcel, M. (2008). The Application of GC–MS and chemometrics to categorize the feeding regime of Iberian pigs in Spain. *Chromatographia,* Vol.68, pp. 593-601, ISSN: 0009-5893.

MAPA. (2001). Real Decreto 1083/2001, de 5 de octubre, por el que se aprueba la Norma de Calidad para el jamón ibérico, paleta ibérica y caña de lomo ibérico elaborados en España. BOE 247: 37830-37833.

MAPA. (2007). Real Decreto 1469/2007, de 2 de noviembre, por el que se aprueba la norma de calidad para la carne, el jamón, la paleta y la caña de lomo ibéricos. BOE 264: 45087-45104.

Marañón, T. (1985). Diversidad florística y heterogeneidad ambiental en una dehesa de Sierra Morena. *Anales de Edafología y Agrobiología,* Vol.44, pp. 1183–1197, ISSN: 0365-1797.

MARM. (2010). Resumen de datos de censos de animales ibéricos y productos comercializados del ibérico en 2009. June 2010, Available from: http://www.marm.es/es/alimentacion/temas/calidad-agroalimentaria/Resumen_censos09_tcm7-8126.pdf

Martín Vicente, A., Infante, J.M., García Gordo, J., Merino, J., Fernández Alés, R. (1998). Producción de bellotas en montes y dehesas del suroeste español. *Pastos,* Vol.28, pp. 237-248, ISSN: 0210-1270.

Medina Blanco, M. (1956). Contribución al estudio del área de la encina en la provincia de Córdoba y de sus posibilidades alimenticias para el ganado. *Archivos de Zootecnia,* Vol. 5, pp. 101–204, ISSN: 0004-0592.

Montero, G., San Miguel, A., Cañellas, I. (1998). Sistemas de selvicultura mediterránea. La dehesa. Agricultura sostenible. Agrofuturo, LIFE, *Ediciones Mundi Prensa,* pp. 519-514, Madrid, Spain.

Montoya, J.M. (1989). Encinas y encinares. *Mundi prensa,* ISBN: 9788471144096, Madrid, Spain.

Montoya, J.M., Mesón, M.L. (2004). Selvicultura: manejo y explotación de las masas de *Quercus*. In: La seca: decaimiento de encinas, alcornoques y otros *Quercus* en España. Tusét, J.J., Sánchez, G., Coord. *Ministerio de Medio Ambiente. Organismo Autónomo de Parques Nacionales,* pp. 125-149, ISBN: 9788480145626, Madrid, Spain.

Olea, L., San Miguel-Ayanz, A. (2006). The Spanish dehesa. A traditional Mediterranean silvopastoral system linking production and nature conservation. *21st General Meeting of the European Grassland Federation,* Badajoz, Spain.

Pineda, F.D., Montalvo, J. (1995). Dehesa systems in the western Mediterranean: biological diversity in traditional land use systems. In: Halladay, P., Gilmour, D.A. (eds). *Conserving Biodiversity outside Protected Areas. The Role of Traditional Agro-ecosystems, IUCN,* pp 107–122, ISBN: 2-8317-0293-3, Gland, Switzerland.

Plieninger, T., Pulido, F.J., Konold, W. (2003). Effects of land-use history on size structure of holm oak stands in Spanish dehesas: implications for regeneratin and restoration. *Environmental Conservation,* Vol.30, pp. 61-70, ISSN: 0376-8929.

Presidencia. (2010). Ley 7/2010, de 14 de julio, para la Dehesa. BOJA 144: 6-11.

Pulido García, F. (2002). La producción animal en la dehesa extremeña. Nuevas tendencias y estrategias de mejora. In: *Libro Blanco de la Agricultura y el Desarrollo Rural. Jornada Autonómica de Extremadura,* Badajoz, Spain.

Pulido, F.J. (1999). Herbivorismo y regeneración de la encina (Quercus ilex L.) en bosques y dehesas. *Doctoral Thesis, Universidad de Extremadura,* Cáceres, Spain.

Rodríguez Estévez, V., Rucabado Palomar, T., Mata Moreno, C. (2007b). La producción ganadera extensiva y la conservación del medio ambiente, en Andalucía. In Patrimonio Ganadero Andaluz Vol. I: La Ganadería Andaluza en el Siglo XXI. Rodero Serrano, E., Valera Córdoba, M. Ed. *Junta de Andalucía - Consejería de Agricultura y Pesca,* Pp. 267-278, ISBN: 978-84-8474-226-5, Sevilla, Spain.

Rodríguez-Estévez, V. (2011). La encina. *La Fertilidad de la Tierra,* Vol.46, pp. 66-69, ISSN: 1576-625X.

Rodríguez-Estévez, V., Díaz Gaona, C., Sánchez Rodríguez, M., Mata Moreno, C. (2010a). La dehesa como ejemplo de biodiversidad en la Ganadería Ecológica. *Agricultura Ecológica,* Vol.0, pp. 24-27, ISSN: In process, Legal deposit: V-2052-2010.

Rodríguez-Estévez, V., García Martínez, A., Mata Moreno, C., Perea Muñoz, J.M., Gómez Castro, A.G. (2008). Dimensiones y características nutritivas de las bellotas de los Quercus de la dehesa. *Archivos de Zootecnia,* Vol. 57(R), pp. 1-12, ISSN: 0004-0592.

Rodríguez-Estévez, V., García Martínez, A., Perea Muñoz, J.M., Mata Moreno, C., Gómez Castro, A.G. (2007a). Producción de bellota en la dehesa: factores influyentes. *Archivos de Zootecnia,* Vol.56(R), pp. 25-43, ISSN: 0004-0592.

Rodríguez-Estévez, V., García, A., Gómez, A.G. (2009b). Characteristics of the acorns selected by free range Iberian pigs during the montanera season. *Livestock Science,* Vol.122, pp. 169–176, ISSN: 1871-1413.

Rodríguez-Estévez, V., García, A., Gómez-Castro, A.G. (2009c). Intrinsic factors of acorns that influence the efficiency of their consumption by Iberian pigs. *Livestock Science,* Vol.122, pp. 281–285, ISSN: 1871-1413.

Rodríguez-Estévez, V., García, A., Peña, F., Gómez, A.G. (2009a). Foraging of Iberian fattening pigs grazing natural pasture in the dehesa. *Livestock Science,* Vol.120, pp. 135–143, ISSN: 1871-1413.

Rodríguez-Estévez, V., Sánchez Rodríguez, M., García, A.R., Gómez-Castro, A.G. (2011). Average daily weight gain of Iberian fattening pigs when grazing natural resources. *Livestock Science,* Vol.137, pp. 292–295, ISSN: 1871-1413.

Rodríguez-Estévez, V., Sánchez Rodríguez, M., Gómez-Castro, A.G. (2009d). El sector del porcino ibérico en Andalucía. In Informe Anual del Sector Agrario en Andalucía 2008. Ed. *Analistas Económicos de Andalucía,* Pp. 483-491, ISSN: 1575-8214.

Rodríguez-Estévez, V., Sánchez-Rodríguez, M., García, A., Gómez-Castro, A.G. (2010c). Feed conversion rate and estimated energy balance of free grazing Iberian pigs. *Livestock Science,* Vol.132, pp. 152–156, ISSN: 1871-1413.

Rodríguez-Estévez, V., Sánchez-Rodríguez, M., Gómez-Castro, A.G., Edwards, S.A. (2010b). Group sizes and resting locations of free range pigs when grazing in a natural environment. *Applied Animal Behaviour Science,* Vol.127, pp. 28–36, ISSN: 0168-1591.

Rupérez Cuéllar, A. (1957). La encina y sus tratamientos. *Gráficas Manero,* Madrid, Spain.

Siebold, M.A. (2009). An analysis of the sustainability of the organic dehesa pig farming systems in Andalusia, Spain, using the multiple criteria decision-making paradigm. *Ph D. Thesis,* University of Reading, Reading, UK.

Standiford, R.B., Huntsinger, L., Campos, P., Martin, D., Mariscal, P. (2003). The bioeconomics of Mediterranean oak woodlands: issues in conservation policy. *XII World Forestry Congress Proceedings,* pp. 111-120.

Telleria, J. L., Santos, T. (1995). Effects of forest fragmentation on a guild of wintering passerines: the role of habitat selection. *Biological Conservation*, Vol.71, pp. 61-67, ISSN: 0006-3207.

Tellería, J.L. (1988). Caracteres generales de la invernada de aves en la peninsula ibérica. In: Tellería JL (ed): *Invernada de aves en la Península Ibérica. SEO monografías 1*, pp 13–22, Madrid, Spain.

Van Wieren, S.E. 1995. The potencial role of herbivores in nature conservation and extensive land use in Europe. In: The National Trust and nature conservation: 100 years on. Ed. Bullock, D.J., Harvey, H.J. *Biológical Journal of the Linnean Societe*, Vol.56(Suppl.), pp. 11-23, ISSN: 0024-4066.

Vázquez, F.M., Doncel, E., Martín, D., Ramos, S. (1999). Estimación de la producción de bellotas de los encinares de la provincia de Badajoz en 1999. *Sólo Cerdo Ibérico*, Vol.3, pp. 67-75, ISBN: B18574063, Badajoz, Spain.

Vázquez, F.M., Peral Pacheco, D., Ramos Maqueda, S. (2001). Historia de la vegetación y los bosques de la Baja Extremadura. Aproximaciones a su conocimiento. *Consejería de Agricultura y Medio Ambiente - Junta de Extremadura*, ISBN: 84-8107-041-6, Mérida, Spain.

Viera Natividade, J. (1950, Reed. 1991). Subericultura. *MAPA*, ISBN: 8474799104, 9788474799101, Madrid, Spain.

2

A Conceptual Model of Carbon Dynamics for Improved Fallows in the Tropics

M. L. Kaonga[1,*] and T. P. Bayliss-Smith[2]
[1]*A Rocha International, Sheraton House, Castle Park, Cambridge,*
[2]*Department of Geography, Downing Place, Cambridge*
UK

1. Introduction

Despite the increasing international sense of urgency, the growth rate of carbon (C) emissions continued to speed up, bringing the atmospheric CO_2 concentration to 383 parts per million (ppm) in 2007 (Global Carbon Project [GCP], 2008). Annual fossil CO_2 emissions increased from an average of 6.4 Gt C yr^{-1} in the 1990s to nearly 10 Gt C yr^{-1} in 2008 (Le Quéré et al., 2009), while emissions from land-use change were estimated to be 1.6 Gt C yr^{-1} over the 1990s. About 45% of annual C emissions (3.5 Pg) remained in the atmosphere each year, while oceans and terrestrial ecosystems assimilated the other 55% (Canadell & Raupach, 2008). Increasing the size and capacity of land-based ecosystems that sequester C in plants and the soil expands the terrestrial C sink. Establishment of agroforestry systems is one of the options of reducing deforestation and increasing the terrestrial C sinks (Kaonga & Bayliss-Smith, 2010; Oelbermann et al, 1997).

Over 1 billion hectares of agricultural land, almost 50% of the world's farmland, have more than 10% of their area occupied by trees, while 160 million hectares have more than 50% tree cover (Zomer et al., 2009). Tree-based farming systems, whether mixed or monocultures, store up to 35% of C stored by a primary forest, compared with only 10% at the most in annual cropping systems. Average C storage by agroforestry systems has been estimated as 9, 21, 50, and 63 Mg C ha^{-1} in semi-arid, subhumid, humid, and temperate regions (Montagnini & Nair, 2004). If agroforestry practices are established immediately after slash and burn agriculture, 35% of the original forest C stocks can be regained (Sanchez, 2000) and a hectare of an agroforestry practice can potentially offset 5 ha of deforestation (Dixon, 1995). Carbon stocks in smallholder agroforestry systems in the tropics ranged from 1.5 to 3.5 Mg C ha^{-1} $year^{-1}$, tripling to 70 Mg C ha^{-1} $year^{-1}$ in a 20-$year^{-1}$ period (Watson et al., 2000). Improved fallows have great potential for increasing the terrestrial C sink through vegetal and soil C sequestration, conservation of forest C, and improved soil productivity (Kaonga & Coleman, 2008; Sanchez, 1999; Sileshi et al., 2007). However, C cycling in agroforestry systems is not clearly understood.

To date, the potential for C sequestration in agroforestry systems has not been adequately described. Despite the large number of publications on C dynamics in land-use systems, it

---

*Corresponding Author

has been difficult to construct a simple C budget of an improved fallow because of marked variations in soil characteristics, climatic factors, plant species, and management practices. Comparisons between reported experiments are complicated by great diversity of analytical techniques used by researchers to study C dynamics in land-use systems (Intergovernmental Panel on Climate Change [IPCC], 2000). In addition, ecological processes, which determine C storage in ecosystems, may themselves be controlled by other factors, most of which may interact strongly. In such situations, a conceptual model can assist to explicitly describe relationships between the various components, explore possibilities for modification of ecosystem processes that underpin C stocks and flows, and to examine the effects of ecosystem drivers and stressors on C pools.

This chapter describes a conceptual model that summarises current knowledge on ecological processes, drivers, and stressors responsible for C cycling, and demonstrates how the conceptual model could be used to estimate major C pools and fluxes in improved fallows using data from eastern Zambia. This model will improve our understanding of C dynamics in ecosystems for strategic C management.

2. Methodology

2.1 Conceptual model development

Published literature on tropical improved fallows in southern Africa (Chintu et al., 2004; Kwesiga et al., 1994; Kwesiga et al., 1999; Mafongoya et al., 1998; Sileshi et al., 2006a) and eastern Africa (Albrecht & Kandji, 2003) and other agroforestry practices in tropical Africa (Young, 1989) and Latin America (Oelbermann et al., 2004) was reviewed to determine major C pools and fluxes, and to describe major ecological processes, drivers, and stressors that determine C stocks in these ecosystems. Major C pools and fluxes, and key ecosystem drivers and stressors determining C dynamics in improved fallows were presented using diagrams and mathematical equations accompanied by detailed narratives.

2.2 Estimation of major carbon pools and fluxes using the conceptual model

2.2.1 Study sites

Data on C stocks were collected from two-, four- and 10-year-old tree fallows, established to study the effect of tree species on soil physical and chemical properties. The experiments were carried out at Kalichero (13°29′S 32°27′E), Kalunga (13°51′S 32°33′E) and Msekera (13°39′S 32°34′E) in eastern Zambia, at altitudes of 1000-1100 m (Table 1), and with a mean annual temperature of 23°C. The sites receive a mean annual rainfall of 960 mm in a single rainy season and 85% of rain falls within four months (December through March). Soils in eastern Zambia are yellowish-red to yellowish-brown loamy sandy or sandy soils - Acrisols. Site-specific soil classes and properties are summarized in Table 1.

2.2.2 Experiments

Aboveground plant biomass and soil samples for C analyses were collected from two-, four- and 10-year old improved fallow experiments at Kalichero, Kalunga, and Msekera research sites (Table 1) in eastern Zambia, from November 2002 to July 2003. The experiments, arranged in a randomized complete block design (RCBD) with four replications, included:

i. two-year-old non-coppicing fallow treatments (2000/02) of *Tephrosia candida* (*T. candida*), *T. candida* 02971, *Tephrosia vogelli* (*T. vogelli*) Chambeshi, *T. vogelli* Misamfu, and *Sesbania sesban* (L) Merr (*Sesbania*) at Kalichero and Kalunga.
ii. two-year old coppicing fallow (2000/03) treatments of *Acacia angustissima* (Mill) (*Acacia*), *Gliricidia sepium* (Jacq.) (*Gliricidia*), *Leucaena collinsii* (*L. collinsii*), *Calliandra callothyrsus* Embu (*Calliandra*), and *Senna siamea* (*Senna*) at Msekera and Kalunga.
iii. four-year old (1999-03) non-coppicing fallow treatments of *Cajanus*, *T. vogelli*, and *S. Sesban* (*Sesbania*) grown sequentially with maize at Msekera. The cropping phase was preceded by a three-year tree phase.
iv. 10-year old (1992-03) treatments of coppicing *L. leucocephala* Lam. deWit, *Gliricidia*, and *Senna* trees intercropped with maize at Msekera. The coppicing fallows comprised two phases: the initial three-year tree phase followed by a seven-year tree-maize intercropped phase. While the initial tree density in the tree phase was 10000 trees ha^{-1}, it decreased by almost 30% during the seven-year tree-maize intercropped phase.

The experiments also included control treatments of continuously cropped maize monoculture with fertilizer (M+F) and without fertilizer (M-F), and natural fallows (NF).

At the end of two-year-old non-coppicing fallows, in October 2002, 18 randomly selected trees at Kalichero and Msekera, and 36 trees at Kalunga, were destructively harvested in each treatment for C analyses. The sampling procedure was derived from published methods (Kaonga & Bayliss-Smith, 2009; Kumar & Tewari, 1999). Data on litterfall, living stem, branch, twig and leaf, and root biomass from two-year old coppiced and non-coppiced fallows, and prunings from 10-year old coppiced trees were collected from improved fallows. Additional data on maize grain yields and crop residues, and weed biomass in four-year old non-coppicing fallows and 10-year old coppiced fallows, provided by the Zambia/ICRAF Project, were also collected from the same experiments. Carbon contents in weed, maize grain and stover, and root biomass were estimated using published conversion factors.

Soil samples for SOC analyses were collected at 0-30 depth in a grid pattern from 10 locations in the centre 49 m^2 of each plot of (i) coppicing fallows (2000/03 and 1992/03) and non-coppicing fallows (1999/02) at Msekera, (ii) coppicing fallows (2000/03) and non-coppicing fallows (2000/02) at Kalunga, and (iii) coppicing fallows at Kalichero from October 2002 to July 2003. Composite soil samples from each plot were air-dried, crushed, passed through a 2 mm sieve, and analyzed for SOC by the Walkley-Black method (Schumacher, 2002). The Zambia/ICRAF Agroforestry Project used the same procedure to collect soil samples in the same experiments from 1997 to 2000. Carbon densities (t ha^{-1}) were determined as a product of bulk density, C concentration, and horizon thickness. The Project also provided data on maize crop, weed, and tree residue inputs for the period 1995-2002.

The conceptual model identifies three major phases of improved fallows - tree, maize cropping, and tree-maize intercropping phases - depending on the spatial or temporal arrangement of trees and the maize crop in a fallow cycle. In non-coppicing fallows, two-three year tree phases alternated with maize monocropping phases of the same duration. However, in coppicing fallows with tree species that re-sprout after cutting, an initial three-year tree phase was followed by a continuous tree-maize intercropping phase, which ended when crop yields dropped below optimal levels (Mafongoya et al., 2006). Trees were pruned two-three times in a cropping season and leaf biomass was applied to the soil as organic fertilizer. Detailed descriptions of management regimes of three-year old coppicing and non-coppicing fallows [Chintu et al., 2004; Kaonga & Coleman, 2008), four-year old non-coppicing fallows (Sileshi & Mafongoya, 2003) and 10-year old coppicing fallows (Sileshi & Mafongoya, 2006a) have been reported in earlier publications.

	Research sites		
Characteristic	Msekera	Kalichelo	Kalunga
Longitude	13°39′ E	13°29′ E	13°51′ S
Latitude	32°34′ S	32°27′ S	32°33′ S
Altitude (m)	1030	1001	1101
Rainfall (mm)	900	800-1000	800-1000
Rain season	Nov - April	Nov-April	Nov-April
Temperature range	15 - 30°C	14 - 28°C	13 - 28°C
Soil classification			
USDA	Ustic Rhodustalf	Typic Kandiustalf	Aridic Kandiustalf
Soil properties			
pH	5.3	5.0	4.8
Organic C	10.0 g kg^{-1}	7.0 g kg^{-1}	4.0 g kg^{-1}
Total N	0.7 g Kg^{-1}	0.7 g Kg^{-1}	0.4 g Kg^{-1}
Clay	26.0 %	22.0 %	8.0 %
Sand	61.0 %	64.0 %	85.0 %

Table 1. Biophysical and climatic conditions, and characteristics of the surface soil (0-15 cm) of research sites in Chipata, eastern Zambia (Kaonga and Bayliss-Smith, 2010)

3. Results and discussion

3.1 Description of the conceptual model of carbon cycling in improved fallows

The model recognizes that C in improved fallows is recycled between the environment and organisms mainly through ecosystem C aggrading processes (e.g. photosynthesis, precipitation, and sediment deposition) and degrading processes (decomposition, respiration, soil erosion, leaching) regulated by drivers (e.g. climate, droughts, hydrology) and stressors (pests, fire, biomass harvesting) (Figure 1). This model, which specifies the boundaries and the scope of C dynamics in tropical improved fallows, comprises diagrams accompanied by detailed narratives. It is based on non-mechanized fallow systems where fauna and microorganisms play a major role in decomposition of SOM and C sequestration. In improved fallows, SOC stocks decrease considerably with depth and the model considers only the soil surface layer (0-30 cm) where vertical variability can be ignored to a reasonable approximation.

3.1.1 Ecosystem processes in improved fallows

Plant C pools represent the difference between primary production through photosynthesis and consumption by respiration, decomposition, and harvest processes (Brown, 1997). Net assimilation of C by plants in improved fallows can be modelled as a function of radiation interception (Q), conversion efficiency (net C fixed/unit radiation intercepted) (E), growth and maintenance respiration (R) (Aber & Melillo, 2001; Vose & Swank, 1990):

$$TPC = \sum_{i=1}^{t} \left(Q_i \times E_i\right) - \sum_{c=1}^{n} R_{i,c} \qquad (1)$$

where TPC (t C ha^{-1} yr^{-1}) is the total plant C gain, the subscript $_c$ in $R_{i,c}$ is respiration rate for specific plant components (leaves, branches, stem, and roots) (Vose & Swank, 1990). However, net C assimilation is influenced by ecosystem drivers (climate, atmospheric deposition, resource availability) and stressors (drought, fire, nutrient deficiencies, herbivory, pests, biomass harvesting). Photosynthetic C intake rates of plants in improved fallows can be estimated as the sum of all plant C fractions expressed as:

$$PCI = C_{HB} + C_{PR} + C_R + C_{RD} \qquad (2)$$

where PCI is photosynthetic C intake (t ha^{-1} yr^{-1}), C_{HB} represents C in harvested biomass, C_{PR} is C in post-harvest plant residues, surface litter, and fresh leaf biomass, C_R is C in root biomass, and C_{RD} depicts rhizodeposit C (Bolinder et al., 1997; Jenkinson et al., 1999). Photosynthetic C intake rates for trees in fallows are derived from NPP by the modified mean annual increment method (Art & Marks, 1971; Brown, 1997]. Data on underground plant C pools in improved fallows are scarce, but fractional allocation of photosynthetic C to different tree components can be approximated using the following formulae (Bolinder et al., 1997; Heal et al., 1997; IPCC, 2000; Young, 1989, 1997):

$$C_{HB} = Y_{HB} \times 0.48 \qquad (3)$$

$$C_{PR} = (Y_{ABG} - Y_{HB}) \times 0.48 \qquad (4)$$

$$C_R = Y_{ABG} \times 0.35 \times 0.48 \qquad (5)$$

$$C_{RD} = C_R \qquad (6)$$

where Y_{ABG} is aboveground biomass (t ha^{-1} yr^{-1}), Y_{HB} is the harvested plant biomass of economic use, 0.35 is tree root C expressed as fraction of aboveground C stock, and C_{RD} is the rhizodeposit C, and 0.48 represents a weighted C content of tree components (Kaonga, 2005):

$$\text{Weighted } \%C = (0.4C_{S+B} + 0.09C_T + 0.12C_L + 0.25C_R + 0.06C_{Lit} + 0.08C_{RD}) \times 100 \qquad (7)$$

where $_S$ = stem, $_B$ = branches, $_L$ = leaves and twigs, $_R$ = root, and $_{Lit}$ = surface litter, and $_{RD}$ = rhizodeposit. Measured standing vegetal C must be adjusted for the dry weight of detached senesced tissues, leachates, herbivory, excreta, grazed or harvested biomass during the production period.

For maize sub-pools, plant C fractions can be estimated using the following formula derived from published methods (Bolinder et al., 1997):

$$C_{HB} = (Y_{ABG} - Y_{PR}) \times 0.45 \qquad (8)$$

$$C_{PR} = Y_{HB}\,(1\text{-}HI)/HI \times 0.45 \qquad (9)$$

$$C_R = Y_{ABG} \times 0.35 \times 0.45 \qquad (10)$$

$$C_{RD} = 0.65 \times C_R \qquad (11)$$

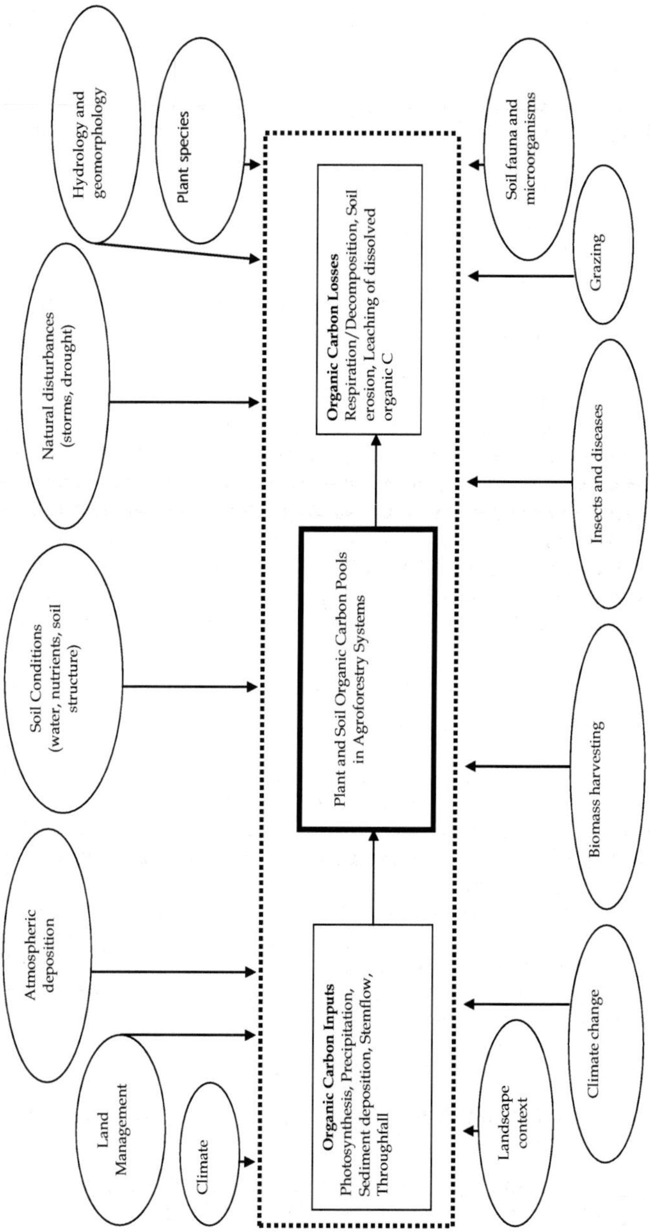

Fig. 1. A diagrammatic presentation of carbon pools and ecosystem drivers, disturbances, and stressors that influence carbon stocks and fluxes

where Y_{ABG} is the total dry matter yield (DM) of aboveground biomass (t ha^{-1} yr^{-1}), HI is the harvest index defined as DM yield of grain/total aboveground DM yield, and C_R = 31% of aboveground maize C stocks was root C (Buyanovsky & Wagner, 1986). Indices vary with maize variety, nutrient status of the soil, climate, pests and diseases, and agronomic practices. Root and rhizodeposit C inputs of weeds (grass) can be estimated by:

$$C_R = 0.31 \times C_{ABG} \quad (12)$$

$$C_{RD} = 0.65 \times C_R \quad (13)$$

Root and rhizodeposit C stocks are determined by various factors, including plant management practices, climate, soil conditions, pests and diseases, and herbivory. Stress factors that limit plant productivity reduce fractional allocation of photosynthesates to the root system and rhizodeposition.

Vegetation often modifies the intensity and distribution of precipitation falling on and through its leaves and woody structures, and chemistry of precipitation passing through agroforest canopies and down the stem. The canopies trap dust, aerosols, and gases in dry deposits and dissolved ions in precipitation and cloud droplets. Intercepted chemicals may be absorbed by plant foliage or microbes living on plant surfaces, or they may be washed off leaves and enter the soil system (Richter et al., 2000). Carbon is transferred to the soil in throughfall (precipitation that drips down through the forest canopy), and stemflow (intercepted precipitation that flows down the stem of a plant). The chemistry of throughfall and stem flow consists of C and nutrients in incident precipitation, soluble organic compounds and nutrients leached from vegetation, and those washed from surface of vegetation.

Products of decomposition and activities of phytophagous insects contribute to organic DOC in stemflow. The primary characteristics of a rainfall event that influence stemflow are rainfall continuity, rainfall intensity, and rain angle (Richter et al., 2000). Tree species determine stemflow through their morphological characteristics (crown size, leaf shape/orientation, flow path obstruction, and bark) and stand characteristics (individual tree species, structure of the forest, and species density). The two primary mechanisms influencing throughfall chemistry are wash-off of dry deposited elements from leaf surfaces, and canopy exchange through leaching of carbon and other organic compounds (Richter et al., 2000). Leaching can reduce soil C sequestration (Wise & Cacho, 1994) and contribute to transportation of C to marine ecosystems. In southern Africa, leaching is not intense because of low rainfall (Brown et al., 1994) and DOC leached below the topsoil is rarely lost from the system and the leaching front is arrested at less than 1m. However, leaching beyond the 0-30 cm depth was estimated using the formula,

$$L = C_i \times 0.05 \quad (14)$$

where C_i is the annual C inputs (t ha^{-1} yr^{-1}) to the soil and 0.05 represents a fraction of C_i that would be leached below the 30 cm depth.

Surface litter protects the soil against erosion, increases infiltration rates, regulates soil moisture, provides food and substrate for the decomposer community (Heal et al., 1997; Waring & Schlesinger, 1995), and cycles C and nutrients through decomposition, mineralization and leaching. The rate of litter decomposition in agroforestry systems (Young, 1989) is given by:

$$\frac{dL}{dt} = A_{Lit} - (K_{Lit} * P_{Lit}) \tag{15}$$

where A_{Lit} = annual litter C input, K_{Lit} = litter decomposition constant, and P_{Lit} = accumulated litterfall. Litter decomposition rates in fallows functionally depend on quality (C:N ratio, polyphenols, and lignin content) and quantity of litter, climate and soil conditions, age and vegetation type, nutrients, and management practices.

Decomposition alters SOM through communition, leaching, and catabolism (Heal et al., 1997). When organic residues are added to the soil, they are enzymatically hydrolysed, mineral elements are released and or immobilized, and humic organic compounds differentially resistant to microbial oxidation are formed through biochemical transformation of SOM or microbial synthesis (Brady & Weil, 1996). Decomposition of SOM depends on soil moisture, soil temperature, clay content and type, soil nutrients, vegetation type, soil microbial activities, and management practices (Brady & Weil, 1996; Jenkinson et al., 1999). Although SOM exists as materials covering a wide range of decomposabilities (Falloon & Smith, 2002; Jenkinson et al., 1999), this model simply partitions SOM into labile, stable, and recalcitrant fractions. The split between humification and oxidation is taken as 15:85 for crop and weed residues and tree prunings, and 33:67 for root biomass (Young, 1989). Soil organic C accretion through decomposition of plant organic inputs is estimated by a method derived from published studies (Bolinder et al., 1997; Young, 1989):

$$C_i = [C_{HB} \times S_{HB}] + [C_{PR} \times S_{PR}] + [C_R \times S_R] + [C_{RD} + S_{RD}] \tag{16}$$

where C_i is the annual C input to the soil, S describes the portion of C pool that is returned to the soil. Relative C input (R_i), expressing C input to the soil as proportion of PCI, is calculated as:

$$R_i = C_i / (C_{HB} + C_{PR} + C_R + C_{RD}) \tag{17}$$

As humus in the soil is oxidized, annual humic C losses are estimated by:

$$C_1 = C_0 - KC_0 \tag{18}$$

where C_0 = antecedent soil humus C, C_1 = C after one year, and K is humus decomposition constant - 3% for the tree phase, and 4% for cropping and tree-maize intercropped phases (Young, 1989).

Soil erosion preferentially removes the light organic fraction of low density SOC (<1.8 Mg m^{-3}), depleting C stocks in the topsoil (Lal, 2003). It alters C stocks and flows in agroforestry systems through removal or deposition of soil particles with humus (IPCC, 2000). Without quantitative data on erosion and the amount of eroded SOC, interpretation of the effects of different land-use systems on SOC dynamics is speculative (van Keulen, 2001). In fallows, erosion C losses are estimated by the formula:

$$E = E_A \times \%SOC \times CEF \tag{19}$$

where E = erosion C losses (t C ha^{-1} yr^{-1}), E_A = achievable erosion rate, %SOC = SOC content in the topsoil, CEF = C enrichment factor (Young, 1989). This model takes E_A as 10 t C ha^{-1} yr^{-1} (Hudson, 1995; Young, 1989) and CEF as 2.0 (Young, 1989). Land-use change from continuous monocropping to improved fallows induces changes in SOC stocks. Such changes can be calculated by a mass-balance equation (Lal, 2003):

$$\Delta SOC = (SOC_a + A) - (E + L + M) \tag{20}$$

where ΔSOC is the change in pool, SOC_a is the antecedent pool, *A* is accretion or input of C through organic additions, and losses due to erosion (E), leaching (L) and mineralisation (M) accentuated by anthropogenic perturbations.

3.1.2 Ecosystem drivers

The major ecosystem drivers of C cycling in improved fallows include climate, hydrology/geomorphology, and soil fauna and microbes. Climatic factors directly relevant to C cycling are rainfall, temperature, potential evaporation, and solar radiation. Climate regulates ecosystem processes and stressors. For example, in ecosystems with low vegetative cover, rainfall intensities may exceed infiltration capacity resulting in infiltration-excess and saturated overland flow, which may carry SOC (IPCC, 2000). The effect of hydrological processes on SOC dynamics depends on antecedent moisture conditions, soil conditions, biological activities, local gradients, and hydraulic conductivity (Brady & Weil, 1996).

Soil fauna, such as earthworms and termites, accelerate catabolism and leaching through communition of litter, mixing and incorporating fragmented products in the soil, changing porosity, and by increasing hydraulic conductivity and water infiltration (Mafongoya et al., 2006). Soil microbes degrade OM reduced by soil fauna. However, populations, activities, and distribution of soil fauna and microorganisms in ecosystems depend on site-specific variables like temperature, soil moisture, nutrients, pH, soil clay content and mineralogy, and vegetation type.

3.1.3 Ecosystem stressors

Productivity of tropical improved fallows is influenced by factors including climate change, air pollution, landscape context, management practices, biomass harvesting, herbivory, fires, and insect attack. Elevated atmospheric CO_2 concentration stimulates photosynthesis and inhibits respiration, increases water use efficiency, and affects feedbacks involving nutrient cycling (IPCC, 2000). By contrast (i) soil warming may increase C losses by accelerating respiration, (ii) increased productivity may deplete nitrogen concentrations leaving vegetation more susceptible to herbivory, (iii) actual plant productivity under field conditions may be constrained by nutrient limitations, and (iv) natural disturbances, insects, and diseases may become more intense and widespread (Sileshi et al., 2007). Droughts reduce ecosystem productivity due to low soil moisture contents and reduced nutrient uptake. However, data on the effect of increasing atmospheric C concentrations on C dynamics in agroforestry systems are scarce.

Carbon pools in improved fallows may be altered by the surrounding landscape depending on the nature of land-use. Widespread de-vegetation due to agricultural production results in a landscape that is windier, exposed to extreme temperatures, accessible to pests and diseases, vulnerable to loss of C through erosion, and favours increased microbial decomposition of SOC (Hudson, 1995; Watson et al., 2000). Management practices that favour C storage in land-use systems also improve soil physical and chemical properties, reduce soil erosion, and increase biodiversity (Dixon, 1995; Sanchez, 1999).

When trees in improved fallows are harvested, photosynthesis ceases and C stored in woody biomass is released to the atmosphere as CO_2, if wood is burned or decays (Albrecht & Kandji, 2003). Similarly, harvesting of agricultural products, such as maize grain, represents a significant C export from the system. In addition, tillage enhances SOM losses through increased microbial decomposition because it destroys soil aggregates which physically protect SOC against decomposers, increases aeration, and it re-distributes bacterial and fungal hyphae in the plough layer thereby increasing contact between microbes and SOM (Paulstian et al., 2000). The effect of management practices on SOC depends on the extent of soil disturbance, quantity and fate of harvested biomass, soil nutrients, water regimes, plant species, and plant cover.

In southern Africa where crop-livestock production systems are common (Kwesiga et al., 1999) grazing reduces green area index (GAI) and NPP, changes fractional C allocation to different plant tissues, and drastically reduces annual C inputs to the soil (Aber & Melillo, 2001). Similarly, insect attack can reduce NPP in agroforestry systems. For example, root nematodes and termites reduced growth and productivity of *Sesbania* and *Cajanus* in eastern Zambia (Mafongoya et al., 2006). Thus, herbivory can reduce overall plant productivity.

3.2 Estimation of major carbon pools using the model

3.2.1 Quantitative estimates of PCI and carbon pools in improved fallows

To illustrate how the conceptual model estimated major C pools using experimental data from improved fallow experiments, the model calculated PCI, and aboveground tree biomass, root and extra root C based on the following assumptions:

a. Trees and the maize crop in improved fallows produce optimal yields in a sub-humid climate with a unimodal rainfall pattern,
b. Fast growing tree legumes in improved fallows produce biomass yields close to those obtainable in other agroforestry systems in similar environments,
c. Carbon inputs and exports in both spatially mixed and rotational tree-crop systems are evenly distributed over a period, but the curve of SOC against time has toothed pattern for rotational fallows (Young,1989; Sanchez, 1999),
d. Root C in the 0 to 30 cm soil layer is taken as 95% for crops (Buyanovsky & Wagner, 1986) and weeds and 70% for tree legumes (Dhyani & Tripathi, 2000).

Using Eqs. (2) - (6), PCI for *L. collinsii* (Table 2) was calculated based on measured harvested aboveground biomass C as follows

$$C_{HB} = (Y_{HB} \times 0.48) / \text{Age of fallow (yrs)} = 5.2/2 = 2.6 \text{ t ha}^{-1}\text{yr}^{-1}$$
$$C_{PR} = (Y_{Lit} \times 0.48) = 1.0 \text{ t ha}^{-1}\text{yr}^{-1}$$
$$C_R = C_{HB} \times 0.35 \times 0.7 = 1.1 \text{t ha}^{-1}\text{yr}^{-1}$$
$$C_{RD} = CR = 1.1 \text{t ha}^{-1}\text{yr}^{-1}$$

Using Eq. (2),

$$\text{PCI for whole tree biomass} = (4.5 + 1.0 + 1.1 + 1.1) = 7.7\text{t ha}^{-1}\text{yr}^{-1}$$

$$\text{PCI for aboveground tree biomass} = (4.5 + 1.0) = 5.5\text{t ha}^{-1}\text{yr}^{-1}$$

Using Eqs. (7) and (16), annual C inputs to the soil in the tree phase were calculated as follows,

$$\begin{aligned} C_i &= [C_{HB} \times S_{HB}] + [C_{PR} \times S_{PR}] + [C_R \times S_R] + [C_{RD} + S_{RD}] \\ &= [4.5 \times 0.21) + [1.0 \times 1.0] + [1.1 \times 1.0] + [1.1 \times 1.0] = 4.2 \text{ t ha}^{-1}\text{yr}^{-1} \end{aligned}$$

The relative C input (R_i) to the soil, calculated using Eq. (17) is given as

$$R_i = 4.2/(2.6 + 1.0 + 1.1 + 1.1) = 0.54$$

Based on Eq. (19), soil erosion C losses were calculated as

$$E = E_A \times \%SOC \times CEF = 10 \times 0.01 \times 2 = 0.2 \text{ t ha}^{-1} \text{ yr}^{-1}$$

Changes in SOC stocks as a result of a shift from maize monoculture to *L. collinsii* improved fallows were quantified by a mass-balance equation Eq. (20) as follows:

$$\begin{aligned} \Delta SOC &= (SOC_a + A) - (E + L + M) \\ &= (35.6 + 4.2) - [0.2 + (4.2 \text{ X}.05) + (2.0 \times .85) + (2.2 \times 0.67)] \\ &= 0.6 \text{ t ha}^{-1}\text{yr}^{-1} \end{aligned}$$

Variables for each species were used to model representative PCI rates and tree C pools in fallows.

3.2.2 Modelled above and belowground carbon pools and fluxes in the tree phase

Figure 2 shows modelled PCI rates, and above- and below- ground C pools, derived from measured and modelled variables in Table 2. Modelled PCI rates (4.1 - 8.1 t ha^{-1} yr^{-1}) for nine tree species in the two-year-old tree phase in eastern Zambia (Table 2) were consistent with those (4.0-8.0 t ha^{-1} yr^{-1}) published for tropical agroforestry systems (Dixon, 1995). Similarly, modelled C stocks in aboveground tree biomass in two-year-old improved fallows (3.4 - 9.4 t ha^{-1}) were within the published range (1.5-12.5 t ha^{-1}) for agroforestry systems in Latin America (Kursten & Burschel, 1993) but lower than those (9.9-21.7 t ha^{-1}) published for 18-22-month old fallows in Kenya (Abrecht & Kandji, 2003). Differences between C stocks in this study and that in Kenya could be attributed to variations in soil and climatic conditions. However, the conceptual model reasonably estimated the PCI rates for, and C stocks in, tree biomass. The quantity of C in tree biomass and the PCI rate differ with tree species. In eastern Zambia, *Gliricidia, L. collinsii, Senna,* and *T. candida* fixed more C in above- and below-ground biomass than other species presumably because of differences between species and their adaptability to site characteristics (Table 2). Carbon sequestration in the tree phase could be increased by selecting superior tree species that are adapted to production sites.

With a modelled PCI rate of 0.7 t ha^{-1} yr^{-1}, weeds in the tree phase stored 0.8 t C ha^{-1} in aboveground biomass, while belowground sub-pools comprised root (0.3 t ha^{-1}) and extra root C (0.2 t ha^{-1} yr^{-1}) (Figure 2). The contribution of weeds to C cycling in improved fallows depended on the species and age of the trees. During the early stages of the tree phase, when the green area index of trees was low, weed density was high. However, after the tree canopy closed and litterfall commenced, the weed population declined probably because of the mulching effect of litter, increased competition for resources, and allellopathic effects of tree-derived organic residues (Sileshi et al., 2007).

Measured total SOC stocks in the soil surface layer (0-30 cm) in two-year-old tree fallows were estimated to be 36.5 t ha^{-1} (Figure 2). With modelled annual humic and erosion C losses estimated at 0.4 and 0.2 t ha^{-1} yr^{-1}, respectively, the modelled net annual assimilation rates of SOC stocks in the topsoil in two-year-old tree fallows was 0.7 t ha^{-1} yr^{-1} compared to 0.7-1.1 t ha^{-1} yr^{-1} in four-year-old non-coppicing fallows at Msekera (Kaonga and Coleman, 2008) and 0.6 t ha^{-1} yr^{-1} in a 10-year-old *Erythrina poeppigiana* alley cropping system in Costa Rica (Oelbermann et al., 2004), suggesting a close fit between modelled and published SOC accretion rates.

3.2.3 Modelled and measured carbon pools and fluxes in the cropping phase

Carbon pools and flows in the cropping phase are influenced mainly by the previous tree phase, and maize and weed biomass inputs. Based on harvest index and rhizodeposit fraction, and C stocks in maize crop residues and root biomass, the calculated PCI for maize in four-year old *Cajanus, Sesbania* and *Tephrosia* rotational fallows (Table 3) ranged from 4.7 to 7.2 t ha^{-1} yr^{-1}. The modelled rate for these fallows (5.4 t ha^{-1} yr^{-1}, Figure 3) was comparable to that (6.6 t ha^{-1} yr^{-1}) calculated for a 10-year-old *Erythrina poeppigiana* alley cropping in Costa Rica (Oelbermann et al., 2004). Differences between the modelled and measured PCI rates may be attributable to differences in age, climate, crop varieties, and approaches to crop biomass measurement.

			Modelled C (t ha^{-1} yr^{-1})		
	Aboveground biomass C	Surface litter	Root biomass	Extra root	PCI*
Treatment	(C_{AB}) (t ha^{-1})	(C_{lit}) (t ha^{-1} yr^{-1})	(C_R)	(C_{RD})	
A. angustissima	5.2	0.7	0.6	0.6	4.5
C. callothyrsus	4.8	0.6	0.5	0.5	4.0
G. sepium	8.2	1.0	1.0	1.0	7.1
L. collinsii	9.0	1.0	1.1	1.1	7.7
S. sesban	5.5	0.7	0.6	0.6	4.8
S. siamea	9.4	1.1	1.1	1.3	8.1
T. candida	7.2	0.9	0.9	0.9	6.2
T. candida 02971	8.9	0.8	1.1	1.1	7.4
T. vogelli	4.5	0.7	0.6	0.6	4.1
Mean	7.0	0.8	0.9	0.9	6.0

Table 2. Modelled tree legume C stocks and photosynthetic C intake (PCI) of the tree phase of fallows (2002/02) in Chipata, Zambia; PCI* = $[(C_{AB}/2) + [(C_{AB}/2) \times 0.35 \times 0.7)] + C_{lit} + C_{RD}$; C_R (0-30 cm depth) = $0.35 \times C_{AB} \times 0.70$; $C_{RD} = C_R$

The plant C pool in the cropping phase in eastern Zambia depends on mainly annual plants and the fate of aboveground biomass. Modelled annual C inputs to the soil consisted of maize crop residues (4.1 t ha^{-1} yr^{-1}) and weed biomass (1.4 t ha^{-1} yr^{-1}). The inputs increased

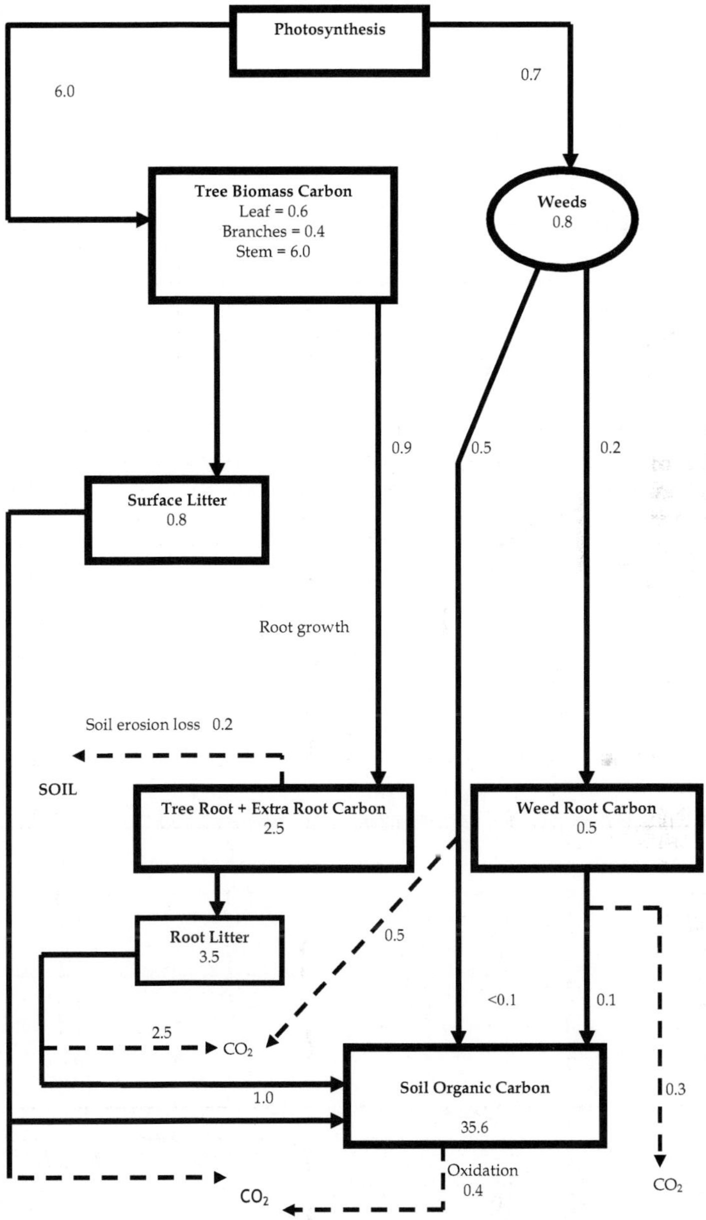

Fig. 2. A conceptual model of the carbon cycle in the tree phase of an improved fallow. Values are in kg C ha^{-1} and kg ha^{-1} yr^{-1}

		Annual C inputs and harvests (t C ha^{-1} yr^{-1})		
		C. cajanus	*S. sesban*	*T. vogelli*
Maize				
	Measured stover (C_{PR})	1.2	1.9	1.5
	Measured grain (C_{HB})	1.1	2.2	1.5
	Modelled root (C_R)	0.7	1.2	0.9
	Modelled rhozodeposit (C_{RD})	0.5	0.8	0.6
Weeds				
	Aboveground biomass (C_{AB})	0.8	0.8	1.1
	Modelled roots (C_R)	0.2	0.2	0.3
	Modelled rhizodeposit (C_{RD})	0.2	0.2	0.2
	Modelled PCI	4.7	7.2	6.1

Table 3. Measured and modelled annual plant C inputs to the soil, photosynthetic C uptake, and biomass C harvests from cropping phase of improved fallows in eastern Zambia

with C and nutrient supply to the soil. An increase of one tonne of SOC in degraded agricultural soils may increase maize crop yield by 10-20 kg ha^{-1} (Lal, 2004). Similarly, restoration of soil fertility using fertilizer trees increases maize biomass production (Mafongoya et al., 2006; Oelbermann et al., 2004). Considering modelled annual humic C inputs and losses, eroded C, and total SOC stocks estimated at 28.0 t ha^{-1} (Figure 3), the net annual SOC assimilation rate in the cropped phase was 0.3 t C ha^{-1} yr^{-1}. Carbon losses through harvested maize grain, estimated at 1.3 t C ha^{-1} yr^{-1} (Figure 3), have a profound effect on ecosystem C pools. In eastern Zambia, where livestock constitute a major component of improved fallows, the existing sequential land tenure system allows livestock to feed on maize stover in the fields. Farmers may also harvest crop residues for fuel or burn them to clear the fields during land preparation to reduce disease and pest infestation, and to return nutrients to the soil. The amount of crop residues returned to the soil depends on the maize variety, climate, soil conditions, agricultural practices, and land tenure.

3.2.4 Modelled and measured carbon pools and fluxes in intercropped phases

Figure 4 shows C pools and flows in intercropped fallows and PCI rates derived from measured and modelled variables in Table 4. In tree-maize intercropping, re-sprouting trees, maize crops and weeds constitute the plant C pool. Trees are periodically pruned and materials are incorporated into the soil as C and nutrient sources. Modelled PCI rates (1.5-3.7 t ha^{-1} yr^{-1}) for 10-year-old *L. leucocephala*, *G. sepium*, and *S. siamea* coppicing trees (Table 4) were consistent with those published for smallholder agroforestry systems (1.5-3.5 t ha^{-1} yr^{-1}) in the tropics [6,9] and tree fallows (1.4 - 4.3 t ha^{-1} yr^{-1}) in eastern Zambia (Sileshi et al., 2007). Modelled PCI rate for maize in coppicing fallows (5.0 t ha^{-1} yr^{-1}, Figure 4) was similar to that (6.6 t ha^{-1} yr^{-1}) calculated for maize in a 10-year-old *Erythrina poeppigiana* alley crop in Costa Rica.

Modelled PCI rates for the whole intercropped phase (7.4-9.4 t ha^{-1} yr^{-1}) were also comparable to published range (4.0-8.0 t ha^{-1} yr^{-1}) for other agroforestry systems (Dixon, 1995). Rates for individual plant species in intercropped phases were not as high as those of pure stands of trees and maize, but the rate for the whole system was either superior or comparable to those of sole cropped phases. Carbon uptake in intercropped phases can be very high because of sequestration by trees and crops (2.0 - 9 t ha^{-1} yr^{-1}) depending on tree rotation (Robert, 2001).

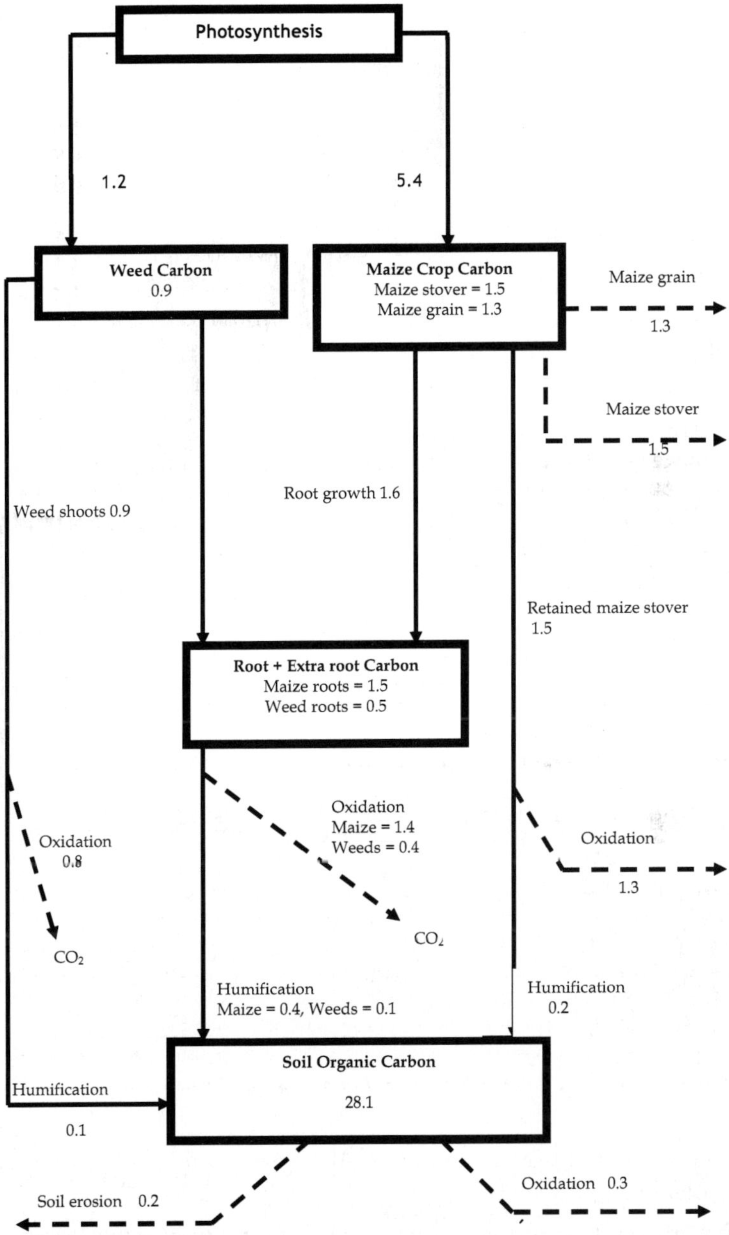

Fig. 3. A conceptual model of carbon cycling in the cropping phase of rotational improved fallows. Values are in kg C ha^{-1} and kg ha^{-1} yr^{-1}.

The maize crop in the intercropped phase in eastern Zambia had the highest PCI rate among plant C sub-pools possibly because high tree pruning intensity, two-three times in a cropping season, reduced total tree DM production. High pruning frequency reduces nodulation efficiency in N_2-fixing species and hence limits overall tree productivity (Chesney, 2000). Pruning intervals of one, two, or three months progressively reduced NPP compared with six monthly pruning (Duguma et al., 1988). In addition, competition for resources between trees and maize, and tree mortality with time can also contribute to reduced tree productivity. However, tree species significantly regulate the productivity of intercropped fallows through the quality and quantity of biomass produced. For example, *Senna* produced almost twice as much biomass as *Gliricidia*, but maize biomass production was still higher in *Gliricidia* than in *Senna* fallows, suggesting that *Gliricidia* produced high quality prunings that readily decomposed releasing nutrients for the maize crop.

	Annual C inputs and harvests (t C ha^{-1} yr^{-1})		
	G. sepium	*L. leucocephala*	*S. siamea*
Maize biomass C			
Measured stover (C_{PR})	1.5	1. 8	1.5
Measured grain (C_{HB})	1.8	1.9	1.6
Modelled root (C_R)	1.0	1.2	1.0
Modelled rhizodeposit (C_{RD})	0.7	0.7	0.6
Weed biomass C			
Aboveground biomass (C_{AB})	1.2	1.3	1.1
Modelled roots (C_R)	0.4	0.3	0.3
Modelled rhizodeposit (C_{RD})	0.2	0.3	0.2
Trees			
Measured prunings (C_{AB})	1.3	1.7	2.1
Modelled Root litter (C_{RD})	0.3	0.3	0.3
Modelled PCI	8.4	9.5	8.7

Table 4. Annual plant C inputs to the soil, photosynthetic C uptake, and biomass C harvests from the Tree-maize intercropped fallow in eastern Zambia

Trees, maize, and weeds constitute the principal sources of annual plant C inputs to the soil. Measured SOC stocks in intercropped fallows in eastern Zambia were estimated at 35 t ha^{-1}, with annual humic C loss of 0.4 t ha^{-1} yr^{-1}. Considering estimates of total SOC, humic C inputs and losses, and eroded C, the net C gain was 1.0 ha^{-1} yr^{-1}. Understanding of long-term C sequestration potential of the intercropped fallows requires studying tree biomass production patterns (as tree population decreases with increasing tree rotation) and biomass removal from the system. Substantial aboveground vegetal C stocks are harvested either as food, fuelwood, or fodder. The intercropped fallow loses C through harvested grain (1.8 t C ha^{-1} yr^{-1}) and tree stems (0.2 kg C ha^{-1} yr^{-1}), and through maize crop residues (1.6 t C ha^{-1} yr^{-1}), if they are removed from the field. In the long-term, SOC stocks in fallows depend on the quantity and quality of above- and below-ground plant residues added to the soil over many rotations.

Modelled PCI rates in improved fallows declined in the order: intercropped phase > cropped phase > tree phase, presumably because of differences in tree species and rotation. Re-sprouting trees in the intercropped phase increased maize biomass production. Net

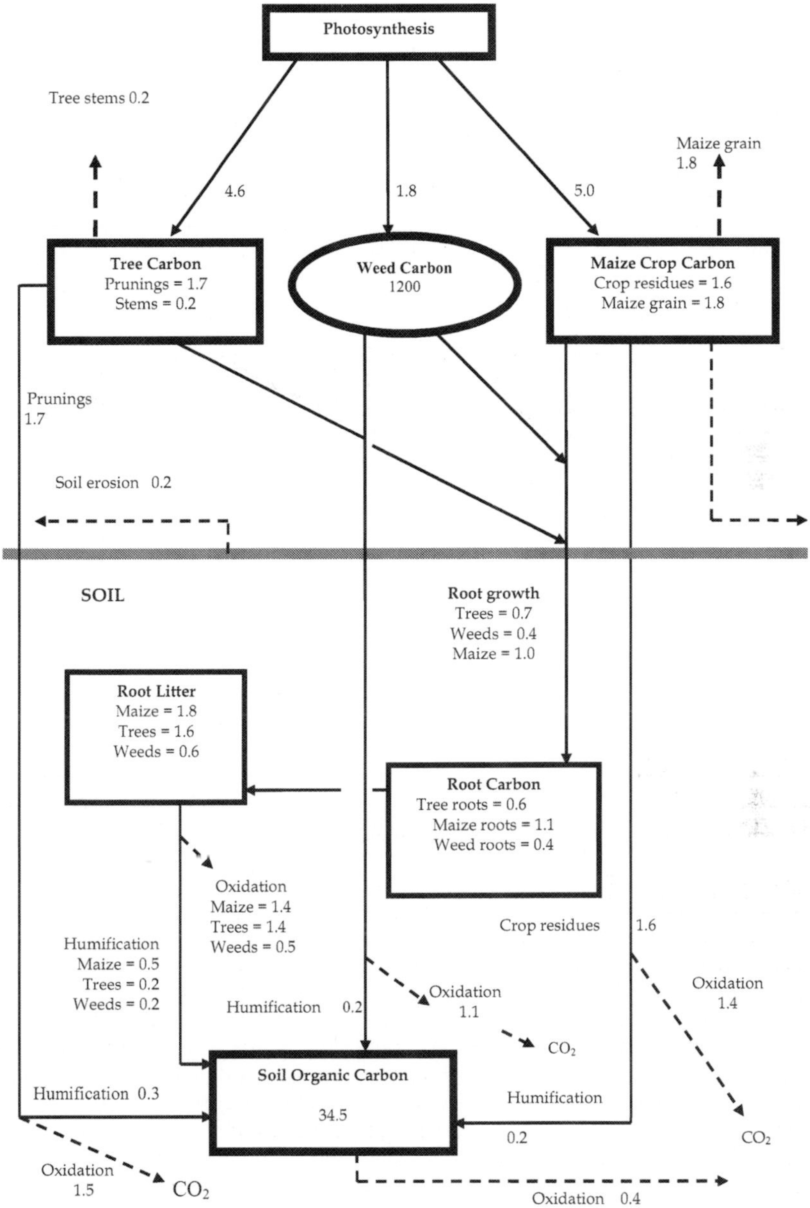

Fig. 4. A conceptual model of the carbon cycle in the tree-maize intercropping phase of a coppicing improved fallow. Values are in kg C ha^{-1} and kg ha^{-1} yr^{-1}

primary production of agroforestry systems is likely to be higher than those of crop-based, tree-based, and animal-based systems (Lal, 1995). However, the long-term sustainability of the system should be investigated.

Land-use change resulted in increased SOC stocks in tree-maize intercropping, tree, and cropping phases by 1.0, 0.7, and 0.3 t ha^{-1} yr^{-1}, respectively. Considering that these changes occur in the top soil, phases with more deeply rooted tree species are likely to deposit more C in the subsoil because of their deep root system (Jobaggy & Jackson, 2000). However, tree roots in the intercropped phase may be shallower than those in the tree phase because of pruning stress and the tendency of roots to be concentrated in the top soil as soil fertility improves. Further research into underground C dynamics in fallows is needed.

4. Conclusion

A conceptual model of carbon dynamics in improved fallows in the tropics is presented. It describes the major C pools and fluxes, ecosystem processes underpinning carbon dynamics, and ecosystem drivers and stressors. It represents a simplified approach to what is a complex biogeochemical cycle, but accounts for major ecosystem processes that determine C turnover in improved fallows to the extent that it can be used to develop practical C management strategies. This model provides a framework for describing the relationships between the various components of the C cycle, exploring possibilities for modification of organic C pools and for examining the consequences of various measures of C management options.

The model, using empirical and published plant and soil C data, estimated major plant and soil C pools in improved fallows, which were used to develop simplified carbon budgets of tree, cropped and intercropped phases of improved fallows. Modelled carbon pools were comparable to measured pools. The model has also revealed gaps in our understanding of C dynamics in improved fallows. Ecosystems stressors and drivers including climate change, atmospheric deposition (C and N fertilization), pest and diseases, natural disturbances, and herbivory, which ultimately reduce plant productivity, are not clearly understood. Similarly, data on soil erosion, underground plant C stocks, and DOC, the longevity of various C pools, and their response to regional climatic changes are needed. This model presents estimates as an initial approximation, recognizing that more reliable estimates emerging from further research can easily be incorporated in the model to improve its accuracy. However, this model provides a useful framework for designing agroforestry systems with a C sequestration function.

5. Acknowledgements

Authors are indebted to the Gates Cambridge Trust at Cambridge University for funding the study. We equally value the professional and logistical support provided by Dr P.L. Mafongoya, and staff of the Zambia/ICRAF Agroforestry Project in Zambia during our field studies.

6. References

Aber, J.D. & Melillo, J.M. (2001). Terrestrial Ecosystems. 2nd Ed. Harcourt Academic Press, London, England, ISBN 0-13-852444-0

Albrecht, A. & Kandji, S.T. (2003). Carbon sequestration in tropical agroforestry systems. Agriculture, Ecosystems & Environment, Vol.99, No.1, (October, 2003), pp. 15-27, ISSN: 01678809

Art, H.W. & Marks, P.L. (1971). A summary of table of biomass and net annual primary production in forest ecosystems of the world. IUFRO working group on Forest Biomass Studies, Life Sciences and Agricultural Experimental Station, pp.3-32, 1971, University of Florida, Gainnesville, USA

Bolinder, M.A.; Angers, D.A. & Dubuc, J.P. (1997). Estimating shoot to root ratio and annual carbon inputs in soils for cereal crops. Agriculture, Ecosystems and Environment, Vol.63, No.1, (May, 1997), pp. 61-66

Brady, N.C. & Weil, R.R. (1996).The Nature and Properties of Soils, Sixth Edition, Prince Hall International Editions, ISBN: 0-9641291-1-6. 2, London, England

Brown, S. (1997). Estimating Biomass and Biomass Change of Tropical Forests: a primer. FAO Forestry Paper, No.134, ISBN: 9789251039557, Rome, Italy

Brown, S.; Anderson, J.M., Woomer, P.L., Swift, M.J. & Barrios, E. (1994). Soil biological processes in tropical ecosystems. In: The Biological Management of Tropical Soil Fertility, P.L. Woomer and M.J. Swift (Eds.), John Wiley & Sons, ISBN-10: 0-471-95095-5, Chichester, England

Buyanovsky, G.A. & Wagner, G.H. (1986). Post-harvest residue input to crop land. Plant & Soil, Vol.93, No.1, (February, 1986), pp. 57-65

Canadell, J. G. & Raupach, M. R. (2008). Managing forests for climate change mitigation," Science, Vol. 320, No. 5882, (June, 2008), pp. 1456–1457, ISSN: 1155458

Chesney, P.E.K. (2000). Pruning effects on roots of nitrogen fixing trees in the humid tropics, Ph.D. Dissertation, CATIE, Turrialba, Costa Rica

Chintu, R.; Mafongoya, P.L., Chirwa, T.S. & Mwale, M. & Matibini, J. (2004). Subsoil nitrogen dynamics as affected by planted coppicing tree legume fallows in eastern Zambia. Experimental Agriculture Journal, Vol.40, No.3, (June, 2004), pp. 327–340

Dhyani, R.C. & Tripathi, R.S. (2000). Biomass and production of fine and coarse roots of trees under agrisilvicultural practices in north-east India, Agroforestry Systems, vol. 50, No,2, (November, 2000), pp. 107-121

Dixon, R.K. (1995). Agroforestry systems: Sources or sinks of greenhouse gases. Agroforestry Systems, Vol. 31, No.2, pp. 99-116

Duguma, B.; Kang, B.T. & Okali, D.U.U. (1988). Effect of pruning intensities of three woody leguminous species grown in alley cropping with maize and cowpea on an Alfisol, Agroforestry Systems, Vol. 6, No. 1, pp. 19-35

Falloon, P. & Smith, P. (2002). Simulating SOC changes in long-term experiments with RothC and Century: model evaluation for regional scale application," Soil Use Manage., vol. 18 no. 2, (January, 2006), pp. 101-111

Global Carbon Project, GCP (September, 2008). Global carbon emissions speed up, beyond IPCC projections. ScienceDaily, Available from http://www.sciencedaily.com/releases/2008/09/080925072440.htm

Heal, O.W.; Anderson J.M., & Swift, M.J. (1996). Plant litter quality and decomposition: An historical overview" in Driven by nature: Plant Litter Quality and Decomposition, G. Cadisch, K.E., Giller, Eds. Cab International, ISBN 9780851991450, Wallingford, England

Hudson, N. (1995). Soil and Water Conservation. B.T. Batsford Ltd., London, England

IPCC (November, 2000). Global perspective. In: IPCC special report on land use, land-use change and forestry, R.T. Watson, I.R. Noble, B. Bolin, N.H. Ravindranath & D.J. Vernado (Eds.), Available from http://www.grida.no/climate/ipcc/land_use

Jenkinson, D.S., Meredith, J., Kinyamario, J.I., Warren, G.P., Wong, M.T.F., Harkness, D.D., Bol, R. & Coleman, K. (1999). Estimating net primary production from measurements made on organic matter. Ecology, Vol.80, (December, 1999), pp. 2762-2773

Jobaggy, E.G. & Jackson, R.B. (2000). The vertical distribution of SOC and its relation to climate and vegetation. Journal of Ecological Applications, vol.10, No.2, (April, 200) pp. 423-436, ISSN 1051-0761

Kaonga, M. L. & Bayliss-Smith, T.P. (2010). Allometric models for estimation of aboveground biomass in improved fallows in eastern Zambia. Agroforestry Systems, Vol. 78, No.3, (July, 2010), pp. 217-232

Kaonga, M.L. & Bayliss-Smith, T.P. (2009). Carbon pools in tree biomass and the soil in improved fallows in eastern Zambia. Agroforestry Systems, Vol.76, No.1, (May, 2009), pp. 37-51

Kaonga, M.L. (2005). Understanding carbon dynamics in agroforestry systems in eastern Zambia. PhD Dissertation, Fitzwilliam College, Cambridge University, Cambridge, UK

Kaonga, M.L. and Coleman, K. (2008). Modelling soil organic turnover in improved fallows in eastern Zambia using the RothC model. Forest Ecology & Management, Vol.256, No.5, (August, 2008), pp. 1160-1166

Kumar V.S.K. & Tewari, V.P. (1999). Aboveground biomass tables for Azadrachta indica a. Juss. In: Sustainable Management of Soil Resources in Humid Tropics, R. Lal (Ed.), United Nations University, Tokyo, Japan

Kursten, E. & Burschel, P. (1993). CO_2 mitigation by agroforestry, Water Air & Pollution, Vol. 70, Nos.1-3, pp. 533-544

Kwesiga, F.; Phiri, D., Simwanza. C.P. (1994). Zambia-ICRAF Research Project Report No. 87, ICRAF, Nairobi, Kenya

Kwesiga, F.R.; Franzel, S., Place, F., Phiri D. & Simwanza, C.P. (1999). Sesbania sesban improved fallows in eastern Zambia: their inception, development, and farmer enthusiasm. Agroforestry. Systems, Vol.47, (December, 1999), pp. 49-66

Lal, R. (1995). Sustainable Management of Soil Resources in Humid Tropics, Tokyo: United Nations University

Lal, R. (2003). Soil erosion and the global carbon budget, Journal Environment International, vol. 29, No.5, (July, 2003), pp. 437-450

Lal, R. (2004). Modelling soil organic matter as affected by erosion, Environment International, vol. 30, No.4, (June 2004) pp. 547-556

Le Quéré, C.; Raupach, M.R., Canadell, J.G., et al. (2009). Trends in the sources and sinks of carbon dioxide. Nature GeoScicience, Vol. 2, No.12, (December, 2009), pp.831-836

Mafongoya, P.L.; Kuntashula, & Sileshi, G. (2006). Managing soil fertility and nutrient cycles through fertilizer trees in southern Africa. In: Biological Approaches to sustainable soil systems, N. Uphoff, A.S. Ball, E. Fernandes, H. Herren, O. Husson, M. Liang, C. Palm, J. Pretty, P. Sanchez, N. Sanginga & J. Thies (Eds.), pp. 274-289, Taylor and Francis, NY, USA

Mafongoya, P.L.; Nair P.K.R. & Dzowela, B.H. (1998). Mineralization of nitrogen from decomposing leaves of multipurpose trees as affected by their chemical composition. Biology & Fertility of Soils, Vol.27, (June, 1998), pp. 143-148

Montagnini, F. & Nair, P.K.R. (2004). Carbon sequestration: An underexploited environmental benefit of agroforestry systems. Agroforestry Systems, Vol.61, (July, 2004), pp. 281-295

Oelbermann, M., Voroney, R. & Gordon, A.M. (2004). Carbon sequestration in tropical and temperate agroforestry systems: a review with examples from Costa Rica and southern Canada. Agriculture, Ecosystems and Environment, Vol.104, (December, 2004), pp. 359-377

Paulstian, J.; Paustian, K., Elliot, E. T. & Combrink, C. (2000). Soil structure and organic matter: I. Distribution of aggregate-sized classes and aggregate-associated carbon. Soil Science Society of America Journal, Vol. 64, No.2, (March, 2000), pp. 681-689

Richter, J.; Lavine, M., Mace, K.A, Richter, D.D. & Schlesinger, W.H. (2000). Throughfal chemistry in a loblolly pine plantation under elevated CO2 concentrations. Biogeochemistry, Vol.50, (July, 2000), pp. 73-93

Robert, M. (2001). Soil carbon sequestration for improved land management, FAO, Rome, Italy

Sanchez, P.A. (1999). Improved fallows come of age in the tropics. Agroforestry Systems, Vol.47, (December, 1999), pp. 3-12

Sanchez, P.A. (2000). Linking climate change research with food security and poverty reduction in the tropics. Agriculture, Ecosystems & Environment, Vol.82, No.1, (December, 2000), pp. 371-383

Schumacher, B.A. (2002). Methods for determination of total organic carbon in soils and sediments, Environmental Science Division National Exposure Research Laboratory, EPA, Las Vegas, U.S.

Sileshi G. & Mafongoya, P.L. (2003). Effect of rotational fallows on abundance of soil insects and weeds in maize crops in eastern Zambia. Journal of Applied Soil Ecology, Vol.23, No.3, (July, 2003), pp. 211-222

Sileshi, G. & Mafongoya, P.L. (2006a). Long-term effects of legume-improved fallows on soil invertebrate and maize yield in eastern Zambia. Journal of Applied Soil Ecology, Vol.33, No.1, (August, 2006), pp. 49-60

Sileshi, G.; Akinnifesi, F.K., Ajayi, O., Chakaredza, S., Kaonga, M. & Matakala, P. (2007). Contributions of agroforestry systems in miombo ecoregion of eastern and southern Africa. African Journal of Environmental Science & Technology, Vol.1, No.4, (November, 2007) pp. 68-80

van Keulen, H. (2001). Tropical soil organic matter modeling: problems and prospects, J. Nutrient Cycling in Agroecosystems, (September, 2001), Vol. 61, Nos.1, pp. 33-39

Vose J.M. & Swank, W.T. (1990). A conceptual model of forest regrowth emphasizing stand leaf area. In: Process Modeling of Forest of Forest Growth Responses to Environmental Stress, R.K. Dixon, R.S. Mendhal, G.A. Ruark & W.G. Warren (Eds.). Portland, Timber Press, Oregon, USA, ISBN: 0881921521

Waring, R.H. & Schlesinger, W.H. (1995). Forest Ecosystems, Concepts and Management. Harcourt Academic Press, London, England

Wise, R. & Cacho, O. (1999). A bio-economic analysis of soil carbon sequestration in agroforests. Available from http://www.une.edu.au/febl/Econ/Carbon

Young, A. (1989). Agroforestry for Soil Conservation. CAB International, Oxford, England, ISBN 085198648X

Young, A. (1997). Agroforestry for Soil Management. CAB International, ISBN 0-85199-189-0, Oxford, England

Zomer, R.J.; Trabucco, A., Coe, R. & Place, F. (2009). Trees on Farm: Analysis of Global Extent and Geographical patterns of Agroforestry. ICRAF Working Paper no. 89, World Agroforestry Centre, Nairobi, Kenya

3

Drivers of Parasitoid Wasps' Community Composition in Cacao Agroforestry Practice in Bahia State, Brazil

Carlos Frankl Sperber[1], Celso Oliveira Azevedo[2], Dalana Campos Muscardi[3], Neucir Szinwelski[3] and Sabrina Almeida[1]
[1]*Laboratory of Orthoptera, Department of General Biology, Federal University of Viçosa, Viçosa, MG,*
[2]*Department of Biology, Federal University of Espírito Santo, Vitória, ES,*
[3]*Department of Entomolgy, Federal University of Viçosa, Viçosa, MG, Brazil*

1. Introduction

The world's total forest area is just over 4 billion hectares, and five countries (the Russian Federation, Brazil, Canada, the United States of America and China) account for more than half of the total forest area (FAO, 2010). Apart from their high net primary production, the world's forests harbour at least 50% of the world's biodiversity, which underpins the ecosystem services they provide (MEA, 2005). Primarily the plants, through their physiological processes, such as evapotranspiration, essential to the ecosystem's energy budget, physically dissipate a substantial portion of the absorbed solar radiation (Bonan, 2002), and sequester carbon from the atmosphere. The carbon problem, considered a trend concern around the world due to global warming (Botkin et al, 2007), can be minimized through the carbon sequestration by forests. Forests have the potential of stabilizing, or at least contributing to the stabilization of, atmospheric carbon in the short term (20–50 years), thereby allowing time for the development of more long-lasting technological solutions that reduce carbon emission sources (Sedjo, 2001).

Brazil's forests comprise 17 percent of the world's remaining forests, making it the third largest block of remaining frontier forest in the world and ranks first in plant biodiversity among frontier forest nations. However, deforestation, mainly due to land-use change, such as conversion of tropical forests to agricultural land, is one of the major threats to terrestrial biomes (Hoekstra, 2005). Globally, around 13 million hectares of forests were converted or lost through natural causes each year between 2000 and 2010. Brazil and Indonesia had the highest annual deforestation rates in the 1990s (FAO, 2010), and one of the most threatened ecosystems in Brazil is the tropical Atlantic Forest. Brazil has lost over 570,000 km^2 of its Amazonian forest.

The Atlantic Forest originally stretched from the Brazilian coastline to Argentina and Paraguay, including around 15% of Brazilian's territory (Rizzini, 1997). A significant portion of the original tropical Atlantic Forest currently supports about 50% of Brazil's human population, resulting in intense habitat degradation and fragmentation (Conde, 2006). Unfortunately, less then 7% of the original Atlantic Forest area is still intact (Tabarelli, 2005), being considered one of the world's 25 biodiversity hotspots due to high rate of conversion and the occurrence of thousands of endemic animals and plants (Myers, 2000). Moreover, most of the original Atlantic Forest areas were cleared and replaced by sugarcane, coffee plantations, cattle ranching, *Eucalyptus* monocultures and cacao plantations (Colombo, 2010). Intensive land use in this biome reduces diversity of several useful species, such as predators, parasitoids and other organisms that are responsible for ecosystem service of pest control, for example (Perfecto, 2004).

Recent emphasis on biodiversity conservation, taking into account the agricultural landscape that surrounds most remnants of tropical forest ecosystems, triggered a revival of agroforestry systems (Perfecto, 2008). Agroforestry systems arose as an important tool for conservation, as far as they provided a high quality matrix habitat for the organisms, allowing for migration among natural habitat and remnant ecosystems (Perfecto, 2008; Stenchly, 2011).

Agroforestry systems can be defined as a set of land-use systems and technologies where woody perennials (trees, shrubs, palms, etc.) are deliberately grown on the same land as agricultural crops and/or animals, in some form of spatial arrangement or temporal sequence. Agroforestry systems provide a variety of ecosystem services beyond the production of food, including nutrients recycling, regulation of microclimate and local hydrological processes, and suppression of undesirable organisms and detoxification of noxious chemicals (Altieri, 1999; Sileshi et al. 2007). Agroforestry systems consisting of traditional cultivars, such as coffee, cacao and banana, are a part of an ancient knowledge and practice (Miller, 2006). For example, planting coffee crops under shade trees in the semi-arid regions of Brazil to avoid extreme micro-climatic fluctuations dates back to the 19th century (Severino, 1999).

Brazil is among the countries in Latin America with the highest cacao (*Theobroma cacao* L., Sterculiaceae) yields (Franzen, 2007) with an estimated production area of 697,420 hectares (Clay, 2004). Most (98%) of Brazil's cacao is produced in Bahia State, northeastern Brazil. These cacao fields are established within the Atlantic Forest domain (Johns, 1999; Schroth, 2007). Cacao is an Amazonic native tree and was introduced in Bahia in the 18th century, causing a fragmentation of the native forest ecosystem, particularly during it's highest production eras, in the 1960's and 1970's (Delabie, 2007).

There are two main cacao management systems in Bahia State (Delabie, 2007): (i) the traditional management system, called *cabruca*, and (ii) the intensive management system, called *derruba total* (total clearing). The *cabruca* system involves planting cacao under a thinned forest canopy, using the native tree's canopy as shade (Greenberg 2000; Sperber, 2004: Franzen, 2007). The *derruba total,* developed in the last 50 years, involves complete clearance of the forest before cacao planting; cacao trees are shaded by introduced trees, planted afterwards. In this management system, the density of cacao plants is twice that attained in the *cabruca* system (Delabie, 2007). Obviously, this second method is not the most conservative for biodiversity because the native forest is completely destroyed, leading to habitat loss. Increased density of cacao plants has similar ecological impacts as other crop monocultures, especially those resulting from high crop density and low plant species richness. The introduction of a monoculture of shading trees, commonly *Erythrina* spp.

(Leguminosae: Papilionoideae) or *Hevea brasiliensis* (Wild.) Muell. - Arg. (Euphorbiaceae), generates overall landscape simplification.

The less management intensive cacao agroforestry system, *cabruca,* is considered a conservation management system because most native trees are maintained above the cacao crop. *Cabruca* allows the maintenance of endangered native tree species such as *Dalbergia nigra* (jacarandá), *Caesalpinia esplinata* (pau-brasil), and *Cariniana brasiliensis* (jequitibá), all important hardwood species (Johns, 1999). Therefore, *cabruca* management system supports high plant species richness and multi-strata structure similar to natural forest (Rolim, 2004; Saatchi, 2001). The fauna is also positively affected in *cabruca* management systems. For instance, the species richness of bats, birds, beetles, ants and a wide range of soil fauna is higher in *cabruca* (Bos, 2007; Delabie, 2007; Moco, 2009; Schroth, 2007) than in *derruba total.* In addition, *cabruca* is frequently visited by mammals, such as the endangered gold lion marmoset (*Leontopithecus rosalia*) (Johns, 1999), and thus can represent a potential habitat for endangered species, contributing to Atlantic Forest species conservation. *Cabruca* systems can work as ecological corridors, linking forest remnants, and allowing organisms' dispersion among habitats (Schroth, 2007). Furthermore, the use of native forest shading trees in *cabruca* systems provides for continuous litter deposition above the soil, affecting the soil's chemical, physical and biotic characteristics, leading to high levels of soil organic matter content and improving soil conservation (Moco, 2009).

Despite both cacao crop systems being less harmful to the environment than herbaceous monoculture crops, they are vulnerable to a large number of pest species. The economically most important pest is generated by a fungus - especially the one called "witches' broom disease", caused by *Moniliophthora perniciosa* and *Moniliophthora roreri* (Oliveira, 2005). Other cacao enemies, like herbivorous insects, can contribute to economic losses in cacao crops. In Brazilian cacao crops, important cacao herbivores are Lepidoptera (e.g. *Stenoma decora, Cerconota dimorpha*), Coleoptera (e.g. *Theoborus villosulus, Taimbezinhia theobromae*), Thysanoptera (e.g. *Selenotnnps rubrocinctus*) and Heteroptera (e.g. *Monalonion annulipes, Toxoptera aurantili*) (Silva-Neto, 2001). There is, also, a diverse insect fauna that has no economic impact or may, even, be beneficial to cacao farmers. Beneficial agents are insects responsible for pollination and pest control. Among pest control agents, there are insect predators, like ants (Delabie, 2007), and parasitoids that control caterpillars' populations (Silva-Neto, 2001).

In this context, the Hymenoptera wasps of the Parasitica series and Chrysidoidea superfamily, may have an important function as parasitoids of cacao pests. Wasps are part of the biodiversity associated to cacao crops, whose maintenance may be differentially linked to the two cacao management systems. Trees, which provide shade to the cacao crop as their direct function, may also attract and maintain wasps (indirect function) (Vandermeer, 1995). Besides, the maintenance of native forest trees may stabilize the microclimate along yearly seasonal changes, dampening insects' diversity and abundance fluctuations (Shapiro, 2000).

The Hymenoptera include more than 115,000 described species, but this is far from being a representative sample of the group's actual diversity (Hanson, 1995). Parasitoid wasps are one of the most species rich and abundant components of terrestrial ecosystems, and represent the highest species richness within the Hymenoptera (LaSalle, 1992). Parasitoids are insects whose larvae develop by feeding on the bodies of other arthropods, usually insects, causing the death of the parasitoid's host (Godfray, 1994) in most of the cases. They play a crucial role in natural pest population regulation (LaSalle, 1992). The world literature on the group is vast, and there was a huge effort to understand parasitoid community structure in Atlantic rain forests (Azevedo, 2000; Azevedo, 2002; Azevedo, 2003; Perioto, 2003; Perioto, 2005; Alencar, 2007; Gnocchi, 2010). We have some knowledge on the environmental drivers of parasitoid wasps' diversity in cacao agroforestry: parasitoid wasp's diversity responds to shading tree species richness and density, and these relationships are altered among seasons (Sperber, 2004). However, there is almost no understanding on the environmental drivers of parasitoid wasp's community composition in agroforestry systems. This work contributes to the understanding of the effect of agroforestry design on biodiversity and the ecosystem services provided by parasitoids. We present original results on the drivers of parasitoid wasps' (Hymenoptera of the Parasitica series and Chrysidoidea superfamily) community composition in cacao agroforestry systems in Brazilian Atlantic Forest.

We evaluated the following potential drivers of parasitoid community composition: (Fig. 1) (i) seasonality (summer *versus* winter *versus* spring); (ii) kind of disturbance ('*cabruca*' *versus* total clearing); (iii) amount of resource availability, estimated by shading tree density; (iv) resource amplitude availability, estimated by shading tree species richness; (v) resource amplitude availability, estimated by herbaceous species richness; (vi) resilience or habitat degradation, estimated by cacao plantation age; (vii) and regional species pool, estimated by cacao plantation area. We expect that the detection of environmental drivers of wasps' community composition may enhance our understanding of the mechanisms driving these organisms' ecology, and provide knowledge which sustainable crop management actions.

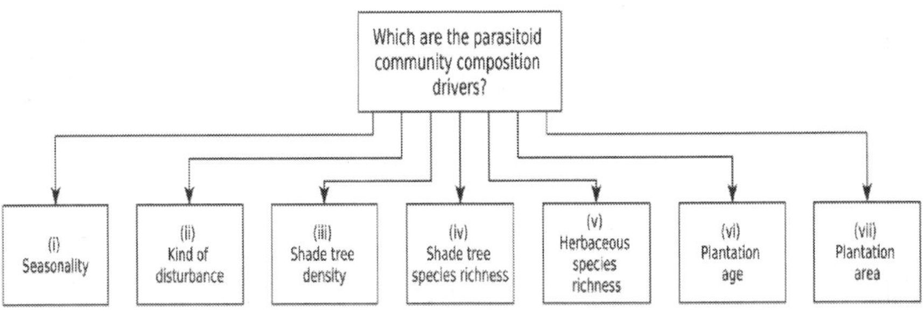

Fig. 1. Hypotheses of the drivers of parasitoid community composition in cacao plantation.

2. Materials and methods

2.1 Study site

The studied cacao plantations were located in Ilhéus, Bahia, Brazil (14°46′ S - 39°29′ W) within the Atlantic Forest ecosystem. Mean annual temperature is 24°C, with lowest temperatures (20°C monthly mean) in June to August (winter) and highest temperatures

(26°C monthly mean) in December to March (summer). Annual precipitation ranges from 2000mm to 2400mm near the coastline, and around 700mm in the hinterland (Santana, 2003).

We sampled 16 cacao agroforestry farms, with areas varying ranging from 16 to 80 ha. The farms were 20 to 60 years old (Table 1). Farm selection was arbitrary, priorizing replication of 'total clearing' management (n=5), and those *cabruca* farms where it was allowed to carry out the study (n=11). Distances between sampled farms ranged from 7 to 55 km. The shade tree species richness in sampled plantations varied from one (total clearing- native forest falling- with either *Erythrina fusca* or *Hevea brasiliensis*) to 22 tree species ha^{-1} (*cabruca* native forest canopy shading trees, Fig 2). Table 1 shows tree species (Lauraceae, Leguminosae, Meliaceae, Moraceae, Sapotaceae, and other, less common, plant families) in the sampled cacao farms. Herbaceous plant species richness was estimated by counting the number of species of herbs in a 1m x 1m plot, located in the core of each sampled 1-ha plot, within each sampled farm. Tree species richness was determined by counting all trees with canopy above the cacao plants, in each sampled 1-ha area. All trees with crowns which over-topped the cacao plants were included. Tree density was determined by counting the number of trees in each sampled 1-ha plot. Tree identification was confirmed by comparing field material with the herbarium collection of CEPLAC (Centro de Pesquisas da Lavoura Cacaoeira - Cacao Crop's Research Center). All collected materials were incorporated in the CEPLAC collection.

Farm	Kind of disturbance	Tree species richness	Plantation age	Area (ha)
1	total clearing	1	27	20
2	total clearing	1	24	18
3	total clearing	1	35	25
4	total clearing	1	40	20
5	total clearing	1	47	20
6	*cabruca*	9	30	50
7	*cabruca*	14	25	16
8	*cabruca*	15	28	80
9	*cabruca*	15	20	20
10	*cabruca*	15	60	20
11	*cabruca*	15	45	20
12	*cabruca*	16	25	60
13	*cabruca*	16	40	70
14	*cabruca*	18	45	20
15	*cabruca*	21	35	30
16	*cabruca*	22	25	20

Table 1. Management system, shading tree species richness, plantation age (years) and planation area of the studied cacao farms.

Fig. 2. Cacao plantation under cabruca management system, CEPLAC (Comissão Executiva do Plano da Lavoura Cacaueira) farm, Ilhéus, BA, Brazil. Photo: Pollyanna Santos.

2.2 Hymenoptera sampling

Each agroforestry farm was sampled using eight Malaise-Townes interception traps (Townes, 1972), erected on the ground for a 24h-period, along a 100m transect, in the core of a 1-ha plot, within each sampled farm. All sites were sampled three times during the year of 2001: summer (March), winter (August) and spring (November - December). The whole study involved an accumulated sampling effort of 16 sites x 8 traps x 3 seasons; two samples from *cabruca* were lost, resulting in 382 sampling days. Since our aim was not to detect area effects (Schoereder et al. 2004), we uniformly sampled farms to avoid sampling effects on diversity estimation (Hill et al., 1994). Parasitoid diversity was estimated as the number of Parasitica and Chrysidoidea (Hymenoptera) families, which are mostly (>95%) parasitoids, and contain most of the hymenopterous parasitoids (Goulet & Huber, 1993). Hymenoptera families were identified using the taxonomic keys provided by Goulet & Huber, (1993) and Gibson et al., (1997). We worked at the family level due to lack of information about taxonomy of genus and species of parasitoids in tropical regions (LaSalle, 1992).

2.3 Data analyses

2.3.1 Parasitoid community composition

To evaluate the effects of selected environmental drivers on parasitoid family composition, we performed longitudinal data analyses for repeated measures, adjusting generalized linear mixed models (GLMM), with binomial errors. Sampling date (March, August and November - December) was adjusted as repeated measure, and sampling site (n=16) as grouping random factor. The use of mixed effects models, adjusting sampling site as random effect, enabled avoidance of pseudo-replication (Crawley, 2007).

We used occurrence in each Malaise trap at each site (n = 128), per sampling date, as binary response variable. Binary logistic analyses are not subject to overdispersion, are robust to zero-inflated data (Zuur, 2009) and the results are more conservative, in comparison to abundance as response variable. Family identity was adjusted as fixed effect, together with the tested environmental variable and an interaction term.

2.3.2 Testing the environmental drivers

To evaluate if any of the environmental variables, presented in Figure 1, worked as drivers of parasitoid comumnnity composition, we adjusted separate statistical models for each variable. A significant effect of an environmental variable on community composition should lead to significance of the interaction term between the environmental variable and the factor 'parasitoid family identity'. Similarly, a significant interaction between a family identity level and an environmental variable should result from differences in the response of wasps families' occurrence to the environmental variable. For example, whereas the occurrence of some families increased with increasing values of the environmental variable, other families' occurrence decreased.

Significance was evaluated by model comparison, deleting non-significant fixed effects (Crawley, 1993). Models were further simplified by amalgamating factor levels, using contrast analyses. To detect which factor levels could be amalgamated, we fitted generalized linear models (GLM), with binomial errors, not considering pseudoreplication, and used the "coms.R" procedure from the RT4Bio package, developed by Ronaldo Reis Jr. (Unimontes, Montes Claros, MG, Brazil). Amalgamation suggested by GLM was tested adjusting the corresponding GLMM. When the substitution of the current by the simplified model did not alter significantly model deviance, we accepted the simplification (Crawley, 2007). Families whose responses were amalgamated within the same factor levels (groups) presented similar occurrence levels and responses to the tested environmental variable.

Seasonality (i) and kind of disturbance (ii) where adjusted as categorical (=nominal) explanatory vairables. Amount of resource availability (iii), resource amplitude availability (iv and v), resilience or habitat degradation (vi), and regional species pool (vii) were adjusted as continuous explanatory variables.

Categorical environmental variables were analyzed through two-way binary logistic analyses of variance (ANOVA); continuous environmental variables (shading tree density, shading tree species richness, plantation age, herbaceous species richness, plantation area), were analyzed through binary logistic analyses of covariance (ANCOVA).

To evaluate if composition was altered by kind of disturbance, we used the whole set of observations (each observation corresponds to the presence or absence of each family, in each trap; n.obs. = 11,460; n.groups = 16). If there was significant effect of kind of disturbance on parasitoid family composition, we tested the remaining environmental variables separately within each kind of disturbance (*cabruca*: n.obs. = 7,860; n.groups = 11); '*derruba total*': n.obs. = 3,360; n.groups = 5). We analyzed the effects of tree density and cacao plantation area, exclusively within *cabruca* management system, as far as total clearing management involved only two tree densities (250 and 476 trees per ha) and three plantation areas (18, 20 and 25ha), whereas in the *cabruca* management systems, there were sites with eleven different tree densities (30 - 137 trees per ha) and seven different plantation areas (16, 20, 30, 50, 60, 70, 80). Effects of shade tree species richness were evaluated exclusively among *cabruca* sites.

Although we considered 5% level of significance, we presented the exact p-values for all analyses, as reccomended by Iacobucci (2005), among others. To visualize the effects of the environmental drivers on the parasitoid wasps' community composition, we plotted the amalgamated families groups' occurrence means (procedure 'interaction plot' within R) of the minimal adequate models. Information criteria indices (Akaike Information Criteria - AIC, and Bayesian Information Criteria - BIC) were used to compare alternative explanatory models. The smallest AIC and BIC values indicated better models (Crawley, 2007). All statistical analyses were done under R (R Development Core Team, 2010).

3. Results

3.1 Parasitoid community composition

We collected a total of 21,346 individuals, of 30 families (Table 2), 16,567 in *cabruca* and 4,779 in 'total clearing' management. Individuals in the Platygastroidea taxa were the most abundant, while those in the Evanioidea family were the least abundant. Two parasitoid families were exclusive of *cabruca*: Gasteruptiidae and Liopteridae.

Taxa	Abundance
Ceraphronoidea	**1049**
Ceraphronidae	983
Megaspilidae	66
Cynipoidea	**1793**
Figitidae	1792
Liopteridae	1
Chalcidoidea	**5019**
Agaonidae	27
Aphelinidae	242
Chalcididae	326
Eucharitidae	12
Encyrtidae	1083
Eulophidae	801
Eupelmidae	136
Eurytomidae	69
Mymaridae	1406
Perilampidae	9
Pteromalidae	368
Signiphoridae	145
Torymidae	53
Trichogrammatidae	342
Chrysidoidea	**1369**
Bethylidae	1178
Chrysididae	57
Dryinidae	104
Sclerogibbidae	24
Evanioidea	**287**
Evaniidae	281
Gasteruptiidae	6
Ichneumonoidea	**3952**

Taxa	Abundance
Braconidae	1921
Ichneumonidae	2031
Platygastroidea	**6486**
Platygastridae	6486
Proctotrupoidea	**1400**
Diapriidae	1130
Monomachidae	99
Proctotrupidae	168

Table 2. Number of individuals of Hymenoptera Parasitica series and Chrysidoidea superfamily in sampled cacao agroforestry systems.

3.2 Evaluation of environmental drivers

3.2.1 Seasonality

Community composition differed among seasons (Figure 3), both for 'total clearing' management ($p < 0.0001$) and *cabruca* shade trees management ($p < 0.0001$). Parasitoid taxa could be amalgamated to a minimum of 11 levels in 'total clearing' (Groups A - K, in Figure 4, and 16 levels in *cabruca* (Groups A - P, in Figure 5) cacao systems. Season levels could not be amalgamated.

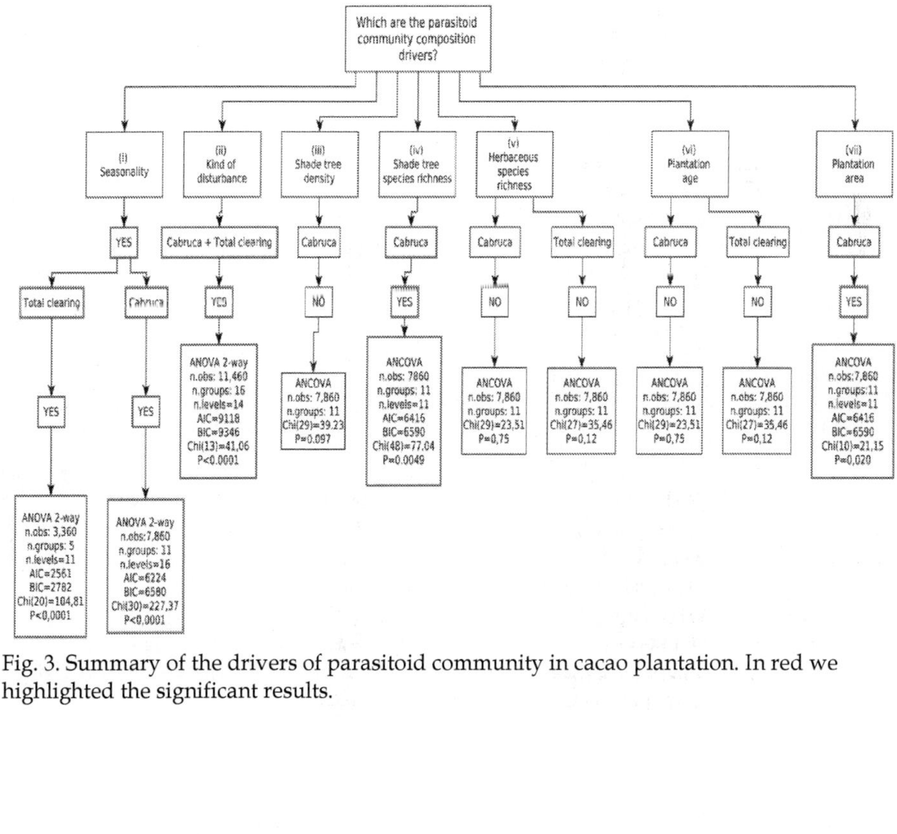

Fig. 3. Summary of the drivers of parasitoid community in cacao plantation. In red we highlighted the significant results.

In 'total clearing' management system, only the parasitoid families Ichneumonidae + Platygastridae did not respond to season (Figure 4, Group A). Most families presented lowest occurrence in winter and highest abundance in summer (Figure 4, Groups B, C, D, E, F, G, H), whereas two wasp families - Proctotrupidae and Monomachidae - presented highest occurrence in winter (Figure 4, Groups I and K). Agaonidae + Eucharitidae + Perilampidae + Sclerogibbidae + Torymidae + Chrysididae (Group J, Figure 4) presented lowest occurrence in both winter and spring.

In *cabruca*, Platygastridae, Figitidae, and Eulophidae were most abundant in spring (Figure 5, Groups A, C, E), while two of them (Platygastridae and Figitidae - were least abundant in summer (Figure 5, Groups A, C). As in 'total clearing', individuals in Proctotrupidae and Monomachidae taxa were observed in largest numbers in winter (Figure 5, Groups J, N) than in other seasons. There were no significant differences in abundance of Braconidae + Ichneumonidae, Encyrtidae + Ceraphronidae, and Gasteruptiidae + Liopteridae + Perilampidae + Eucharitidae (Figure 5, Groups B, F, O) across seasons. Other parasitoid families were least abundant in winter, and most abundant in summer (Figure 5, Groups D, G, H, I, K, L, M, P).

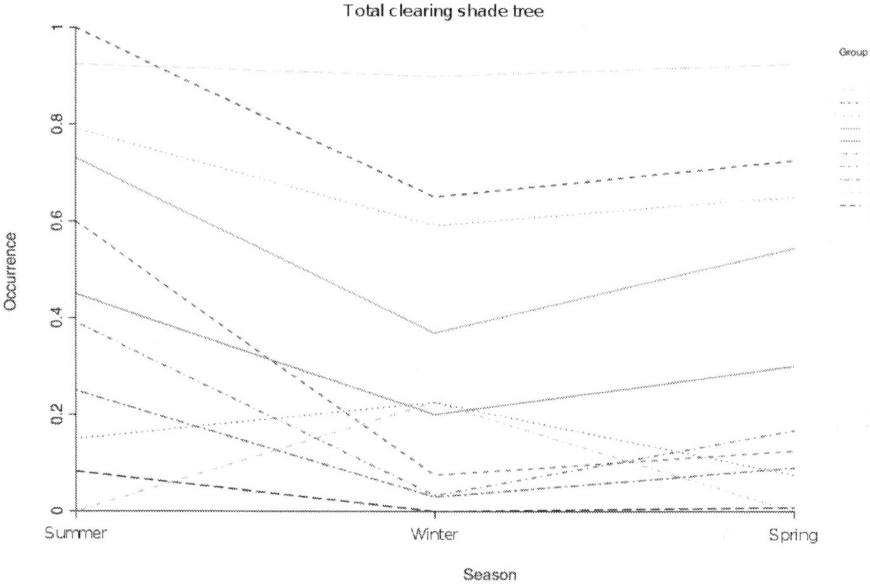

Fig. 4. Changes in occurrence (p < 5%, mean of presence (1)/absence (0) per trap) of parasitoid families in monospecific 'total clearing' shading trees' cacao management, along three seasons. Groups are A: Ichneumonidae + Platygastridae, B: Braconidae, C: Bethylidae + Mymaridae + Figitidae , D: Encyrtidae + Ceraphronidae + Eulophidae + Diapriidae, E: Trichogrammatidae, F: Dryinidae + Aphelinidae + Chalcididae, G: Pteromalidae, H: Eurytomidae + Ceraphronidae + Eulophidae + Diapriidae, I: Proctotrupidae, J: Agaonidae + Eucharitidae + Perilampidae + Sclerogibbidae + Torymidae + Chrysididae, K: Monomachidae.

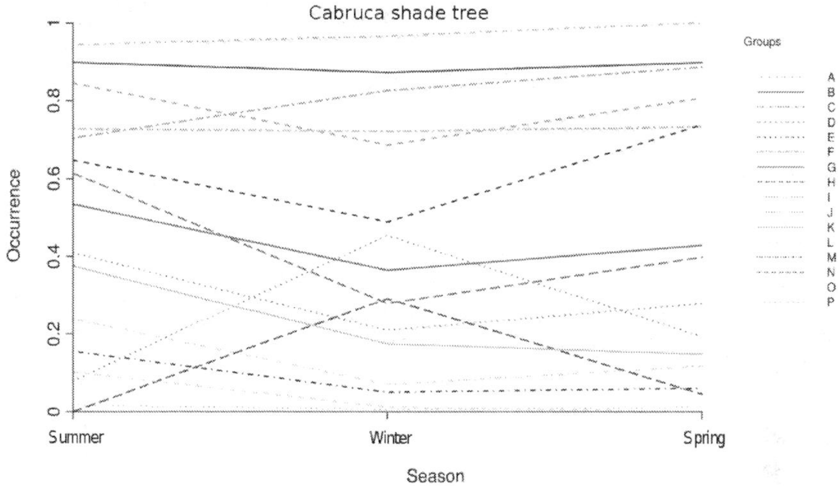

Fig. 5. Changes in occurrence (p < 5%; mean of presence (1)/absence (0) per trap) of parasitoid families in *cabruca* shading trees' cacao management across seasons. Groups are A: Platygastridae, B: Braconidae + Ichneumonidae, C: Figitidae, D: Mymaridae + Bethylidae + Diapriidae, E: Eulophidae, F: Encyrtidae + Ceraphronidae, G: Pteromalidae + Trichogrammatidae + Evaniidae, H: Chalcididae, I: Aphelinidae + Eupelmidae, J: Proctotrupidae, K: Signiphoridae, L: Torymidae + Eurytomidae + Dryinidae. M: Agaonidae + Chrysididae + Megaspilidae, N: Monomachidae, O: Gasteruptiidae + Liopteridae + Perilampidae + Eucharitidae, P: Sclerogibbidae.

3.2.2 Kind of disturbance

Parasitoid family composition differed between cacao management systems (p < 0.0001, Figure 3). Parasitoid taxa could be amalgamated to a minimum of 14 levels (Groups A - N, in Figure 6). Whereas Ichneumonidae and Dryinidae were more abundant in 'total clearing' management (Groups A and H, in Figure 6), other parasitoid families were less abundant in 'total clearing' management (see Groups C, D, F, G, I and J, in Figure 6). Platygastridae, Eucharitidae + Sclerogibbidae, and Gasteruptiidae + Liopteridae + Perilampidae did not differ significantly (p > 0.0001) between systems (Groups A, L and N, in Figure 6).

3.2.3 Shade tree density and plant species richness

Shade tree density had no significant effect on parasitoid community composition (p=0.097). Shade tree species richness affected parasitoid community composition (p = 0.0049; Figure 7). Parasitoid taxa could be amalgamated to a minimum 11 levels (Groups A - K, in Figure 7). The abundance of Aphelinidae + Chalcididae + Trichogrammatidae + Evaniidae + Pteromalidae, Agaonidae + Megaspilidae + Chrysididae + Monomachidae, and Gasteruptiidae + Liopteridae + Eucharitidae + Perilampidae, increased with increasing tree species richness (Figure 7, Groups F, I, K); other families decreased in their occurrence with increasing tree species richness (Figure 7, Groups A - E, G, H, J). Herbaceous plant species richness had no effect on parasitoid community composition in both agroforestry systems (p = 0.058).

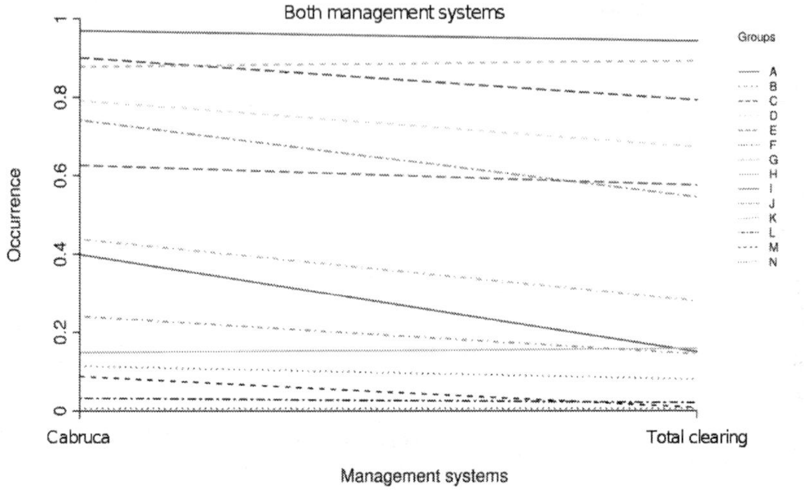

Fig. 6. Effect of cacao management system (cabruca versus 'total clearing') on the occurrence (mean of presence (1)/absence (0) per trap) of parasitoid families in both cacao management systems. Groups are A: Platygastridae, B: Ichneumonidae, C: Braconidae, D: Mymaridae + Diapriidae + Figitidae, E: Eulophidae, F: Encyrtidae + Ceraphronidae + Bethylidae, G: Chalcididae + Trichogrammatidae + Pteromalidae, H: Dryinidae, I: Aphelinidae + Evaniidae, J: Signiphoridae + Proctotrupidae + Eupelmidae, K: Megaspilidae + Chrysididae + Monomachidae + Torymidae + Eurytomidae, L: Eucharitidae + Sclerogibbidae, M: Agaonidae, N: Gasteruptiidae + Liopteridae + Perilampidae.

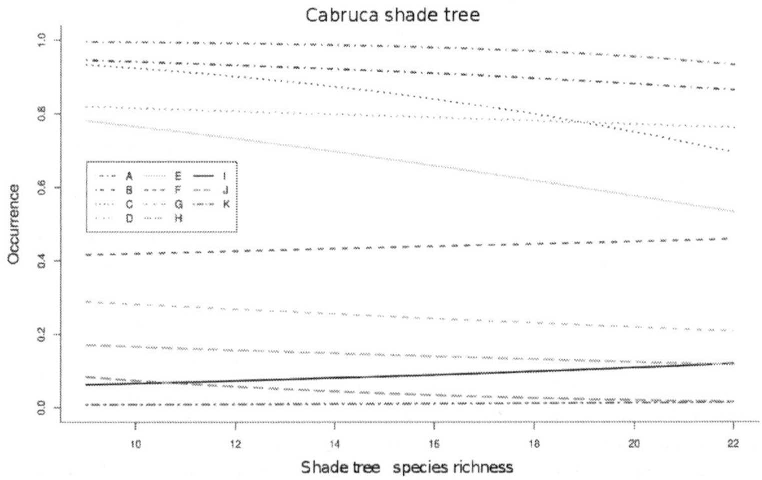

Fig. 7. Effect of shading tree species richness on the occurrence (mean of presence (1)/absence (0) per trap) of parasitoid families in cabruca shading trees' cacao management.

Groups are A: Platygastridae, B: Ichneumonidae + Braconidae, C: Figitidae, D: Encyrtidae + Ceraphronidae + Mymaridae + Bethylidae + Diapriidae, E: Eulophidae, F: Aphelinidae + Chalcididae + Trichogrammatidae + Evaniidae + Pteromalidae, G: Signiphoridae + Proctotrupidae + Eupelmidae, H: Torymidae + Dryinidae + Eurytomidae, I: Agaonidae + Megaspilidae + Chrysididae + Monomachidae, J: Sclerogibbidae, K: Gasteruptiidae + Liopteridae + Eucharitidae + Perilampidae.

3.2.4 Cacao plantation age and area

Cacao plantation age did not significantly affect parasitoid community composition in both 'total clearing' ($p = 0.12$) and *cabruca* ($p = 0.75$) shade tree management systems. By contrast, cacao plantation area significantly affected parasitoid community composition ($p = 0.020$; Figure 8). Parasitoid taxa could be amalgamated to a minimum 11 levels (Groups A - K, in Figure 8). The abundance of most parasitoid families increased with increasing plantation area (Figure 8, Groups A - C, E - H, J). The abundance of Ceraphronidae and Agaonidae + Megaspilidae + Chrysididae (Groups D and I, in Figure 8) decreased with increasing plantation area, whereas the abundance of Gasteruptiidae + Liopteridae + Perilampidae (Group K, in Figure 8) was not significantly affected by plantation area.

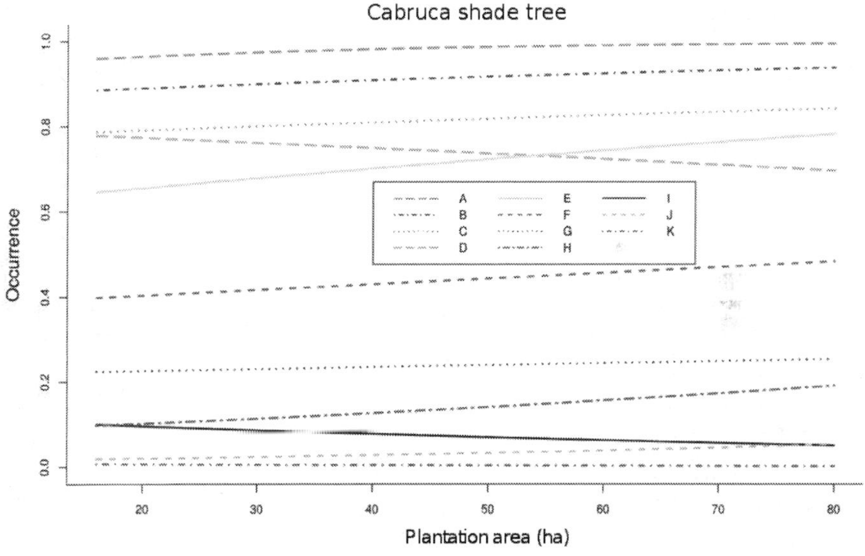

Fig. 8. Effect of cacao plantation area (ha) on the occurrence (mean of presence (1)/absence (0) per trap) of parasitoid families in cabruca shading trees' cacao management. Groups are A: Platygastridae, B: Ichneumonidae + Braconidae, C: Mymaridae + Bethylidae + Diapriidae + Figitidae, D: Ceraphronidae, E: Eulophidae + Encyrtidae, F: Aphelinidae + Chalcididae + Trichogrammatidae + Evaniidae + Pteromalidae, G: Signiphoridae + Proctotrupidae + Eupelmidae, H: Monomachidae + Torymidae + Dryinidae + Eurytomidae, I: Agaonidae + Megaspilidae + Chrysididae, J: Eucharitidae + Sclerogibbidae, K: Gasteruptiidae + Liopteridae + Perilampidae.

Management system, seasonality, shade tree species richness and plantation area affected parasitoid community composition (Figure 3). For *cabruca* management system, we were able to compare the effects of alternative environmental Drivers - seasonality, tree species richness and plantation area - by comparing the information criteria values of the alternative models. The best models, depicted by the lowest AIC and BIC values, were those for tree species richness and plantation area, which presented exactly the same AIC and BIC values (Figure 3).

4. Discussion

In our statistical approach, we avoided the use of multivariate analyses, as commonly recommended for community composition studies (Hammer, 2001). The multivariate approach considers each taxon's occurrence as one dimension of a multidimensional 'entity', which would represent the ecological community (Manly, 1986; Harris, 2001). An assumption that is implicit in such an approach is that the set of studied taxa represents an actual interacting community. The multivariate approach would evaluate if the 'shap' of this abstract 'entity' differs among factor levels (e.g. non-metric multidimensional scaling - NMDS), or along a continuous variable's variation (e.g. multivariate regression). With our approach, we do not require such an abstract entity. Each taxon varies as a separate response variable, but this variation is not independent. In inserting 'sample site' as the random effect, we include a correlation structure for the errors (Zuur, 2009), such that sites with a high wasp occurrence will not generate a false effect related to more abundant wasp taxa in this site. Such an approach allowed us to attain a high statistical power, as depicted by the contrast between the amalgamation results obtained with pseudo-replicated GLM and the significant contrasts in GLMM analyzes. Furthermore, the amalgamation of family identity levels allowed us to distinguish families with differing occurrence levels, from those with similar occurrences, and the analyses of the 'interaction plots' allowed us to visualize and compare the different responses of community composition to each environmental driver. Therefore, we think our approach permits less stringent assumptions on the existence of interactions among the components of the assumed ecological community.

We separated the parasitoid wasps' families into groups of differing frequencies and responses to the environmental drivers. Whereas responses among some of these groups were different, responses for some of the parasitoid families could not be distinguished. A higher parasitoid family richness in both cacao management systems than found in natural Atlantic rain forest areas was evident. In four studies carried out in preserved forest areas, in the Espírito Santo state, an average of 28 families of parasitoid wasps was found (Azevedo, 2000; Azevedo, 2002; Azevedo, 2003; Alencar, 2007). In forest areas impacted by human activities, this number falls down to 19, as found by Perioto et al. (2000); Perioto, Lara, Santos & Selegatto (2002); Perioto, Lara, Santos & Silva (2002) in intensive management agroecosystems (soybean, cotton and coffee), suggesting that the current cacao agroforestry systems has a high conservation role for the parasitoid fauna.

Cacao plantations also keep the relative abundance of the families of parasitoid wasps. Platygastridae, Braconidae, Ichneumonidae, Diapriidae, Bethylidae and Figitidae are usually abundant families in native forest, as we found in cacao plantations. For instance, Bethylidae is an uncommon family in intensive management agroecosystems, such as soybean, cotton and coffee, probably because these agroecosystems do not preserve the soil structure, as

Bethylidae are parasitoids of insects which depend somehow on the litter (Mugrabi, 2008). Intensive management of agroecosystems attracts less species and families of parasitoid wasps from the neighborhoods, which results in lower parasitoid family richness than in cacao plantations. For instance, according to Perioto et al., (2002), 54.2% of the total of parasitoid wasps in soybean crop belonged to three genera, *Telenomus, Trissolcus* and *Copidosoma*; the two formers are Platygastridae, known as parasitoids of soybean bugs (*Nezara viridula, Piezodorus guildinii* and *Euschistus heros*), and the latter is an Encyrtidae known as parasitoid of soybean defoliator. This means that cacao plantation is better to conserve parasitoid fauna when compared to other crops cited above.

Although both cacao management systems sustained high parasitoid diversity, we detected that total clearing, followed by monospecific shading tree plantation, alters parasitoid wasps' community composition, in comparison to the more conservative *cabruca* management. Overall, frequency of the parasitoid families diminished, suggesting lower resource availability in these more intensively managed systems.

We detected an effect of seasonality on both 'total clearing' and *cabruca* shade tree systems, but changes in the more intensive management system were more pronounced. This may result from a higher denpendency of immigration from neighboring forest areas to the more intensely managed 'total clearing' system, especially in winter. In contrast, the less altered *cabruca* habitat seemed to have a dampening effect on parasitoid occurrence. The higher availability of resource types in *cabruca* may be involved in this dampening, like that expected by the portfolio effect (Figge, 2004; Schindler, 2010).

Although insect seasonality has been studied for a long time, it is not settled which seasonal factors drive Hymenoptera communities, particularly in the tropics (Shapiro, 2000). Factors that affect these communities include host availability, adult food resource, habitat type and climate (English-Loeb, 2003; Tylianakis, 2004; Hoehn, 2008). In tropical forests, temperature varies little throughout the year, contrasting to the wide variation in rainfall and moisture, which explains the major importance of moisture as a key factor driving parasitoid wasps' community composition (Shapiro, 2000). Although the available studies on the effects of seasonality on Hymenoptera in the tropics have no replication of seasons among years (Shapiro, 2000; Sperber, 2004), both point to the conclusion that seasonality alters Hymenoptera communities.

In this study, most families' occurrence decreased during winter. However, two families of Proctotrupoidea - Monomachidae and Proctotrupidae - were most prevalent in winter. Monomachidae are often found during the winter time (Azevedo, 2001), in high altitudes or early in the morning (Masner, 1996). The Proctotrupidae are more abundant in high moisture and elevated areas (Masner, 1996). Both families are typical of low temperature areas, within the Neotropical region. The findings of this study were consistent with those published previously for these ecosystems.

The shade tree species richness altered the parasitoid composition mostly because the frequency of uncommon families increased and the frequency of common families decreased with shading tree species richness. This means that rare families benefited, probably because higher tree species richness enables more niches for those parasitoid species which are host species-specific. One example that supports such argument is Agaonidae. Members of Agaoninae are the fig-wasps which act as pollinators of the internal fig flowers (the syconium) (Gibson, 1993), so the more fig-tree species, the more Agaoninae species and the more their abundance. The size of plantation area also altered the parasitoid composition, probably because an increase in *cabruca* plantation area correlates to increase in available shade tree species richness, especially as far as parasitoids are good flyers, being able to explore large plantation areas. The convergence of statistical models' AIC and BIC of plantation area and shade tree species richness supports this assertion.

5. Conclusion

Our results showed that cacao agroforestry provides suitable habitat for parasitoid communities. The drivers of parasitoid community composition include seasonality, kind of disturbance, shade tree species richness and plantation area, ranging from local spatial scale, at the farm's management system, through regional spatial scale, at the cacao plantation area. Further, our result highlight temporal (seasonal), categorical (management system) and continuous (tree species richness and plantation area) environmental drivers.

6. Acknowledgement

We thank CNPq, CAPES and Fapemig, for financial support, Comissão Executiva do Plano da Lavoura Cacaueira (CEPLAC) Ilhéus, for institutional support. We especially thank Kazuo Nakayama for managing all field expeditions, sorting laboratory labor and gently providing the data. We would like to thank the editor for the invitation.

7. References

Alencar, I., Fraga, F., Tavares, M. & Azevedo, C. (2007). Perfil da fauna de vespas parasitóides (Insecta, Hymenoptera) de uma área de Mata Atlântica do Parque Estadual de Pedra Azul, Domingos Martins, Espírito Santo, Brasil, Arquivos do Instituto Biológico Vol. 74(No. 2): 111–114. ISSN: 0020-3653.

Altieri, M. A. (1999). The ecological role of biodiversity in agroecosystems, Agriculture, Ecosystems and Environment Vol. 74(No. 1): 19–31. ISSN: 0167-8809.

Azevedo, C. & Santos, H. (2000). Perfil da fauna de himenópteros parasitóides (Insecta, Hymenoptera) em uma área de Mata Atlântica da reserva biologica de duas bocas, Cariacica, ES, Brasil, Boletim do Museu de Biologia Mello Leitão Vol. 11/12(No. 1): 117–126. ISSN: 0103-9121.

Azevedo, C. & Santos, H. (2001). Seasonality of Monomachus Klug (Hymenoptera, Monomachidae) in the biological reserve of duas bocas, Espírito Santo state, Brazil, Revista Brasileira de Zoologia Vol. 18(No. 2): 395–398. ISSN: 0085-5626.

Azevedo, C., Corrêa, M., Gobbi, F., Kawada, R., Lanes, G., Moreira, A., Redighieri, E., Santos, L. & Waichert, C. (2003). Perfil das famílias de vespas parasitóides (Hymenoptera) em uma área de Mata Atlântica da estação biológica de Santa Lúcia, Santa Teresa, ES, Brasil, Boletim do Museu de Biologia Mello Leitão Vol. 16(No. 1): 39–46. ISSN: 0103-9121.

Azevedo, C., Kawada, R., Tavares, M. & Perioto, N. (2002). Perfil da fauna de himenópteros parasitóides (Insecta, Hymenoptera) em uma área de Mata Atlântica do Parque Estadual da Fonte Grande, Vitória, ES, Brasil, Revista Brasileira de Entomologia Vol. 46(No. 2): 133–137. ISSN: 0085-5626.

Bos, M., Steffan-Dewenter, I. & Tscharntke, T. (2007). The contribution of cacao agroforests to the conservation of lower canopy ant and beetle diversity in Indonesia, Biodiversity and Conservation Vol. 16(No. 8): 2429–2444. ISSN: 1572-9710.

Clay, J. (2004). World Agriculture and the environment: A commodity-by-commodity guide to impacts and practices, Island Press,Washington. ISBN: 978-1559633703.

Colombo, A. & Joly, C. (2010). Brazilian Atlantic Forest lato sensu: The most ancient brazilian forest, and a biodiversity hotspot, is highly threatened by climate change, Brazilian Journal of Biology Vol. 70(No. 3): 697–708. ISSN: 1519-6984.

Crawley, M. (1993). Glim for Ecologists, Blackwell Scientific Publications. Oxford.

Crawley, M. (2007). The R book, JohnWiley & Sons, West Sussex. ISBN: 0470510242.

Delabie, J., Jahyny, B., Nascimento, I., Mariano, C., Lacau, S., Campiolo, S., Philpott, S. & Leponce, M. (2007). Contribution of cocoa plantations to the conservation of native ants (Insecta: Hymenoptera: Formicidae) with a special emphasis on the Atlantic forest fauna of southern Bahia, Brazil, Biodiversity and Conservation Vol. 16(No. 8): 2359–2384. ISSN: 1572-9710.

English-Loeb, G., Rhainds, M., Martinson, T. & Ugine, T. (2003). Influence of flowering cover crops on Anagrus parasitoids (Hymenoptera: Mymaridae) and Erythroneura leafhoppers (Homoptera: Cicadellidae) in New York vineyards, Agricultural and Forest Entomology Vol. 5(No. 2): 173–181. ISSN: 1461-9563.

FAO, (2010). Global forest resources assessment 2010, Main report 163, Food and Agriculture Organization of the United Nations Publisher, Rome - Italy. ISBN: 978-92-5-106654-6.

Figge, F. (2004). Bio-folio: Applying portfolio theory to biodiversity, Biodiversity and Conservation Vol. 13(No. 1): 827–849. ISSN: 0960-3115.

Franzen, M. & Mulder, M. (2007). Ecological, economic and social perspectives on cacao production worldwide, Biodiversity and Conservation Vol. 16(No. 1): 3835–3849. ISSN: 0960-3115.

Gibson, G. (1993). Superfamilies Chalcidoidea and Mymarommatoidea, in H. Goulet & J. Huber (eds), Hymenoptera of the world: An identification guide to families, Research Branch Agriculture Canada, Ottawa, Ontario, Canada, pp. 570–655. ISBN: 9993997331.

Gibson, G., Huber, J. & Woolley, J. (1997). In annotated keys to the genera of nearctic Chalcidoidea (Hymenoptera), NRC Research, Ottawa, Ontario, Canada. ISBN: 0-660-16669-0.

Gnocchi, A., Savergnini, J. & Gobbi, F. (2010). Perfil da fauna de vespas parasitóides (Insecta, Hymenoptera) em uma área de Mata Atlântica de João Neiva, ES, Brasil, Episteme Vol. 1(No. 1): 72–75. ISSN: 1413-5736.

Godfray, H. (1994). Parasitoids, behavioral and evolutionary ecology, Princeton University Press, New Jersey - USA. ISBN: 0691033250.

Goulet, H. & Huber, J. (1993). Hymenoptera of the world: An identification guide to families, Agriculture Canada Research Branch, Ottawa, Ontario, Canada. ISBN: 9993997331.

Greenberg, R., Bichier, P. & Angon, A. (2000). The conservation value for birds of cacao plantations with diverse planted shade in Tabasco, México, Animal Conservation Vol. 3(No.,1): 105–112. ISSN: 1469-1795.

Hammer, O. y., Harper, D. A. T. & Ryan, P. D. (2001). PAST: Paleontological statistics software package for education and data analysis, Palaeontologia Electronica 4(1): 1-9.

Hanson, P. & Gauld, I. (1995). The Hymenoptera of Costa Rica, Oxford University Press, USA. ISBN: 0198549059.

Harris, R. (2001). A Primer of multivariate statistics, Lawrence Erlbaum Assoc. Inc., Mahwah - USA. ISBN: 0805832106.

Hill, J.L., Curran, P.J. & Foody, G.M. (1994) The effects of sampling on the species-area curve. Global Ecology and Biogeography Letters, 4, 97–106.

Hoehn, P., Tscharntke, T., Tylianakis, J. & Steffan-Dewenter, I. (2008). Functional group diversity of bee pollinators increases crop yield, Proceedings of the Royal Society B Vol. 275(No. 1648): 2283-2291. ISSN: 1471-2954.

Hoekstra, J., Boucher, T. & Roberts, C. (2005). Confronting a biome crisis: Global disparities of habitat loss and protection, Ecology Letters Vol. 8(No. 1): 23–29. ISSN: 1461-0248.

Iacobucci, D. (2005). From the editor - On *p* values. Journal of Consumer Research, *32*, 1-6.

Johns, N. (1999). Conservation in Brazil's chocolate forest: The unlikely persistence of the traditional cocoa agroecosystem, Enviromental Management Vol. 1(No. 1): 31–47. ISSN: 1432-1009.

LaSalle, J. & Gauld, I. (1992). Parasitic Hymenoptera and the biodiversity crisis, Insects Parasitoids Vol. 74(No. 3): 315–334. ISSN: 0370-4327.

Manly, B. (1986). Multivariate statistical methods: A primer, Chapman and Hall, London - UK. ISBN: 0-412-28620-3.

Masner, L. (1996). The proctotrupoid families, in P. Hanson & I. Gauld (eds), The Hymenoptera of Costa Rica, Oxford University Press/Natural History Museum, London - USA, pp. 209–246. ISBN: 0198549059.

Miller, R. & Nair, P. (2006). Indigenous agroforestry systems in Amazonia: From prehistory to today, Agroforestry Systems Vol. 66(No. 2): 151–164. ISSN: 0167-4366.

Miller, S. (2007). An environmental history of Latin America (New Approaches to the America), Cambridge University Press, United Kingdom. ISBN: 978-0521612982.

Moço, M., Gama-Rodrigues, E., Gama-Rodrigues, A., Machado, R. & Baligar, V. (2009). Soil and litter fauna of cacao agroforestry systems in Bahia, Brazil, Agroforestry Systems Vol. 76(No. 1): 127–138. ISSN: 1572-9680.

Mugrabi, D. F., Alencar, I. D. C. C., Barreto, F. C. C. & Azevedo, C. O. (2008). Os gêneros de Bethylidae (Hymenoptera: Chrysidoidea) de quatro áreas de Mata Atlântica do Espírito Santo, Neotropical Entomology Vol. 37(No. 2): 152–158. ISSN: 1519-566X.

Myers, N., Mittermeier, R., Fonseca, C. & Kent, A. (2000). Biodiversity hotspots for conservation priorities, Nature Vol. 403(No. 1): 853–858. ISSN: 0028-0836.

Oliveira, M. & Luz, E. (2005). Identificação e manejo das principais doenças do Cacaueiro no Brasil, Cambridge University Press, Ilhéus, Bahia, Brasil. ISBN: 85-99169-01-7.

Perfecto, I. & Vandermeer, J. (2008). Biodiversity conservation in tropical agroecosystems, a new conservation paradigm, Annals of New York Academy of Science Vol. 1134(No. 1): 173–200. ISSN: 1749-6632.

Perfecto, I., Vandermeer, J., Batista, G., Nunez, G., Greenberg, R. & Bichier, P. (2004). Greater predation in shaded coffee farms: The role of resident Neotropical birds, Ecology Vol. 85(No. 10): 2677–2681. ISSN: 1749-6632.

Perioto, N. & Lara, R. (2003). Himenópteros parasitóides (Insecta, Hymenoptera) da Mata Atlântica. I. Parque Estadual da Serrra do mar, Ubatuba, SP, Brasil, Arquivos do Instituto Biológico Vol. 70(No. 4): 441-445. ISSN: 0020-3653.

Perioto, N., Lara, R. & Selegatto, A. (2005). Himenópteros parasitóides da Mata Atlântica. II. Núcleo Grajaúna, Rio Verde da estação ecológica Juréia-Itatins, Iguape, SP, Brasil, Arquivos do Instituto Biológico Vol. 72(No. 4): 81-85.

Perioto, N., Lara, R., Santos, J. & Selegatto, A. (2002). Himenópteros parasitóides (Insecta, Hymenoptera) coletados em cultura de algodão (Gosypium hirsutum L.) (Malvaceae), no município de Ribeirão Preto, SP, Brasil, Revista Brasileira de Entomologia Vol. 46(No. 2): 165-168. ISSN: 0020-3653.

Perioto, N., Lara, R., Santos, J. & Selegatto, A. (2005). Himenópteros parasitóides (Insecta, Hymenoptera) coletados em cultura de café Coffea arabica L. (Rubiaeae) em Ribeirão Preto, SP, Brasil, Arquivos do Instituto Biológico Vol. 71(No. 1): 41-44. ISSN: 0020-3653.

Perioto, N., Lara, R., Santos, J. & Silva, T. (2002). Himenópteros parasitóides (Insecta, Hymenoptera) coletados em cultura de soja (Glicine max (L.)) Merril (Fabaceae), no município de Nuporanga, SP, Brasil, Revista Brasileira de Entomologia Vol. 46(No. 2): 185-187. ISSN: 0085-5626.

R Development Core Team (2010). R: A language and environment for statistical computing, R Foundation for Statistical Computing, Viena - Austria. URL: http://www.r-project.org.

Rice, R. & Greenberg, R. (2000). Cacao cultivation and the conservation of biological diversity, Ambio Vol. 29(No. 3): 167-173. ISSN: 0044-7447.

Rizzini, C. T. (1997). Tratado de fitogeografia do Brasil: Aspectos ecológicos, sociológicos e florísticos, 2 edn, Âmbito Cultural, Rio de Janeiro.

Rolim, S. & Chiarello, A. (2004). Slow death of Atlantic Forest trees in cocoa agroforestry in southeastern Brazil, Biodiversity and Conservation Vol. 13(No. 14): 2679-2694. ISSN: 1572-9710.

Saatchi, S., Agosti, D., Alger, K., Delabie, J. & Musinski, J. (2001). Examining fragmentation and loss of primary forest in the southern bahian Atlantic Forest of Brazil with radar imagery, Conservation Biology Vol. 15(No. 4): 867-875. ISSN: 0888-8892.

Santana, S., Ramos, J., Ruiz, M., Araújo, Q., Almeida, H., Faria-Filho, A., Mendonça, J. & Santos, L. (2003). Zoneamento agroecológico do município de Ilhéus, Bahia, Brasil, Boletim Técnico n. 186, CEPLAC/CEPEC, Ilhéus, Bahia, Brasil. ISBN: 0100-0845.

Schindler, D., Ray, H., Brandon, C., Christopher, P., Thomas, P., Lauren, A. & Webster, S. (2010). Population diversity and the portfolio effect in an exploited species, Nature Vol. 465(No. 3): 609-612. ISSN: 0028-0836.

Schroth, G. & Harvey, C. (2007). Biodiversity conservation in cocoa production landscapes: An overview, Biodiversity and Conservation Vol. 16(No. 8): 2237-2244. ISSN: 1572-9680.

Severino, L. & Oliveira, T. (1999). Sistema de cultivo sombreado do cafeeiro (Coffea arabica L.) na região de Baturité, Ceará, Revista Ceres Vol. 46(No. 268): 635-652.

Shapiro, B. & Pickering, J. (2000). Rainfall and parasitic wasp (Hymenoptera: Ichneumonoidea) activity in sucessional forest stages at Barro Colorado nature monument, Panama, and la selva biological station, Costa Rica, Agricultural and Forest Entomology Vol. 2(No. 1): 39-47. ISSN: 0034-737X.

Sileshi, G., Akinnifesi, F.K., Ajayi, O.C., Chakeredza, S., Kaonga, M. & Matakala, P.W. (2007). Contributions of agroforestry to ecosystem services in the miombo eco-region of eastern and southern Africa. African Journal of Environmental Science and Technology Vol. 1(No. 4): 68–80. ISSN: 1996-0786.

Silva-Neto, P., Matos, P., Martins, A. & Silva, A. (2001). Sistema de produção de cacau para a Amazônia brasileira, CEPLAC, Belém, Brasil. ISBN: 0102-5511.

Sperber, C., Nakayama, K., Valverde, M. & Neves, F. (2004). Tree species richness and density affect parasitoid diversity in cacao agroforestry, Basic and Applied Ecology Vol. 5(No. 3): 241–251. ISSN: 1439-1791.

Stenchly, K., Clough, Y., Buchori, D. & Tscharntke, T. (2011). Spider web guilds in cacao agroforestry: Comparing tree, plot and landscape-scale management, Diversity and Distributions Vol. 17(No. 4): 748–756. ISSN: 1366-9516.

Tabarelli, M., Pinto, L., Silva, J., Hirota, M. & Bede, L. (2005). Challenges and opportunities for biodiversity conservation in the brazilian Atlantic Forest, Conservation Biology Vol. 19(No. 3): 695–700. ISSN: 0888-8892.

Townes, H. (1972). A light-weight malaise trap, Entomological News Vol. 82/83(No. 1): 239–247. ISSN: 0013-872X.

Tylianakis, J., Didham, R. &Wratten, S. (2004). Improved fitness of aphid parasitoids receiving resource subsidies, Ecology Vol. 85(No. 3): 658–666. ISSN: 1749-6632.

Vandermeer, J. & Perfecto, I. (1995). Breakfast of biodiversity: The truth about rainforest destruction, Food First Books, Oakland. ISBN: 978-0935028669.

Vera y Conde, C. F. & Rocha, C. (2006). Habitat disturbance and small mammal richness and diversity in an Atlantic rainforest area in southeastern Brazil, Brazilian Journal of Biology Vol. 66(No. 4): 983–990. ISSN: 1519-6984.

Zuur, A., Ieno, E., Walker, N., Saveleiev, A. & Smith, M. (2009). Mixed effects models and extensions in ecology with R, Springer Press, New York - USA. ISBN: 978-0-387-87457-9.

4

The Effects of Tree-Alfalfa Intercropped Systems on Wood Quality in Temperate Regions

Hamid Reza Taghiyari[1] and Davood Efhami Sisi[2]
[1]*Shahid Rajaee Teacher Training University,*
[2]*The University of Tehran*
Iran

1. Introduction

Agroforestry is a dynamic, ecologically based, natural resource management system that, through the integration of trees in farm and rangeland, diversifies and sustains production for increased social, economic and environmental benefits (Leakey, 1996). Apart from the social and cultural advantages of growing trees, recreational benefits for human being, as well as improvement in wildlife, there are other advantages associated with planting trees with crops. There are five mechanisms through which trees contribute to the agricultural environment (Yin, 2004). These include reducing wind velocity and wind erosion, controlling sheet and rill erosion, mediating solar radiation and regulating soil and air temperatures, increasing field moisture, and improving soil nutrients.

In low forest cover countries, development of tree-based intercropping is necessary to reduce the dependence on natural forests. Such an agroforestry system can encourage farmers to produce wood along with annual crops (Efhami Sisi et al., 2010). However, a tree plantation is usually considered a long-rotation activity in comparison with agricultural crops. This discouraged farmers from adopting tree farming (Asadi, 1994). Agroforestry encompasses several systems; among which alley intercropping is considered a common practice in this regard. More than 40% of research projects in international agroforestry research institutes focus on this practice (Singh et al. 2001).

Alley cropping is an agroforestry management system that permits the production of a variety of crops in alleys between widely spaced rows of trees (Asadi et al., 2005). Alley cropping (hedged agroforestry) increase tree cover, fuelwood supplies and infiltration of rain, provide protection against wind, and reduce runoff (Otengi et al., 2000). In alley cropping systems where timber is a major ecosystem service, initial spacing between the trees is of great importance because it influences anatomical, physical, and morphological characteristics of wood. For woody components in agroforestry systems, there are some desirable characteristics, such as adaptability, straight bole, thin crown, appropriate leafing phenology, deep root, little or no negative effect on crop, and economical and social traits (Muthuri et al., 2005; Singh et al., 2001). Interplanting of trees with crops requires management practices, which affect wood characteristics of timber trees in alley cropping.

However, little is known about the properties of timber sourced from agricultural lands (Shanavas & Kumar, 2006).

In agroforestry systems, farmers are interested in increasing initial spacing between trees to achieve higher crop yields. Two factors are considered of vital importance in an alley agroforestry to study the quality of the wood cultivated: the crops and their effects on the soil fertility and tree growth, and the initial spacing between the trees. DeBell et al. (2002) found that interplanting nitrogen-fixing *Albizia* spp. increased the mean stem diameter of *Eucalyptus saligna* by 37% but did not alter wood density. Similarly, growth rate of trees generally increases with wider initial-spacing because of the decreased competition with surrounding trees for soil moisture and nutrients (Wodzicki, 2001). The goal of silvicultural practices such as thinning, spacing, interplanting, weeding, and fertilizing is to increase tree height and diameter growth (Chen et al., 1998). In turn, any change in the growth pattern and growth rate of a tree may result in wood property variation (Zobel & van Buijtenen, 1989).

All forestry practices may influence tree growth in one way or another, and consequently, wood properties would also be altered (Fig. 1). It should be justified if the changes in wood properties such as the size of log, proportion of juvenile wood, density, fiber length, etc., are technically accepted by the wood industry. The economical aspects of the silvicultural practices should also be taken into account (Bowyer et al .2007).

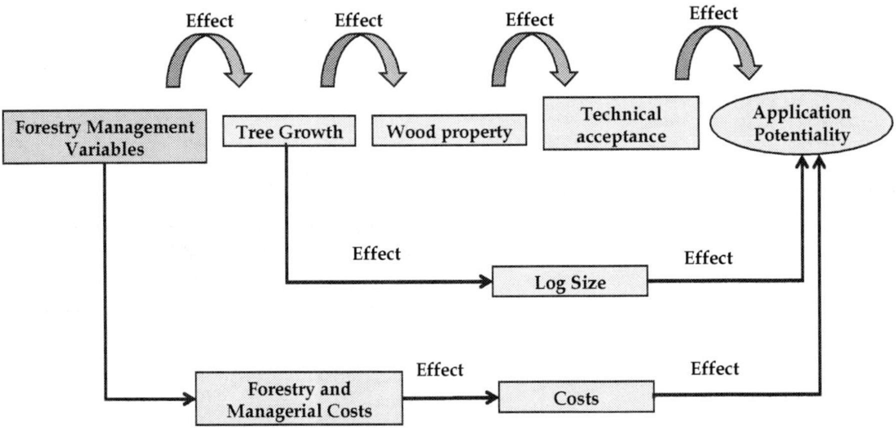

Fig. 1. Relationship between silvicultural practices and its effects on wood quality (Bowyer et al., 2007)

The influence of growth rate on wood quality is very complicated. In many cases, a tree species may be positively affected by a certain forestry practice that shows a completely opposite effect on another species (Kollmann & Cötè, 1968). For example, increase in growth rate of a tree may cause some changes in tree ring structures (Fig. 2). In softwoods, increase in tree ring width does not have any effect on dense latewood width; it would therefore be predicted that the density of wood would naturally decrease. In ring-porous hardwoods such as oak, this effect would be quite the opposite; that is, increase in tree ring width does not have any effect on porous early wood width; therefore, the density would naturally increase. In diffuse-porous hardwoods such as poplar, however, no clear relationship between ring width and wood density is observed (Kollmann & Cötè, 1968). Similarly, growth rate may have significant effects on wood anatomy (Efhami Sisi et al. 2010, 2011a), physical and mechanical properties (Taghiyari & Sarvari Samadi, 2010; Taghiyari, 2011; Taghiyari et al., 2010, 2011; Taghiyari & Efhami Sisi, 2011; Shanavas & Kumar, 2006). Some researchers believe that, regardless of the cause of increase in growth rate, it may have similar effects on wood quality (DeBell et. al., 1998).

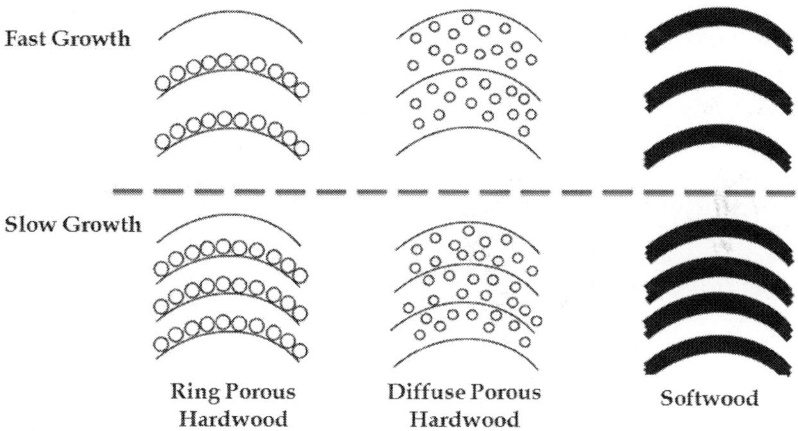

Fig. 2. Schematic diagram of growth rate effects on tree ring structure

There are many complicated interactions between wood properties and technical acceptance that need to be taken into account when studying growth rate effects on wood quality. Improvement in tree growth properties should not necessarily have similar results on technical acceptance of the wood (Fig. 3). In ring-porous species for instance, increase in density by higher growth rates would ultimately improve mechanical properties; while increase in diameter and the number of branches showed negative effect on it (Zobel & van Buijtenen, 1989).

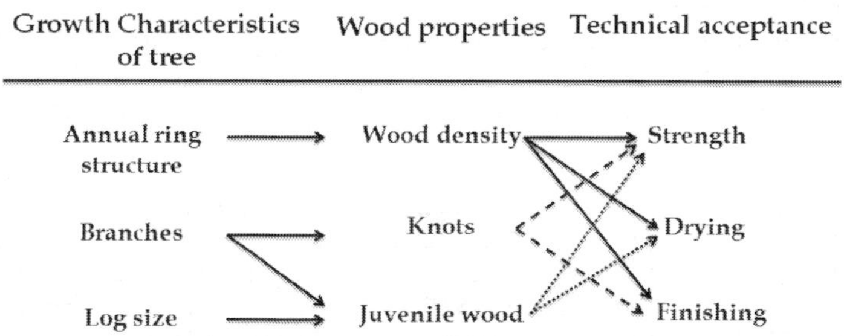

Fig. 3. Effects of tree growth characteristics on wood quality and technical acceptance (Zobel & van Buijtenen, 1989)

Based on the above literature review, alley cropping and N-fixing crops improve the growth rate of trees. Changes in growth rate by forestry management variables (Fig. 1) are reported to alter wood properties. However, not many studies have so far assessed the extent to which alley cropping would affect wood properties from anatomical, physical, and mechanical points of view. Therefore, this chapter evaluates the effects of initial spacing and intercropping on growth rate and wood quality.

2. Effects of agroforestry on growth rate and bole form

Increases in soil organic matter and total organic nitrogen are reported to explain the increase in growth rate of trees in agroforestry systems (Eaglesham et al. 1981; Sea-Lee et al. 1992). DeBell et al. (2002a) evaluated the effects of chemical fertilizer, spacing, and interplanted nitrogen-fixing trees on diameter growth of 15-year-old *Eucalyptus saligna* trees and concluded that diameter growth (hence, productivity) can be increased substantially through supplemental nitrogen and increased growing space. In a separate study, 8 years after establishment, *P. deltoides* intercropped with wheat-fodder maize had larger diameter, crown width and wood volume (m^3/ha) than pure tree stands (Chaudhry et al., 2003). Other studies have also shown that (i) an intercropped agroforestry system was more economical at the rotations of 4 and 6 years compared to pure stands (Chaudhry et. al., 2003), (ii) there was more growth in poplar trees under agroforestry conditions than that of forest conditions (Singh et al., 1988), and (iii) *Acacia auriculiformis, Acacia mangium,* and *Grevillea robusta* trees grown in agroforestry systems had better growth rate (Shanavas & Kumar, 2006).

Efhami Sisi et al. (2008) studied the effects of *Populus nigra*-alfalfa intercropping and initial spacing on growth rate of poplar trees. They found that (i) tree diameter in tree-crop intercropped systems was greater than in pure tree stands, and (ii) tree diameter increased with decreasing tree density. General trends of diameter growth in relation to age were similar for all treatments (Fig. 4), but the greatest difference in diameter growth values occurred from age 3 to about age 7.

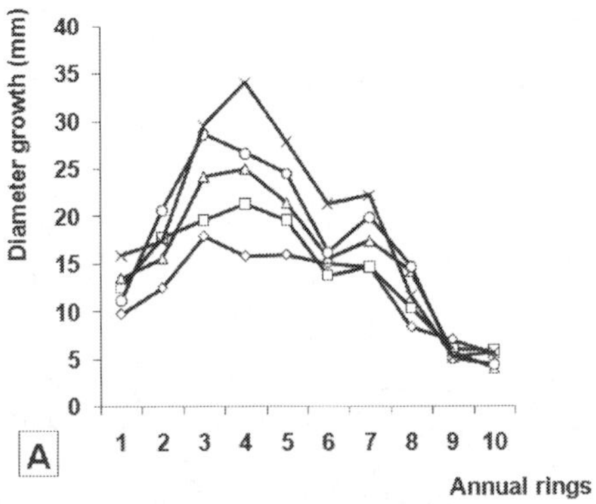

Fig. 4. Diameter growth as a function of ring number from pith to bark
◊ = 3 m × 4 m without alfalfa; □ = 3 m × 4 m with alfalfa; Δ = 3 m × 6.7 m with alfalfa; ○ = 3 m × 8 m with alfalfa; × = 3 m × 10 m with alfalfa

With regard to the early rising and the consequent falling trend of tree growth (Fig. 4), in any plantation, the ring width generally decreases with age because of the increased competition with the surrounding trees (Wodzicki, 2001); in poplar plantations, this decrease in ring width is usually observed in rings 3 to 5. The pointer year at age 6 found only in trees of the treatments with alfalfa might be due to the termination of alfalfa cultivation at age 5 which could be beneficial to trees (Fig. 4).

Alfalfa, a nitrogen(N)-fixing plant, has the capacity of fixing about 230 kg N ha^{-1} yr^{-1} and does not need annual plowing and sowing (Tisdal & Nelson, 1974). In tropical and sub-tropical forests, trees of legume family such as *Albizia, Pterocaria,* and *Gleditchia* spp are the main source for N-fixing in the soil (Tisdal & Nelson 1974).. Use of N-fixing plants is one of the methods for fertilizing plantation trees (Zobel and van Buijtenen, 1989). Legumes have the synergistic effect of improving soil health through biological N-fixation and adding nutrient-rich residues to the soil (Skelton, 2002). Intercropping trees with alfalfa may increase in soil N content and fertility resulting in an increase in tree diameter (Saarsalmi et al., 2006; Skelton, 2002; Tisdal & Nelso, 1974). Moreover, a wider initial-spacing would decrease competition among individual trees (Wodzicki, 2001) and consequently increase growth rate. Overall wood production and basal area can decrease although wider initial spacing increases growth rate. While intercropping trees with alfalfa can increase basal area, wider initial spacing could decrease it (Fig. 5).

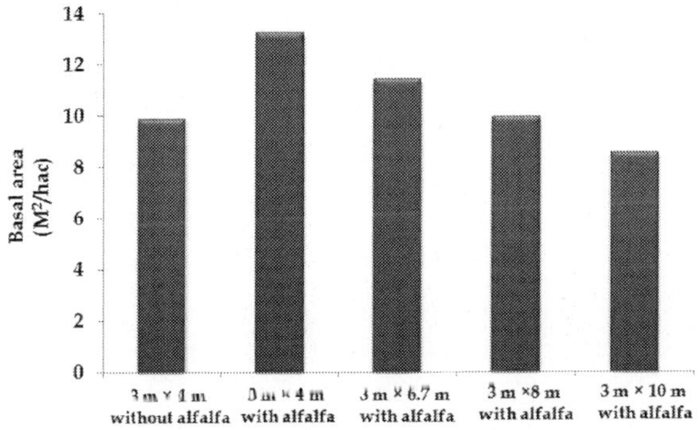

Fig. 5. Basal area of poplar trees influenced by initial spacing and alfalfa-intercropping (Efhami Sisi et al., 2008)

Although the trees in plantations with wide initial spacing grew at a significantly rapid rate and quickly reached merchandisable diameter, the increase in growth rate of trees did not compensate for low tree density (Lundgren, 1981). There is always an optimum initial spacing for a certain tree species - given specific climatic conditions and stand quality in which biomass does not change with initial spacing. Sjolte-Jorgensen (1967) presented data showing quality trends for Norway spruce (Table 1). The biomass of 47-year-old Norway spruce did not change between 2 m and 3 m spacing regimes while mean diameter of trees increased. In fact, this is an optimum initial spacing in which rapid growth rate and wider initial spacing may compensate for a lower tree-density. Finding this optimum point is of great importance in agroforestry system. Larger diameter logs yield significantly more revenue than smaller logs (Barbour and Kellogg's, 1988).

Spacing (m)	Mean Diameter (cm)	Taper Whole stem (cm/m)	Percentage of Knots	Total Production (Tones/ha)
1.25 × 1.40	20.1	0.98	0.191	261
1.40 × 1.65	20.5	1.02	0.236	240
2.00 × 2.00	24.1	1.04	0.260	218
3.00 × 3.00	26.0	1.13	0.340	218
3.50 × 3.50	28.3	1.26	0.335	166

Table 1. Stand characteristics of 47-year-old *Picea abies* as influenced by initial spacing (Data cited in Sjolte-Jorgensen 1967)

Table 1 shows that initial spacing could influence bole quality; that is, an increase in initial spacing could decrease bole quality because of a higher percentage of knots and taper. Trees with significant taper have relatively low lumber yields and they are unacceptable for manufacturing some of the specialty products such as poles. Knot size is an important factor for poles and lumber. The greater the proportion of knots, the lower the strength and the lower the value of clear wood produced (Zobel & van Buijtenen, 1989).

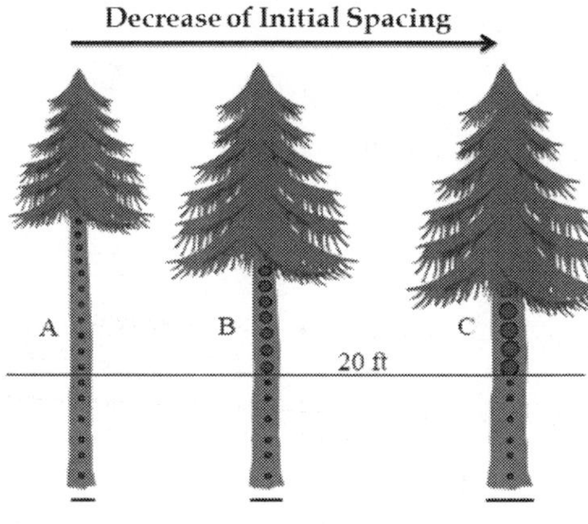

Fig. 6. Schematic diagram of the effects of initial spacing on crown and branch expansion

Taper is largely a crown effect. Since the cambium activates first within the crown, growth rings tend to be widest here, and maximum diameter growth often occurs. Thus, trees with large crowns tend to have highly conical stems, while stems of trees whose crowns have receded gradually become more cylindrical (Fig. 6). High-taper trees have smaller scaling diameters (because diameter is measured at the log's small end). Knot size is directly impacted by crown size. Persistent, live crowns give branches more time to grow, and knot size increases. Receding crowns limit branch size, thus limiting knot size (Ballard & Long, 1988).

Efhami Sisi et al. (2008) studied the effects of initial spacing and intercropping (with alfalfa) on bole form factors such as taper, eccentric, roundness and number, diameter, length and angle of branches, as well as height of trees (Table 2).

Treatments	Taper (cm/m)	Eccentric	Roundness (%)	Branches				height
				Number	Diameter (cm)	Length (m)	Angle	
3 m × 4 m without alfalfa	1.37	6.17	1.10	11	3	3.4	40	10.8
3 m × 4 m with alfalfa	1.34	8.9	1.09	12	4	4.2	40	11.8
3 m × 6.6 m with alfalfa	1.42	8.63	1.10	12	4	4.3	45	11.8
3 m × 8 m with alfalfa	1.59	13.63	1.38	12	4.6	5	45	12.1
3 m × 10 m with alfalfa	1.76	11.83	1.28	13	5.6	6	47	12.9

Table 2. Bole form of poplar trees influenced by initial spacing and alfalfa-intercropping (Efhami Sisi et al., 2008)

There was no significant difference in tree height across treatments. Taper, eccentric and roundness increased with increasing inter-tree spacing, while integration of alfalfa did not. Number, length, diameter and angle of branches increased in widely spaced and intercropped treatments. Roundness is also considered as an important and influential parameter of yield in veneer and plywood industries (Mäkinen, 1998). Stand density and thinning accounted for 2 – 9% of roundness (Mäkinen, 1998). Also, eccentricity is considered a sign of reaction wood formation in tree stem. Its measurement was based on maximum radius and minimum radius at breast height, showing an increase by initial spacing (Efhami Sisi et al., 2008).

At a close spacing, the sample trees had somewhat less branches in a whorl than more in widely spaced plots. The most pronounced effect of initial spacing was the increase in branch diameter with increasing initial spacing (Mäkinen & Hein, 2006; Ulvcrona et al., 2007). The effects of initial spacing on straightness of tree bole, diameter, and number of branches in each inter-node, are more pronounced than on intrinsic wood properties (Malinauskas, 1999). Planting trees in widely spaced plots reduces establishment costs and accelerates diameter growth of individual trees, resulting in larger, but fewer, trees at any given age with lower bole quality. The more trees established per acre, the higher the total cubic-foot volume yield. However, this increased volume must be harvested from more and smaller trees (Lundgren, 1981).

3. Effects of agroforestry on wood anatomy

3.1 Vessel properties

Vessel diameter and frequency in trees affect wood quality traits such as permeability which in turn determines, among other variables, wood preservation, wood drying, pulp and paper making (Chen et al., 1998). Efhami Sisi et al. (2010) studied the effects of intercropping *Populus nigra* with alfalfa and initial tree spacing on vessel element attributes by measuring the proportion of each ring relative to the whole disc area to obtain weighting coefficient for every growth ring. The study showed that intercropping *Populus nigra* with alfalfa and increasing initial spacing increased vessel diameter and frequency; while wider initial spacing decreased the vessel frequency (VF), and to some extent the vessel lumen area percentage (VLA %), but increased vessel lumen diameter (VLD) (Table 3; Figs. 7 & 8).

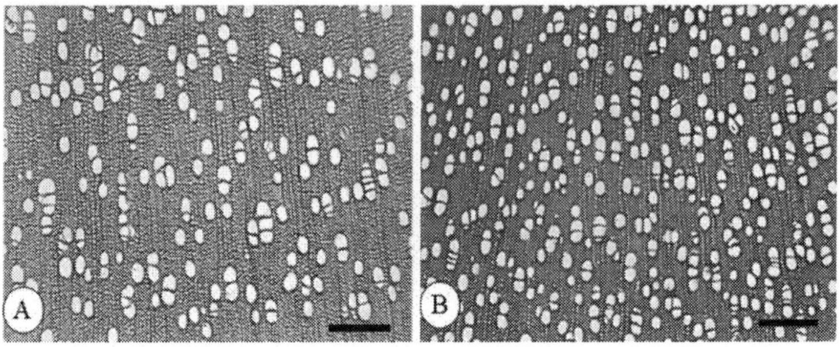

Fig. 7. Microscopic images of cross-section of the third tree-ring in trees harvested in 3 × 4 and 3 × 10 meter inter-tree spacing in tree- alfalfa intercropping (scale bar: 300μ). **A:** 3 × 10 with alfalfa: vessels with low frequency but more diameters resulting in lower vessel lumen area. **B:** 3 × 4 with alfalfa: vessels with more frequency but lower diameter resulting in high vessel lumen area

Vessel lumen diameter increased more or less linearly from pith to bark in all treatments (Fig. 8-A). The rate of increase of VLD in the outer rings was comparatively lower in tree stands without alfalfa than in tree-alfalfa intercropped systems. Vessel Frequency per unit area (mm^2) decreased as cambial age increased (Fig. 8-B), but rates were similar across treatments. Vessel Lumen Area (%) increased consistently from pith to bark in treatments with alfalfa (Fig. 8-C). Zobel and van Buijtenen (1989) reported that N fertilization increases the period of juvenile wood production. Considering the definition of juvenile wood as the part of wood that shows severe radial change in wood properties (Zobel & Sprague, 1998), it may be expected that intercropping trees with alfalfa may increase the period to reach wood maturity.

Treatments	Annual Diameter Growth (mm)	Based on the area of tree rings		
		Vessel Diameter (μm)	Vessel frequency per mm	Vessel lumen area percentage
3 m × 4 m without alfalfa	12.2 (d)	62 (c)	94 (b)	28 (b)
3 m × 4 m with alfalfa	13.8 (cd)	67 (b)	103 (ab)	35 (a)
3 m × 6.7 m with alfalfa	14.9 (bc)	69 (ab)	90 (ab)	33 (ab)
3 m × 8 m with alfalfa	16.4 (b)	68 (ab)	89 (ab)	33 (ab)
3 m × 10 m with alfalfa	19.3 (a)	72 (a)	79(a)	32 (ab)

( ) Duncan's separation grouping results

Table 3. Mean values for annual diameter growth rate and vessel properties of poplar trees

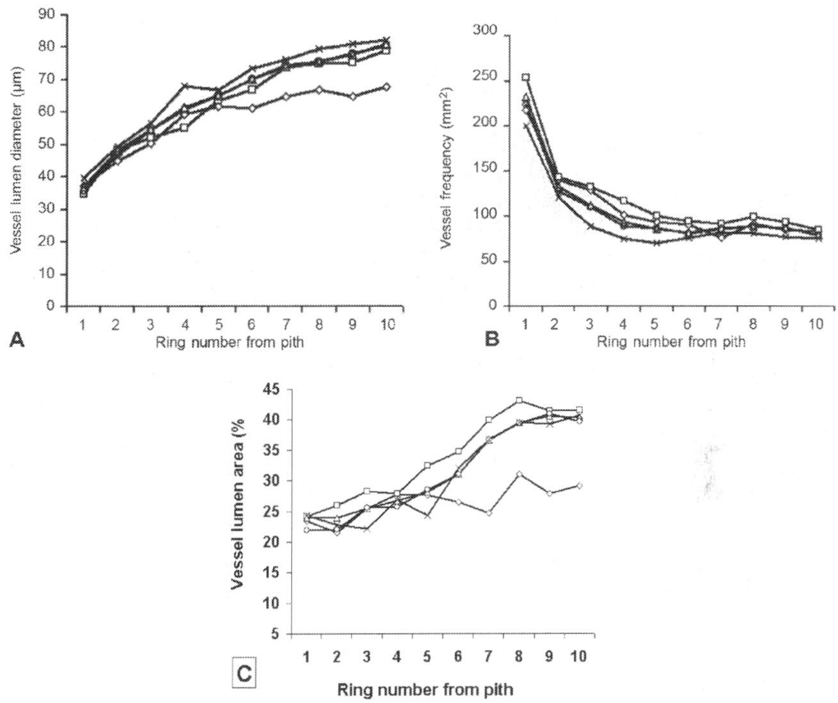

Fig. 8. Radial dimensions of vessel lumen diameter, vessel frequency, and vessel lumen area as a function of ring number from pith to bark in young poplar trees after different treatments; ◊ = 3 × 4 without alfalfa; □ = 3 × 4 with alfalfa; Δ = 3 × 6.7 with alfalfa; ○ = 3 × 8 with alfalfa; × = 3 × 10 with alfalfa; A= Vessel lumen diameter; B= Vessel frequency in mm2; C= Vessel lumen area percentage

Although agroforestry systems were found to have positive effects on growth rate, no correlation was found between growth rate and wood properties of six-month-old poplar stems (Jourez *et al.* 2001). However, Doungpet (2005) reported a positive correlation between growth rate (ring width) and vessel lumen diameter (VLD), but negative correlations with VF. Peszlen (1993) investigated three different clones of 10- to 15-year-old poplars and reported that wood properties had no consistent and significant relationship with growth rate. Arnold and Mauseth (1999) reported that low N fertilizer caused reduction of VLD and VF in the cactus species *Cereus peruvianus*. In *Populus deltoides*, deficiencies of nitrogen and sulfur resulted in reduced fiber and vessel diameter (Zobel & van Buijtenen, 1989). These studies suggest that agroforestry systems have the potentiality to significantly affect wood properties.

3.2 Fiber properties

Fiber attributes in trees determine, to some extent, the final quality of pulp and paper (Dinwoodie, 1965). Efhami Sisi et al. (2011a), studying the effects of intercropping *Populus nigra* with alfalfa and initial tree spacing on fiber element attributes, found that fiber diameter and wall thickness significantly increased in tree harvested from tree-alfalfa intercropped plots (Table 4). However, initial-spacing had no significant effect on fiber properties.

Cluster analysis on fiber wall thickness and fiber diameter showed that all three trees of treatment without alfalfa are clustered together (Fig. 9). Although results of Duncan test on fiber length showed the treatment without alfalfa is grouped quite separately, individual trees of this treatment were clustered differently. Also, different trees of treatments with alfalfa were clustered separately. Fiber lumen diameter was not significantly different among treatments. Consequently, fiber wall thickness was the main source of fluctuations in fiber diameter (Table 4).

Table 4 shows that (i) tree diameter and fiber morphological properties of poplar trees in poplar-alfalfa intercropped plots were significantly greater than those in pure poplar stand at all initial tree spacings, (ii) properties of trees in intercropped systems were not significantly different across different initial inter-tree spacings. Therefore, tree-alfalfa intercropping, rather than initial spacing, determined fiber properties in these agroforestry systems.

Treatments	Tree Diameter (cm)	Fiber length (μm)	Fiber wall thickness (μm)	Fiber lumen diameter (μm)	Fiber diameter (μm)
3 m × 4 m without alfalfa	11.4 (c)	895.3 (b)	3.19 (b)	16.8 (ab)	22.2 (b)
3 m × 4 m with alfalfa	14.5 (b)	936.7(ab)	3.91 (a)	17.1 (a)	24.4(a)
3 m × 6.7 m with alfalfa	17.2 (ab)	958.9 (a)	3.88 (a)	17.1 (a)	24.8 (a)
3 m × 8 m with alfalfa	17.5 (ab)	961.0 (a)	3.87 (a)	16.5 (a)	24.9 (a)
3 m × 10 m with alfalfa	18 (a)	957.8(a)	3.93 (a)	16.4 (a)	24.7 (a)

Table 4. Mean values for diameter and fiber morphological parameters of poplar

Fiber length in all treatments increased rapidly from pith to bark. However, fiber diameter and wall thickness showed mild fluctuation (Figs. 10-A & B). The treatment without alfalfa showed a slightly less steep, but still significant, increase in fiber attributes, especially in fiber length. As to the milder changes of fiber attributes in treatment without alfalfa, and considering the definition of juvenile wood as the part of wood that shows severe radial changes in wood properties (Zobel & Sprague, 1989), it may be concluded that intercropping with alfalfa may increase the period to reach wood maturity. However, final decision would be made when older trees are studied. Similar results were also found in vessel attributes of the same treatments (Efhami Sisi et al. 2010). Zobel & Van Buijtenen (1989) reported that nitrogen fertilization increases the period of juvenile wood production. Therefore, it is expected that those trees obtaining more nitrogen would show a more intensified increase in their fiber-length trend.

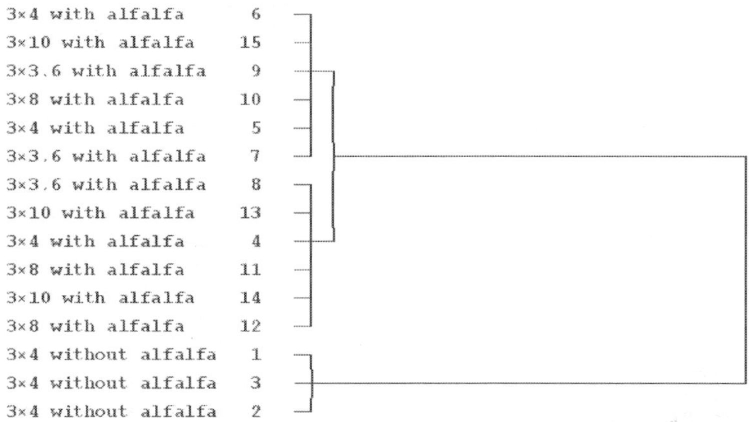

Fig. 9. Cluster analysis of all 15 trees based on wall thickness of fibers

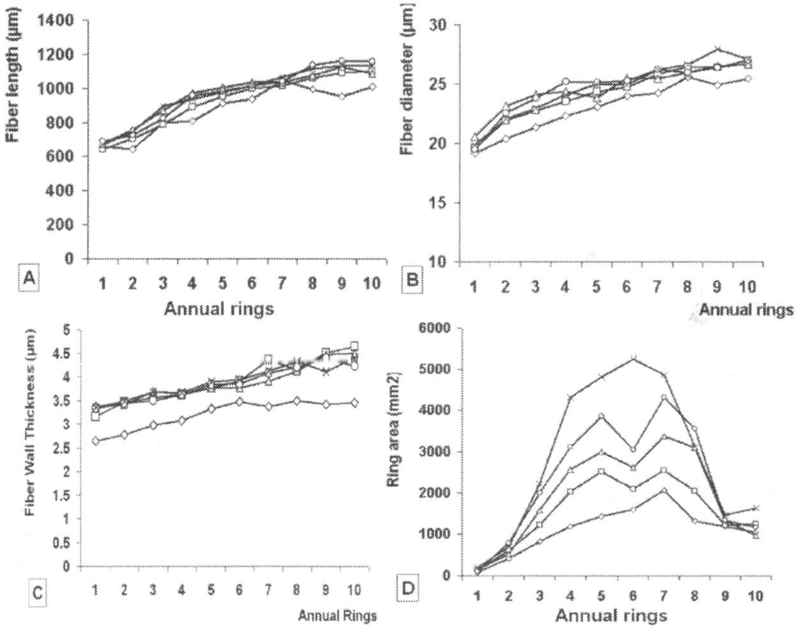

Fig. 10. Mean characteristics as a function of ring number from pith to bark. **A**: Fiber length; **B**: Fiber diameter; **C**: Fiber wall thickness; **D**: Ring area. ◊ = 3 m × 4 m without alfalfa; □ = 3 × 4 with alfalfa; Δ = 3 × 6.7 with alfalfa; ○ = 3 × 8 with alfalfa; × = 3 × 10 with alfalfa

Efhami Sisi et al. (2011) observed that the whole-disk fiber length increased with growth rate caused by agro-silvicultural practices as correlated by stem diameter (Fig. 11-A).

Furthermore, weighted fiber diameter and wall thickness showed an increasing trend by stem diameter (Fig. 11-B and C).

Focusing on a positive relationship between whole-disk fiber attributes and growth rate, DeBell et al. (1998) and Doungpet (2005) found that fast-growing trees have more of their basal area concentrated in rings further from the pith than do slower growing trees, and these rings have longer and thicker fibers compared with rings closer to the pith. Thus, whole-disk fiber attributes increased with overall growth rate. Therefore, under similar conditions and with the same age and species, fast-growing young trees have longer and thicker fibers.

A negative effect of growth rate on fiber length was expected, given the existing knowledge about lateral divisions and how they may affect the length of cambial initials, i.e., high rate of anticlinal division is accompanied by short cells (Bannan, 1967). It has been proposed that the cell length in juvenile wood is related to age (Fujiwara & Yang, 2000). However, most of relationships between growth rate and fiber length were not significant at the earlier ages; at the older ages, although some significant relationships were observed, but there were not outstanding (Table 5).

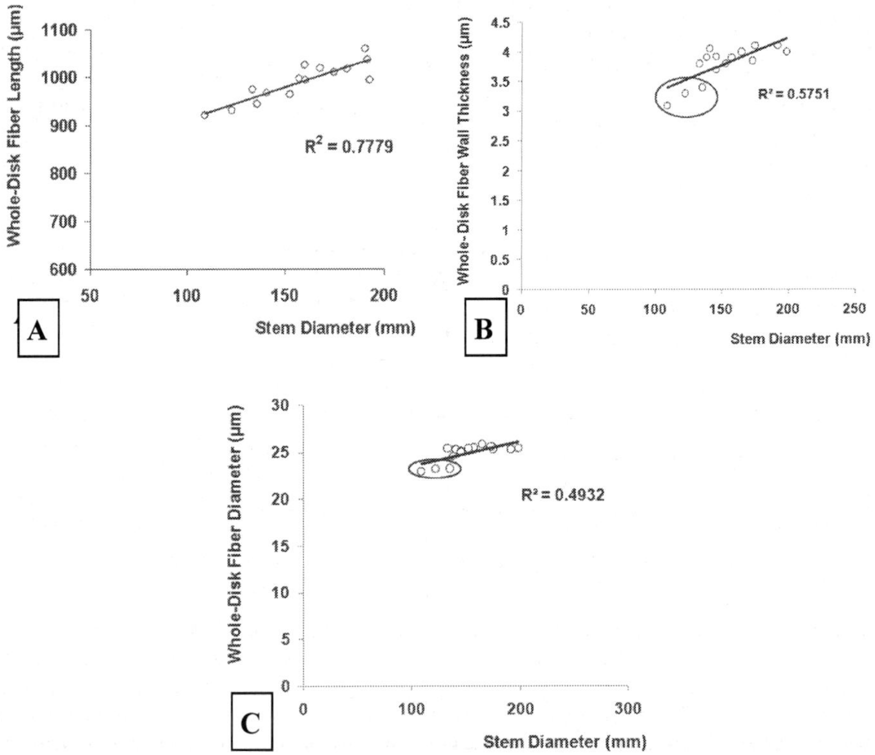

Fig. 11. Mean whole-disk fiber attributes as a function of stem diameter

	Ring 1	Ring 2	Ring 3	Ring 4	Ring 5	Ring 6	Ring 7	Ring 8	Ring 9	Ring 10
Significance level	0.128 NS	0.154 NS	0.018 NS	0.012 NS	0.046 S(+)	0.278 NS	0.008 S (+)	0.076 NS	0.030 S(-)	0.461 NS
R square	0.169	0.150	0.209	0.193	0.273	0.190	0.326	0.222	0.315	0.046

S Statistically significant at the 5% level.
NS Not significant at the 5% level.
( ) positive (+) or negative (-) correlation

Table 5. Regressions analysis results for correlations between ring width and fiber length (Efhami Sisi et al., 2011a)

The effect of growth rate on shortening the cambial initials would be overshadowed by the subsequently greater elongation of daughter cells in the fast-growing trees (Fujiwara & Yang, 2000; Debell et al. 1998). For example, daughter-cell elongation of fibers in hardwoods averages 140% (Panshin & deZeeuw 1980). It was reported that fiber length was not influenced by growth rate in poplar plantations that are cultivated under different silvicultural practices and had dissimilar growth rates (Snook et al., 1986; DeBell et al., 2002a). Although intercropping and initial spacing have significant effects on fiber dimensions, their effects on tree growth are more influential (Efhami Sisi et al., 2011a). Also, agro-silvicultural practices increase growth rate; but considering the existing knowledge on lateral divisions and how they may affect the length of cambial initials, this increase in growth rate should not necessarily end up in shorter fiber length in young poplar trees as was previously believed.

Debell *et al.* (1998) found that growth rate under different initial spacing had no consistent effect on fiber length within rings of the same age for rings 2-6 of young poplar hybrids although for ring 7 there were positive correlation. They believed that this general relationship will hold for most cultural practices (e.g., increased growing space and supplemental nutrition) that are applied to enhance growth rate. Fujiwara and Yang (2000) reported that there was a positive relationship between fiber length and ring width in mature wood of *Populus tremuloides* Michx. Koubba et al. (1998) reported the correlation between fiber length and growth rate in poplar hybrids varied over the age of the tree. At early ages, correlation between ring width and fiber length was not significant; at older ages, slight negative but significant correlation was found between these two traits. Other studies reported in cultured poplars have concluded that growth rate have no effect on fiber length (Snook et al. 1986; DeBell et al. 2002b). Despite several studies undertaken to assess the effects of growth rate on fiber dimension, the results have been inconclusive.

Under high-nitrogen exposure, xylem fibers were 17% wider and 18% shorter compared to the low nitrogen treatment, and very significant thickening of the fiber cell walls was also observed throughout the stem of trees receiving the high-N treatment (Pitre et al. 2007). Zoble and Van Buijtenen (1989) concluded that N may reduce cell size, wall thickness and specific gravity in hardwoods and increase volume growth, but no generalizations can be made due to interspecific variations especially in the diffuse porous hardwoods.

4. Effects of agroforestry on wood physical properties

4.1 Density and shrinkage of wood

Concerns regarding the physical and mechanical properties of timber harvested from fast growing tree species have been articulated, still more studies should be done because such data from the agroforestry systems are scarce (Shanavas & Kumar, 2006). Evaluation of the effects of chemical fertilizer, spacing, and interplanted nitrogen-fixing trees on wood density of 15-year-old *Eucalyptus saligna* trees showed that (i) wider spacing increased mean diameter by 34%, (ii) the level of chemical fertilization did not affect wood density, and mean diameter of trees, (iii) interplanting of N-fixing *Albizia* trees increased mean diameter by 37%, but did not alter wood density (DeBell et al., 2002). Pith-to-bark profiles of wood density revealed that trees with rapid growth had more uniform wood density patterns across the radius. They conclude that diameter growth (hence, productivity) can be increased substantially through supplemental N and increased growing space without decreasing wood density. Moreover, rapid growth - whether associated with improved nutrition or increased growing space - will result in wood with a more uniform density from pith to bark.

Shanavas & Kumar (2006) evaluated physical and mechanical properties of *Acacia auriculiformis, Acacia mangium,* and *Grevillea robusta* trees grown in agroforestry systems and suggested that agroforestry practices per se do not exert any negative impact on wood properties. In another experiment, in older pine and spruce trees, wood density was about the same after as before planting lupines. More growth with more earlywood was obtained but also more latewood was formed. In young pine and spruce though, intercropped with lupines, specific gravity of the wood produced declined (Pechmann and Wutz, 1960). Seven years after establishment of Eucalyptus-Leucaena mixtures, in Brazil, showed that there were no major differences in wood density or holocellulose yields of the eucalypts in the mixture although there was growth response (De Jesus et al., 1988).

The effects of intercropping with alfalfa as well as initial tree spacing on physical variations of *Populus betulifolia* wood were also reported (Efhami Sisi et al., in press). Trees were harvested from an agroforestry trial described in details in Efhami Sisi et al. (2010). Wood density and shrinkage were decreased with alfalfa- *Populus nigra* intercropping while increased by initial spacing (Figs. 12 & 13; Efhami Sisi et al., 2011b). In another study, alfalfa-*Populus nigra* intercropping and initial spacing increased vessel lumen diameter (VLD) and vessel lumen area (VLA), resulting in lower density in this treatment. On the other hand, VLA decreased with increase in initial spacing resulting in higher density. Decrease in wood density caused by direct N-fertilizer was also reported in *Eucalyptus globules* and *P. deltoides* (Raymond & Muneri, 2000). Arnold and Mauseth (1999) reported that low nitrogen fertilizer caused reduction of VLD and VF in the cactus species *Cereus peruvianus*. In *Populus deltoides,* deficiencies of nitrogen and sulfur resulted in reduced fiber and vessel diameter (Zobel & van Buijtenen, 1989). Thus, it can be concluded that the decrease in wood density by alfalfa-intercropping resulted in increase in woody cell-lumen and the consequent wood porosity.

Density had a decreasing trend from pith to bark at breast height, showing similarity with the results of other researcher on different poplar species (Karki, 2001; Doungpet, 2005). Low lumen area of fibers and vessels in the early years of tree growth (Peszlen, 1994; Efhami Sisi et al. 2011a, 2010; Efhami Sisi & Sarayeian, 2009), as well as more extractives in this section of the stem, may have caused this decrease in density from pith to bark (Zobel & van Buijtenen, 1989).

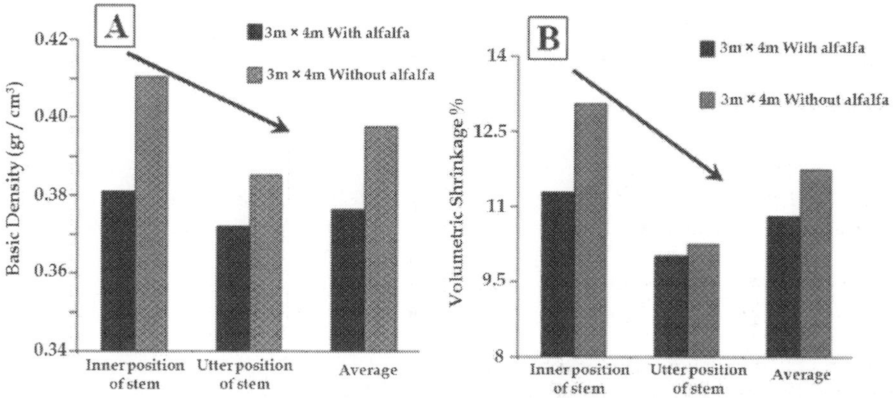

Fig. 12. Density and volumetric shrinkage variations in wood for 3 × 4 meters treatments with and without alfalfa

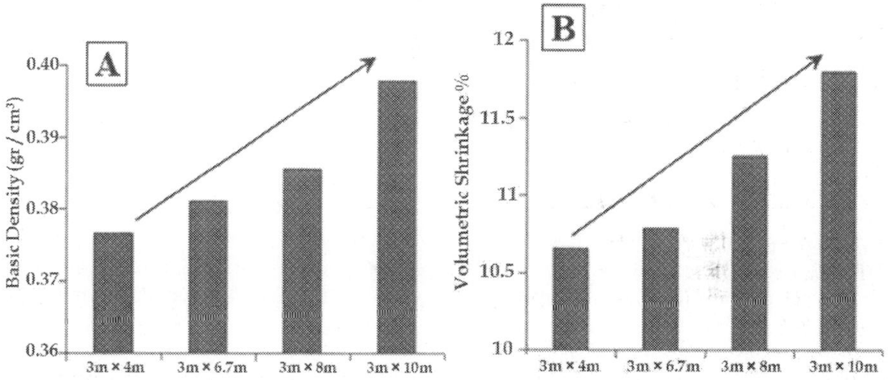

Fig. 13. Density and volumetric shrinkage variations in wood for different initial spacings intercropped with alfalfa

4.2 Permeability of wood

Wood permeability, as a physical property, is of vital importance and has great impact on wood and its utilization in different industries (Chen et al., 1998). Permeability is a critical property of porous materials that have continuous-porosity. Many industries need to know how permeable their porous material is so that they could use permeability values in decision-making processes for impregnation, drying, filtration, as well as other purposes. In hardwoods, longitudinal permeability is more important than transversal (radial and tangential) values because of vessel elements orientation along longitudinal axis of trees (Siau, 1971).

Intercropping and initial spacing significantly influences the vessel properties and capillary structures of wood (Efhami Sisi et al., 2010). Permeability is itself influenced by porosity and capillary structure of wood (Siau, 1995). Thus, the effects of agroforestry practices on permeability were investigated on the same treatments (Efhami Sisi et al., 2010).

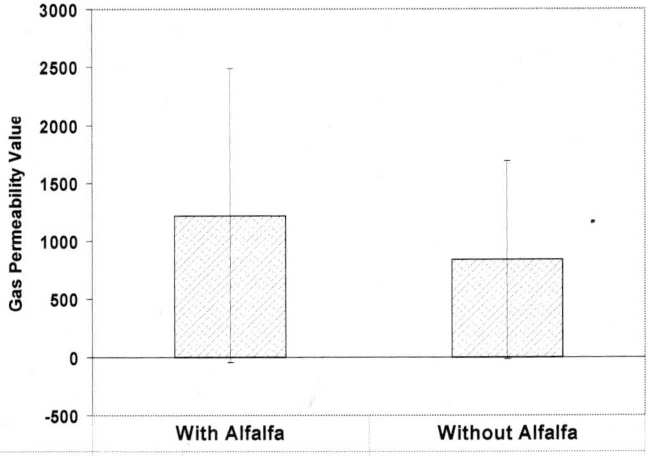

Fig. 14. Specific longitudinal gas permeability values ($\times 10^{-13}$ m^3 m^{-1}) for the two treatments of 3 × 4 meters with and without alfalfa

Longitudinal gas permeability values for tree stands with, and without, alfalfa were 1,220.4 and 840.2 $\times 10^{-13}$ (m^3 m^{-1}) (Fig. 14), respectively. There were no significant differences ($p < 0.05$) in longitudinal gas permeability between tree stands with and without alfalfa which is characteristic of permeability in solid woods (Taghiyari et al., 2010) (Fig. 14). As to the increase in vessel lumen area and vessel lumen diameter caused by intercropping with alfalfa (Table 3), the increase in permeability could have been expected. Furthermore, wider initial spacing showed an increasing effect on both longitudinal and radial gas permeability (Fig. 15).

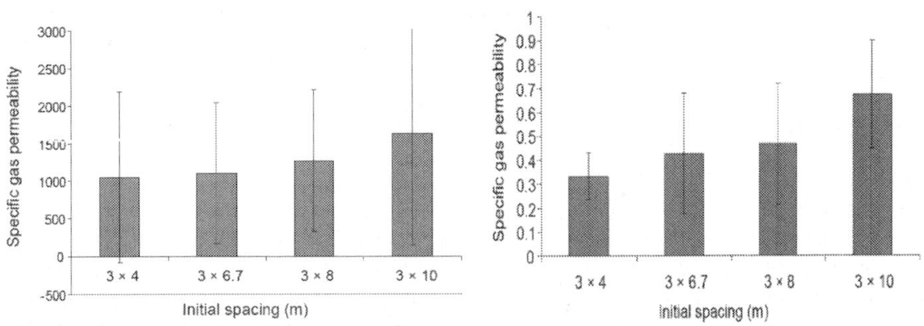

Fig. 15. Specific longitudinal (left) and radial (right) gas permeability values ($\times 10^{-13}$ m^3 m^{-1}) for the four initial spacings intercropped with alfalfa

A study of longitudinal gas permeability at different tree densities in intercropped treatments (Fig. 15) showed significant growth, caused by increase in initial-spacing, increased VLD and naturally gas permeability would be expected to improve. Longitudinal gas permeability increased by as much as 55% from 3×4 to 3×10, but VLD increased by only 7.2%. Poiseuille's law of viscous flow, which applies to gases through hardwood vessels, proves that there is positive relationship between permeability value and the fourth exponent of the radius of capillary (radius of vessels) (Equation 1) (Siau, 1971).

$$k_l = \frac{n\pi R^4}{8\eta} \times 1.013 \times 10^6 \qquad (1)$$

Where:

k_l = longitudinal permeability [cm^3 (fluid) cm^{-1} atm^{-1} sec^{-1}]
1 atm = 1.013×10^6 [dyne cm^{-2}]
R = radius of vessels [cm]
n = N/A = number of vessels per cm^2 of cross section
η = viscosity of fluid [dyne sec cm^{-2}]

The fourth exponent of the radius implies that a slight increase or decrease in vessel radius may have a high impact on gas permeability. A similar conclusion was made for longitudinal gas permeability values in *Populus deltoides* (69/55) and 5 trees of *Populus × euroamericana* (cv. I-214) (Taghiyari et al., 2010). However, VLA decreased by 10.2% from 3×4 to 3×10. But, there is a considerable increase in specific gas permeability (55%). Therefore, VLD had a greater effect on gas permeability than VLA.

Chen et al. (1998) studied correlation between different diameter growth rates caused by tree-tree competition and percentage of vessel lumen area (VLA%) in hardwoods, and found no significant correlation in three hardwoods (northern red oak, black walnut, and yellow poplar). However, they still found an increase in permeability in yellow poplar as growth rate increased. They concluded that other factors may also be involved in the increase in longitudinal sapwood permeability. These factors might include VLD and the type of perforation plates between vessel elements. Doungpet (2005) reported correlation coefficient between growth rate and VLA%, vessel frequency (VF), and VLD in six-year old *Populus deltoides* trees to be -0.137, -0.426, and 0.338 respectively. Therefore, an increase in growth rate may eventually result in more vessel diameter and consequently increases permeability values.

5. Conclusion

Current agroforestry practices (intercropping and initial spacing) may significantly influence the growth rate of trees rather than internal wood properties. In agroforestry systems, wider initial spacings are usually used to provide better sunlight for the agricultural crops. However, the wider spacings may have negative effects on the bole form of trees. In order to prevent this negative effect, narrower spacing may be used at the time of stand establishment; while the stand grows and crown of the trees expand, thinning and/or pruning may be used to provide enough sunlight for the agricultural crops. More growth rate induced by intercropping systems may influence wood properties. As to poplar-based agroforestry systems intercropped with alfalfa in particular, this increase in growth rate should not necessarily end up in shorter fiber length in young poplar trees as was previously believed. In the meantime, intercropping with alfalfa and wider initial spacing may alter the capillary structure of poplar wood in a way that its permeability is increased leading to some improved technical acceptance of wood.

6. Acknowledgment

Authors are grateful to all the contributing people helping us in the compiling of this chapter; Prof. Ali Karimi from UPM for his scientific support; Dr. Farhad Asadi for procurement of the sample trees; Prof. Peter Baas from IAWA journal, Prof. Roshafiza Mohamad and KA Sarifah from The Journal of Tropical Forest Science, Prof. Hubert Hasenauer from The Austrian Journal of Forest Science, and Prof. Ulrich Lüttge and Rob Guy From Trees - Structure and Function Journal for their great help. Also, we would like to deeply thank Dr. Hamid Reza Azemati and Dr. Mohammad Shams from Shahid Rajaee Teacher Training University for their intellectual support.

7. References

Arnold, D. H. & Mauseth, J.D. (1999). Effect of Environment Factors on Development of Wood. *American Journal of Botany*, Vol.86, No.3, pp. 367-371, ISSN 0002-9122

Asadi, F. (1994). Investigation of economic-society reasons on decline area cultivated of Poplar in marginal of Zanjan-rood River. M.Sc thesis. Natural Resources College, University of Tehran. 109 pp.

Asadi, F., Calagari, M., Ghasemi, R., & Bagheri, R. (2005). Investigation of Spacing Effect on Production of Poplar and Alfalfa in Intercropping. *Iranian Journal of Forest and Poplar Research*, Vol.12, No.4, pp. 455-480, ISSN 0883-1735

Ballard, L.A. & Long, J.N. (1988). Influence of Stand Density on Log Quality of Lodgepole Pine. *Canadian Journal of Forest Research*, Vol.18, No. 7, pp 911-916, ISSN 0045-5067

Bannan, M.W. (1967). Sequential Changes in Rate of Anticlinal Division, Cambial Cell Length, and Ring Width in the Growth of Coniferous Trees. *Canadian Journal of Botany*, Vol. 45, pp 1359–1369, ISSN 0008-4026

Barbour, R. J. & Kellogg, R. M. (1990) Forest management and end-product quality: a Canadian perspective. *Canadian Journal of Forest Research*. Vol.20, No. 4, pp 405-417, ISSN 0045-5067

Barna, M. (2011) Natural regeneration of *Fagus sylvatica* L.: a Review. *Austrian Journal of Forest Science*, Vol.128, No.2, pp 71–91, ISSN 03795292

Bowyer, J., Shmulsky, R. & Haygreen, J.G. (2007). *Forest products and wood science: an introduction*. Blackwell Publishing Ltd, ISBN-13: 978-0813820361, Oxford, UK.

Chaudhry, A.K. (2003). Comparative Study of Different Densities of Poplar in Wheat Based Agroforestry System in Central Punjab. PhD thesis, University of Agriculture, Faisalabad, Pakistan.

Chaudhry, A.K., Khan, G. S., Akhtar, M & Aslam, Z. (2003). Effect of Arable Crops on the Growth of Poplar (*Polpulus deltoides*) Tree in Agroforestry System. *Palestinian Journal of Agricultural Science*, Vol. 40, No.(1-2), pp 82-85, ISSN 0552-9034

Chen, P.Y.S., Zhang, G., & Van Sambeek, J.W. (1998). Relationships Among Growth Rate, Vessel Lumen Area, and Wood Permeability for Three Central Hardwood Species. *Forest Products Journal*. Vol.48, No.3, pp 87-90. ISSN: 0015-7473

De Jesus, R. M., Dias, G. B. N & Cardoso, E.M. (1988). Eucalyptus/Leucaena Mixture Experiment - Growth and Yeild. *IPEF journal*. Vol.39, No.2, pp 41-46, ISSN 0100-4557

DeBell, J.D.; Gartner, B.L. & DeBell, D.S. (1998). Fiber Length in Young Hybrid *Populus* Stems Grown at Extremely Different Rates. *Canadian Journal of Forest Resource*, Vol.28, No.4, pp 603-608, ISSN 0045-5067

DeBell, D.S., Christopher R.K. & Barbara L.G. (2002a). Wood density of *Eucalyptus saligna* Grown in Hawaiian Plantations: Effects of Silvicultural Practices and Relation to Growth Rate. Australian Forestry, Vol. 64, No. 2, pp. 106-110, ISSN 0004-9158

DeBell D.S., Singleton, R., Harrington, A. & Gartner, L.B. (2002b). Wood Density and Fiber Length in Young *Populus* Stems: Relation to Clone, Age, Growth rate, and Pruning. *Wood and Fiber Science*, Vol.34, No. 4, pp 529-539, ISSN 0735-6161

Dinwoodie, J.M. (1965). The Relationship between Fiber Morphology and Paper Properties: A Review of Literature. *Tappi*, Vol.48, pp 440– 447, ISSN 0039-8241

Doungpet, M. (2005). Environment and Genetic Effects on Wood Quality of *Populus*. PhD thesis. NCS University. Department of wood and paper science. USA.

Eaglesham, A. R. J.; A. Ayanaba; V. R. Rao & Eskew, D. L. (1981). Improving the Nitrogen Nutrition of Maize by Intercropping With Cowpea. *Soil Biology & Biochemistry*, Vol.13, pp 169-171, ISSN 0038-0717

Efhami Sisi D., Asadi F., Karimi A., & Pourthamasi K. (2008). Study on the Initial Spacing and Intercropping of Alfalfa on Bole Form and Annual Growth Rate of *Populus nigra betulifolia*. *Proceedings of The 1st Iranian Conference on supplying raw materials and development of Wood and Paper Industries*, Gorgan University of Natural Resources & Agriculture, Iran, December 3-4, 2008

Efhami Sisi, D & Saraeyan, A.R. (2009). Evaluation of Anatomical and Physical Properties of Juvenile/Mature Wood of *Populus alba* and *Populus × euramericana*. *Iranian Journal of Wood and Paper Science Research*, Vol.24, No.1, pp. 138-151, ISSN 1735-0913

Efhami Sisi, D.; Karimi, A.N.; Pourtahmasi, K.; Taghiyari, H.R & Asadi, F. (2010). The Effects of Agroforestry Practices on Vessel Properties in *Populus nigra* var. *betulifolia*. *IAWA Journal*, Vol.31, No.4, pp. 781-487, ISSN 0928-1541

Efhami Sisi D.; Karimi A.N.; Pourtahmasi K.; Taghiyari H.R (2011a). The Effects of Agroforestry Practices on Fiber Attributes in *Populus nigra* var. *betulifolia*. *Trees-Structure and Function*. DOI 10.1007/s00468-011-0604-4. ISSN 0931-1890

Efhami Sisi, D.; Karimi, A.N.; Pourtahmasi, K.; Asadi, F. & Mohamadzadeh, M. (2011b). The Effect of agroforestry practices on wood physical properties in Radial and Longitudinal Axis of *Populus nigra*. *Iranian Journal of Scientific Association of Wood & Paper*, (Accepted In Press)

Fujiwara, S. & Yang, K. C. (2000). The Relationship between Cell Length and Ring Width and Circumference Growth Rate in Five Canadian Species. *IAWA Journal*, Vol. 21, No.3, pp.335-345, ISSN 0928-1541

Jourez, B., A. Riboux & A. Leclercq. 2001. Anatomical Characteristics of Tension Wood and Opposite Wood in Young Inclined Stems of Poplar (*Populus euramericana cv 'Ghoy'*). *IAWA Journal*. Vol. 22, No. 2, pp 133–157, ISSN 0928-1541

Karki, T. (2001). Variation of Wood Density and Shrinkage in European Aspen, *Holz als Roh- und Werkstoff*, Vol.59, No. 1/2, pp 13-25. ISSN 0018-3768

Kollmann F.F.P, Cötè W.A. (1968). *Principles of Wood Science and Technology*. I. Solid Wood. Springer, ISBN-10 0387042970, Berlin Heidelberg, New York, 592 pp

Koubaa, A., R. E. Hernandez, M. Beaudoin & Poliquin, J. (1998). Interclonal, Intraclonal, and Within-Tree Variation in Fiber Length of Poplar Hybrid Clones. *Wood and Fiber Science*. Vol.30, No.1, pp 40–47, ISSN 0735-6161

Leakey, R. 1996. Definition of Agroforestry Revisited. *Agroforestry Today*, Vol. 8, No.1, pp 5-7, ISSN 1013-9591

Lundgren, A. L.1981. The Effect of Initial Number of Trees Per Acre and Thinning Densities on Timber Yields From Red Pine plantations the Lake States. Research Paper NC-193. St. Paul, MN: U.S. Dept. of Agriculture, Forest Service, North Central Forest Experiment Station

Mäkinen, H. (1998). Effect of thinning and natural variation in bole roundness in Scots Pine (*Pinus sylvestris*). *Forest Ecology and Management*, Vol.107, pp 231–239, ISSN: 0378-1127

Makinen, H. & Hein, S. (2006). Effect of Wide Spacing on Increment and Branch Properties of Young Norway Spruce. *European Journal of Forest Research*, Vol.125, No.3, pp 239–248, ISSN 1612-4669

Malinauskas, A. (1999). The Influence of the Initial Density and Site Conditions on Scots Pine Growth and Wood Quality. *Baltic Forestry*, Vol.5, No.2, pp 8-19, ISSN 1392 - 1355

Muthuri, C.W., Ong, C.K., Black, C.R., Ngumi, V.W., Mati B.M. (2005). Tree and Crop Productivity in *Grevillea, Alnus* and *Paulownia*-Based Agroforestry Systems in Semi-Arid Kenya. *Forest Ecology and Management*, Vol.212, No.1–3, pp 23–39, ISSN 0378-1127

Otengi, S.B.B., Stigter, C.J., N'ganga, J.K. & Mungai, D.N. (2000). Wind Protection in a Hedged Agroforestry System in Semi-Arid Kenya. Agroforestry Systems. Vol.50, No.2, pp 137–156, ISSN 0167-4366

Panshin,A.J. & C,Dezeeuw. (1980). *Text book of wood technology*, 4th edition, Mc Graw -Hill Publishing Co., ISBN ISBN 0-942391-04-7, New York

Pechmann, H. Von & Wutz, A. (1960). Haben Mineraldungung und lupinenaubau einen Kiefernholz? (Do Mineral fertilizer and Planting of Lupines Have any Effect on the Properties of wood of Spruce and Pine?). *Forestswiss. CBL*. Vol.79, No.2, pp 91-105, ISSN 1104-2877

Peszlen, I. (1993). Influence of site, clone, age, and growth rate on wood properties of three *Populus× euramericana* clones. PhD dissertation. Virginia Polytechnic Institute and State University, Blacksburg, Virginia.

Peszlen, I. (1994). Influence of Age on Selected Anatomical Properties of *Populus* clones. *IAWA Journal*, Vol.15, No.3, pp 311-321, ISSN 0928-1541

Pitre, E.F., Cooke, J. E. K., & Mackay, J. J. (2007). Short-Term Effects of Nitrogen Availability on Wood Formation and Fiber Properties in Hybrid Poplar. *Trees- Structure & function*, Vol.21, No. 2, pp 249–259, ISSN 0928-1541

Raymond, C.A. & Muneri, A. (2000). Effect of Fertilizer on Wood Properties of *Eucalyptus globules*. *Canadian Journal of Forest Resource*. Vol.30, No, pp 136–144, ISSN 0045-5067

Saarsalmi, A., Kukkola, M., Moilanen, M. & Arola, M. (2006). Long-Term Effects of Ash and N Fertilization on Stand Growth, Tree Nutrient Status and Soil Chemistry in a Scots Pine Stand. *Forest Ecology Management*, Vol.235, pp 116–128, ISSN: 0378-1127

Sea-Lee, S.; P. Vityakon & Prachaiyo, B. (1992). Effects of Erees on Paddy Bunds on Soil Fertility and Rice Growth in Northeast Thailand. *Agroforestry Systems*. Vol.18, No.3, pp 213-223, ISSN: 0167-4366

Shanavas, A. & Kumar, B.M. (2006). Physical and Mechanical Properties of Three Agroforestry Tree Species from Kerala, India. *Journal of Tropical Agriculture, Vol.*44, No.1–2, pp 23–30, ISSN 0973-5399

Siau, J.F. (1971). *Flow in Wood*, Syracuse University Press, ISBN 0815650280, New York, pp. 131.

Siau, J.F. (1995). Wood: Influence of Moisture on Physical Properties; Blacksburg, VA, Department of Wood Science and Forest Products Virginian Polytechnic Institute and State University, 1-63.

Singh, H. P., Kohli, R. K., & Batish, D. R. (2001) Allelophatic Interference of *Populus deltoides* With Some Winter Season Crop. *Agronomie*, Vol.21, No. 2, pp 139-146, ISSN 0249-5627

Singh, K., Ram, P., Singh, A. K. & Hussain, A. (1988). Poplar (*Populus deltoides* Batram Ex. Marshall) in forest and agroforestry systems. *Indian Forester*. Vol.114, No.11, pp 814-818, ISSN 0019-4816

Sjolte-Jorgensen, J. (1967). The Influence of Spacing on the Growth and Development of Coniferous Plantations. *International Reviwe of Forest Research*. Vol.2, pp 43-94, ISSN 1465-5489

Skelton, L. E. (2002). A Comparison of Conventional and Alternative Cropping System Using Alfalfa (*Medicago sativa*) and Winter Wheat (*Triticum aestovim*): An Agroecosystem Analysis. M.S thesis. The University of Georgia.

Snook, S.K., Labosky, P.l., Bowersox, T.W. & Blankenhorn, P.R. (1986). Pulp and Paper Making Properties of a Hybrid Poplar Clone Grown Under Four Management Strategies and Two Soil Sites. *Wood and Fiber Science*, Vol.18, No.1 , pp 157-167, ISSN 0735-6161

Taghiyari, H.R. & Sarvari Samadi, Y. (2010). Ultimate Length for Reporting Gas Permeability of *Carpinus betulus* Wood; *Special Topics & Reviews in Porous Media*, Vol.1, No.4, pp 345 - 351, ISSN Print: 2151-4798, ISSN Online: 2151-562X.

Taghiyari, H.R., Karimi, A.N., Parsapajouh, D. & Pourtahmasi, K. (2010). Study on the Longitudinal Gas Permeability of Juvenile Wood and Mature Wood; *Special Topics & Reviews in Porous Media*, Vol.1, No.1, pp 31 - 38, ISSN Print: 2151-4798, ISSN Online: 2151-562X

Taghiyari H.R., Efhami Sisi, D., Karimi, A. & Pourtahmasi, K. (2011) The Effect of Initial Spacing on Gas Permeability of *Populus nigra*. *Journal of Tropical Forest Science*, Vol.23, No.3, pp 305-310, ISSN 0128-1283

Taghiyari HR (2011) Effects of nano-silver on gas and liquid permeability of particleboard. Digest Journal of Nanomaterials and Bioresources, Vol. 6, No 4, October-December, pp 1509 - 1517; ISSN 1842 - 3582

Taghiyari HR, Talaei A., Karimi A. (2011) A correlation between th gas and liquid permeabilities of beech wood heat-treated in hot water and steam mediums. *Maderas. Ciencia y tecnologia*, 13(3): 329 - 336, ISSN 0717-3644 and e-ISSN 0718-221X

Taghiyari, H.R., Efhami Sisi, D. (2011) Diameter Increment Response of *Populus nigra* var. *betulifolia* Induced by Alfalfa. *Austrian Journal of Forest Science*, Vol.128, No.2, pp 113–127, ISSN 03795292

Taghiyari HR (2012) Correlation between Gas and Liquid Permeabilities in some Nano-Silver-Impregnated and Untreated Hardwoods. Journal of Tropical Forest Science, Accepted: JTFS 24(2): in press on April, 2012 issue, ISSN 0128-1283

Tisdal L. S., & Nelson L. W. (1974). *Soil Fertility & Fertilizers. Third edition.* Collier Macmillan. pp 402.

Ulvcrona, K.A., Claesson, S., Sahlen, K. & Lundmark, T. (2007). The Effects of Timing of Pre-Commercial Thinning and Stand Density on Stem Form and Branch Characteristics of *Pinus sylvestris*. *Forestry Advance Access*, Published May 21

Wodzicki, T.J. (2001). Natural Factors Affecting Wood Structure. *Wood Science and Technology*, Vol.35, No.1-2, pp 5-26, ISSN 0043-7719

Yin, R.S. (2004). Valuing the Impacts of Agroforestry in Northern China. Valuing Agroforestry Systems. pp. 259-280. The Netherlands: Kluwer Academic Publishers.

Zobel, B.J. & Spargue, J. R. (1998). *Juvenile Wood in Forest Trees*. Springer-Verlag, ISBN-10: 3540640320, New York. 300 pp.

Zobel, B.J., van Buijtenen, J.P., (1989). *Wood Variation: Its Causes and Control*, Springer-Verlag, ISBN-10: 038750298X, New York, 363 p

5

Shoot Pruning and Impact on Functional Equilibrium Between Shoots and Roots in Simultaneous Agroforestry Systems

Patrick E. K. Chesney
*United Nations Development Programme**
Guyana

1. Introduction

Shoot pruning of the woody components in simultaneous agroforestry systems with annuals and perennials enhances the services they provide to the ecosystem functions and to human livelihoods. These services include organic inputs, such as biomass and plant nutrients. Shoot pruning of the woody components is now an essential management practice in simultaneous agroforestry systems to avoid competition for growth factors, such as light and nutrients.

The purpose of this chapter is to review the biophysical science of shoot pruning of the woody components in simultaneous agroforestry systems with annual crops. The evidence from field experiments carried out mainly in the humid tropics is used to examine the impact of this management practice on the functional equilibrium between the shoots and roots of the woody component and to elucidate how the tree recovers from shoot pruning.

Research has shown that the outcome of the ecological interactions between woody and non-woody components in a simultaneous agroforestry system depends on species selection, shoot pruning management and spatial and temporal association of the components. This chapter focuses on shoot pruning management.

This review chapter is important because shoot pruning management of service trees - woody components - for the benefit of associated annual crops, and at the same time, for the maintenance of soil fertility and reduced environmental impact, remains an important determinant of the adoption of agroforestry systems.

Adoption of simultaneous agroforestry systems

Almost a quarter of a century ago, Raintree (1987) suggested that the adoptability of agroforestry technology depended on how well the technology is fitted to the social and environmental characteristics of the land use system. Further, this technology should possess the essential elements of productivity and sustainability. About one decade later,

* The views expressed in this publication are those of the author and do not necessarily represent those of the United Nations or UNDP.

Kass et al. (1997) analysed the evidence from the field and identified seven biophysical elements which could be manipulated to make alley cropping, a very popular simultaneous agroforestry system with annual crops, more productive, sustainable and acceptable to small producers. Around the same time, Current et al., (1995), in assessing farmer adoption of agroforestry in Central America and the Caribbean, reported mixed results for the rate of adoption of alley cropping technology, suggesting that the technology was not yet well fitted to the social and environmental characteristics of the land use systems of the farmers.

Current and colleagues (1995) went on to report that many farmers who adopted agroforestry systems, practiced shoot pruning of the woody components to rejuvenate them, increase productivity and reduce their environmental impact, indicating that there was understanding of the importance of the biophysical elements of productivity and sustainability. A better understanding of the biophysical science of shoot pruning management may lead to greater adoption of agroforestry systems in the tropics where poverty rates are high and land management for food and agriculture remains a major concern to governments and development partners.

What is known about the biophysical science of shoot pruning?

In his review of the merits of alley cropping, Sanchez (1995) argued that the failure of this system has been the inability to demonstrate that competition between the trees and associated crops for growth factors can be managed.

Since 1995, a number of field studies have been carried out to elucidate the mostly negative biophysical interactions aboveground between agroforestry trees and associated crops, and the required tree management by shoot pruning to avoid the negative interactions. The intensity of shoot pruning to preserve the service attributes of agroforestry trees, relative to the associated crops, has also been reviewed.

The operating premise of shoot pruning management is that managing perennial tree species by frequent pruning is possible because affected plants tend to restore the functional balance between above- and below-ground plant organs through reducing root respiration, slowing or ceasing root growth or reallocating carbon from storage organs in roots and stems to shoot meristems to support tree regrowth (Chesney & Vasquez, 2007; Eissenstat & Yanai, 1997). The consequence of acropetal movement of carbon from roots and stems to shoot meristems to provide energy for new shoot growth and restoration of photosynthetic capacity is the death of roots and nodules and contribution of carbon and nitrogen to soil pools (Chesney & Vasquez, 2007; Nygren & Campos, 1995; Nygren & Ramirez, 1993). This response mechanism by pruned trees is essential to recovery and sustainability of the tree-crop system.

What is not known about the biophysical science of shoot pruning?

What has not been reviewed in a cogent way is the evidence from the field on the effects of aboveground tree management (primarily shoot pruning) on tree roots and nodules and the regrowth of pruned trees. A review of the correlative processes between shoots and roots as a result of shoot pruning will increase understanding of shoot pruning as an important management practice in agroforestry systems and enhance the contribution of trees to agro-ecosystems.

2. Shoot pruning

2.1 What is pruning?

In the horticultural sense, pruning is the mechanical removal of vegetative and/or flowering and fruiting growth from a plant to regulate its size (Soule, 1985). This could take the form of thinning, the complete removal of individual branches or, heading, the trimming off of ends of branches. In the agroforestry literature, several manifestations of tree pruning are used and are reported as pollarding, coppicing or lopping, sometimes used interchangeably in the same article. For example, Islam et al., (2008) reported that *Sesbania grandiflora* L. can be pruned, lopped or pollarded for shoot development, forage production and green manuring purposes. That might be so, but it is important to understand each type of pruning and to associate them with their proper use.

The following definitions should provide some clarity as to the distinct practices these pruning terms refer to:

- Pollarding is the repeated pruning of branches at or near the same point, which results in a distinctive thick bushy appearance of the trees (Soule, 1985). This practice involves cutting off the crown of a tree. Typically, depending on pruning height and the needs of associated crops, pollarding allows a time window of 3-4 months where there is near zero completion for light. However, fine roots and nodules start to regrow at 2-3 months after pruning and competition for nutrients may occur.
- Coppicing is the periodic heading back of a small wood or thicket grown for this purpose in like manner from forest trees or shrubs (Soule, 1985). Essentially, this practice involves cutting the tree down to the stump and allowing it to regrow to maximise biomass production. This type of pruning provides a longer time window (4-6 months depending on species) in which there is near zero competition for light between coppiced tree and crop.
- Lopping is the cutting off e.g. of leafy branches or twigs from a tree (Akunda & Huxley, 1990). The time window for renewal of interspecific competition for light is similar to trees managed by pollarding but may be less depending on branch autonomy for carbon uptake.

Comparatively speaking, coppicing is the most extreme of the tree cutting practices, usually involving cutting to a height of 10-30 cm above ground. Lopping, cutting off branches, commonly leaves stubs of about 30-100 cm long on 150 - 200 cm main stems, whilst pollarding is usually done at a height of 75-150 cm depending on the service function of the agroforestry tree.

In alley cropping, the pollard height of 75 cm is commonly used (Kass et al., 1997). When trees are used as live stakes for vegetables such as tomato, a pollard height of 150 cm is preferred (Chesney et al., 2000). In shaded coffee (*Coffea arabica* L.) systems, shade trees made up predominantly of *Erythrina poeppigiana* (Walp.) O.F. Cook, are both lopped and pollarded usually at a height of 1.5 - 2 m (Beer et al., 1998; Muschler et al., 1993).

Therefore, pollarding, coppicing and lopping are tree cutting practices used for different purposes and care should be exercised in the use of these terms in the agroforestry literature. Each practice exerts a different physiological stress on the service tree and this has implications for the correlative mechanism involved in tree recovery, time to restoration of service attributes to the tree and contribution to enhancing the agro-ecosystem. For instance it is importance to understand the organ source of carbon for regrowth. On one hand, if the tree stem is the organ source of carbon then tree pruning management by coppicing may contribute to decline and eventual death of the coppiced trees. On the other hand, lopping or partial pollarding (e.g. leaving one branch on the pruned stump) may lead to the growth of the retained branch at faster rate than other branches from shoots on the pruned stump (Chesney, 2008; Chesney & Vasquez, 2007). This may be due to branch autonomy for carbon uptake independent of the needs of other developing shoots on the pruned stump and this may be species and season dependent (Sprugel, 2002; Sprugel et al., 1991).

2.2 Why prune trees in agroforestry systems?

Pruning agroforestry trees in simultaneous agroforestry systems, particularly in the humid tropics, enhances resource (mainly light) supply (Cannell, 1983) and controls the competitive ecological interaction between the trees and associated crops (Siriri et al., 2010; Bayala et al., 2008). Use of the available growth resources is by competitive interaction between species (Anderson & Sinclair, 1993).

In alley cropping, tree-crop interaction for light exceeds or nullifies the positive contributions to soil fertility made by the service trees (Rao et al., 1998). Analysis of alley cropping data from Turrialba, Costa Rica (Kass, 1987) has shown negative (-3%) or near neutral (1%) estimates of overall interaction effect for commonly used *E. poeppigiana* and *G. sepium* hedgerow trees, respectively. In home gardens in the humid areas of Kerala, India, Chandrashekara (2007) recommended shoot pruning for 10 important tree species to avoid competition with associated understorey crops. Hedgerow pruning of mimosa (*Albizia julibrissin* Durazz) increased light interception and reduced water stress in maize crops (Kang et al., 2008). There is no doubt that shoot pruning of the service tree in a simultaneous agroforestry system with annual crops is a necessary management practice to avoid competition for light between the tree and crop and to enhance the performance of the crop, maintain the service attributes of the tree species and enhance contribution of residual fertility to the agro-ecosystem.

Pruning as a management practice, while widely practised, has received little analytical attention in agroforestry research and extension. About 15 years ago, van Noordwijk et al. (1996) acknowledged the need for more research on aboveground tree management (shoot pruning), particularly the effects on tree roots. Timmer and colleagues (1996) investigated the reasons why farmers prune trees and found that, rejuvenation and improvement of tree survival and productivity as well as a reduction of tree influence on its environment were the more important ones. More than one-half of the farmers interviewed applied intensive pruning i.e., cutting all main branches to or at the same distance from the trunk. Over the fifteen year period (1996-2011), a number of field experiments were carried out on the effect of aboveground tree management on tree roots and nodules as well as the correlative processes involved in tree regrowth. The results of these studies are examined below.

2.2.1 Importance of branch retention on the pruned stump

Before 1996, shoot pruning management tended to be the complete removal of tree canopy to a certain tree height (pollarding, coppicing) at least twice per year to coincide with the planting of annual crops. Marginal increases in crop performance and poor survival of the pruned trees, especially when pruning was more than twice a year, led researchers to realise that the preservation of service attributes of the tree when pruning frequency is more than twice per year required a change in pruning intensity from complete removal of all branches (complete pruning) to retaining at least a single leafy branch (partial pruning). Partial pruning when applied twice or more per year to the service tree was found to be better than increasing the frequency of complete pruning or leaving too many branches on the pruned tree stump at pruning.

Depending on the desired height of the retained stump, complete pruning may be achieved by coppicing, pollarding or lopping. On the other hand, partial pruning may be achieved through pollarding and lopping with the slight modification of retaining foliage on the intact branch. There is a history to partial pruning. Leaving one or two branches on the pruned tree stump is a traditional partial pruning practice in Costa Rican coffee farms (Somarriba et al., 1996), a practice that is sometimes referred to as 'lung branch' pruning in Asian tea (*Camellia sinensis* (L.) O. Kuntze) farms (Kandiah et al., 1984). Its utility to simultaneous agroforestry systems was scientifically investigated towards the end of the 20th century.

In a series of experiments carried out at Turrialba, Costa Rica, Chesney & Nygren (2002) and Chesney (2008) found that partial pruning (retention of a single branch representing about 5% of foliar biomass before pruning) conserved fine roots. The authors argued that this result may have been due to the maintenance of a sequence of axes leading from leaves to stem and root system for allocation of photosynthates. Partial pruning nearly doubled the total above-ground biomass and increased nitrogen accumulation in the above-ground biomass by 60 kg ha^{-1} yr^{-1} compared to complete pruning. In accordance with the principle of branch autonomy for carbon uptake (Sprugel et al. 1991), 75% of new shoot growth occurred on the retained branch of partially pruned *E. poeppigiana* (Chesney, 2008). Sprugel (2002) posits that the critical characteristics of a branch's carbohydrate economy (e.g. photosynthesis, respiration, growth) are largely independent of the tree to which the branch is attached as long as light is the primary factor limiting photosynthesis and growth.

2.2.2 Key species evaluated in agroforestry systems managed by shoot pruning

The selection and use of suitable trees and shoot pruning regime remain important to successful annual crop production in simultaneous agroforestry systems in the humid tropics.

In terms of the woody component, the fast growing nitrogen-fixing leguminous trees that have shown tolerance to shoot pruning and that are used extensively in simultaneous agroforestry systems with annual crops include: *G. sepium*, *Grevillea* spp, Casuarina spp, *Leucaena leucocephala* (Lam.) de Wit, *Erythrina* spp, *Eucalyptus* spp and *Sesbania* spp.

Most of the studies done on simultaneous agroforestry systems with annual crops have disproportionately focused on maize (*Zea mays* L.) and beans (*Phaseolus vulgaris* L.), although some examples of studies on vegetables in simultaneous agroforestry systems have been reported. For example, work with vegetable crops associated with N-fixing leguminous trees has been reported in various growing environments in the tropical zones of Africa (Nigeria, Ivory Coast), Asia (Philippines, India and Papua New Guinea) and the Americas (Costa Rica, Peru). The production of such crops like pepper (*Piper nigrum* L.) in

India and yam (*Dioscorea alata* L.) in Nigeria and Costa Rica, are mainly in bush fallows although some form of alley cropping is practised, e.g. with tomato (Chesney et al. 2000). Sweet potato (*Ipomoea batatas* (L.) Poir) has been evaluated in an agroforestry system in Papua New Guinea (Brook, 1992).

In these systems, the shoot pruning height and frequency of pruning of the woody component depend on the needs of the associated crop and the tolerance of the woody component to frequent shoot pruning.

2.2.3 Implications of shoot pruning

In classical horticulture, the manner in which pruning cuts are made may extend or shorten the longevity of a tree while the invigorating effect of pruning depends on the time of year it is done and how much is pruned. For example, when a thinning cut is made to reduce density, care should be taken not to leave short stubs as these either dieback to the base or give rise to shoots from dormant buds located at the base of the stubs. These vigorous stubs divert energy from the tree.

Architecturally, branches are structurally attached to the trunk by a series of trunk collars that envelope the branch collars every growing season. When the trunk collar is injured or removed by branch pruning, the trunk xylem above and below the cut is rapidly and extensively infected and decay develops (Shigo, 1990). This is common in pruning management of agroforestry trees and is unavoidable as the benefits from more careful pruning may not offset the incident costs of pruning.

In agroforestry, it is the propensity of pruned stumps to regrow shoots from dormant buds that is exploited to ensure tree survival through shoot regrowth and restoration of physiological function to the tree. Dieback associated with shoot pruning cannot be avoided in managed agroforestry systems because of the objective and cost of shoot pruning, the latter being the main factor in situations where there is a shortage of labour.

In one of the few reported estimation of the cost of shoot pruning, van Noordwijk et al. (1997) calculated that pruning and maintenance of hedgerows (row 4 m; pruning height 0.5-1 m; regular pruning) require 80-100 person-days per year which may represent a large fraction of total amount of annual household labour available for farming (ICRAF, 1996). Brook (1992) reported that 108 man-days were required to manage the hedges of an experimental area of 0.24 ha in a single cropping season. This labour requirement could conflict with the farmer's peak demand for labour (Sanchez, 1995) and the opportunity cost inherent in delayed or less frequent pruning and increased competition may be too high. The cost: benefit analysis of shoot pruning has not been examined.

The deleterious effect of dieback is avoided when fast growing, nitrogen fixing trees are used in managed agroforestry systems and they are pollarded or lopped to retain at least one branch. The fast growth rate of the trees, and especially shoots on the retained branch, allow for rapid restoration of photosynthetic capacity to the tree in the regrowing vegetation on tree stumps. Dieback can be selectively removed in subsequent pruning.

There is an effect of season on shoot pruning. Trees pruned during the dry season resprout more vigorously compared to the response during the rainy season. Chesney & Vasquez

(2007) reported that pruned *E. poeppigiana* and *G. sepium* trees mobilised similar amounts of starch in roots and stems in the rainy season but more starch in stems in the dry season because sink demand was greater in the dry season when greater and faster resprouting occurred compared to the wet season. In that experiment, resprouting occurred two weeks earlier during the dry season compared to the wet season.

2.2.4 How much aboveground biomass to prune?

In horticulture, whatever the pruning regime, the rule of thumb is that pruning trees for delivering service functions to crop production should be done in a way to retain the correlative processes of apical dominance or apical control as well as the allocation mechanism to maintain feedback among the sources and sinks (Wilson, 1990), particularly with respect to biomass and nitrogen availability and use. These correlative processes are examined in section 3.2.

In agroforestry systems, shoot pruning removes apical dominance and attention is more focussed on the allocation mechanism between sources and sinks for carbon and nitrogen. How much to prune depends on species, canopy size, light needs of the crop and rate of recovery of the tree species. Shoot pruning amount is a function of height of pruning, shoot biomass at time of pruning and frequency of pruning in a cropping year.

Of three legume trees tested for rotational alley cropping, *G. sepium* appeared to be a suitable candidate species owing to its superior tolerance to long term pruning compared to *E. orientalis* and *Calliandra calothyrsus* Benth., which died back after 3 and 6 years, respectively (van Noordwijk et al., 1995). The physiological reason appears to be the rapid replenishment of starch in roots of *G. sepium*. In a study of the dynamics of non-structural carbohydrates reserves in pruned *E. poeppigiana* and *G. sepium* in Costa Rica, Chesney and Vasquez (2007) found that replenishment of starch in roots of *G. sepium* reached 70% of its initial concentration by 12 weeks after pruning. Root stores of starch in this species play an important role in its post-prune recovery and tolerance to pruning.

Increasing lopping height (1-1.5 m) and reducing pruning frequency (2-3 times per year) not only maintain high biomass production over the long term albeit, with a decreasing tendency over time (Keerthisena, 1995) but do lead to increased survivability of the trees. For example, Duguma et al. (1988) recommended that *G. sepium* should be pruned fewer than four times per year since this frequency of pruning could reduce tree stand by as much as 25%. In a field experiment with Leucaena in Bangladesh, Tipu et al., (2006) found that pruning at 1.5 m height yielded the highest biomass compared to lower pruning heights.

Tree survivability to frequent pruning may be related to tree age. Duguma et al. (1988) opined that further studies are needed to examine the relationship between age of seedlings and pruning intensity on survival and biomass production. Although the elucidation of this relationship remains unrealised, some insights in research results have been provided. Chadhokar (1982) reported that frequent cuttings of young trees had a negative yielding effect on Gliridicia in later years. Chesney (2008), who reported that completely or partially pruned two year old *E. poeppigiana* tree yielded less aboveground biomass (4.4 or 7 Mg ha^{-1} yr^{-1}) than eight-year-old trees (5.5 or 9Mg ha^{-1} yr^{-1}), similarly pruned although there is a higher investment in root growth in younger trees. Figures represent wet or dry season. Shoot pruning was carried out four times per year, during the two cropping seasons.

Partial shoot pruning is better than complete shoot pruning insofar as preserving tree survival, continuing ecosystem function and contributing biomass and nutrients in pruned shoots, nodules and fine roots to the agro-ecosystem (Chesney, 2008).

3. Shoot pruning and correlative processes in trees

3.1 Functional equilibrium hypothesis

The functional equilibrium hypothesis proposed by Brouwer (1962, 1983) contends that plants display a tendency to maintain a constant balance between growth rates of shoots and roots. The balance is regulated by the demand for plant resources such as non-structural carbohydrates and nitrogen. When nitrogen limits growth, root growth is relatively favoured and when the limiting factor is non-structural carbohydrate, which can occur after shoot pruning, aboveground growth is relatively favoured. Using these two growth factors to illustrate the point, the typical plant response in the restoration, or the establishment, of a new functional equilibrium between shots and roots, is to mobilise non-structural carbohydrate reserves in the stem or roots to support resprouting and early shoot growth. Research carried out by a number of researchers support this contention (Chesney & Vasquez, 2007; von Fircks & Snnerby-Forsse, 1998; Erdmann et al., 1993).

Kang (1993) posited that competition between trees and crops may be sufficient to outweigh the positive benefit of mulching especially on highly acidic and low moisture status soils. The selection of N-fixing and fast growing trees may not be the solution rather there is an urgent need to look for complementarity in rooting of trees and crops. From the limited root studies undertaken with leguminous trees in vegetable production, *G. sepium* presented little competition when associated with a yam crop (Budelman, 1990). Soil tillage in planting strips of crops could reduce competition from superficially rooted trees or covercrop in addition to facilitating contribution of organic matter and nutrients from cut roots. There is an insufficient body of published literature on this topic to evaluate its usefulness as a management practice or to compare with shoot pruning.

3.2 Shoot pruning and correlative processes

The previous sections have established that shoot pruning management of the woody component in simultaneous agroforestry systems such as alley cropping is a standard practice to avoid competition for growth resources (e.g. light, water, nutrients) between the woody and non-woody components. Field research support the contention that shoot pruning enhances resource (such as light) supply and use of the resource is by competitive interaction between species (Anderson & Sinclair, 1993). In some simultaneous agroforestry systems such as alley cropping, without tree pruning management, the tree-crop competition for light exceeds or nullifies the positive contributions to soil fertility made by the service trees (Ong et al., 1996).

Reviews of alley cropping have shown that there is soil improvement through mulch effect (Oelbermann & Voroney, 2010; van Noordwijk et al., 1997) but competition for light, water (especially in the dry tropics) and nutrients could outweigh its advantage (Sanchez, 1995; van Noordwijk et al., 1997). This finding led to a system-based approach to avoid the negative tree-crop interaction in simultaneous agroforestry systems was pursued. Rotational alley cropping where trees are still in hedgerows but cropping is not continuous, in other words, a phasic alternation of tree and crop, was introduced. During the crop phase, trees are severely cut back by shoot pruning near to ground level (coppicing) to reduce interspecific competition as well as labour for pruning, yet the tree stumps are supposed to survive and allow a quick regrowth of trees after 1-3 years of cropping. Candidate trees for this system must survive the setback of pruning and develop a proper tree canopy when left to grow (van Noordwijk et al., 1997). This approach may reduce competition for light between tree and crop but the required frequent soot pruning of the woody component may affect its survivability, and therefore the choice of shoot pruning method assumes high importance.

For that kind of intensive shoot pruning management (coppicing), it is important to select trees species that store adequate amounts of carbohydrates in the roots to provide the energy for resprouting and rapid regrowth of above ground parts. Shoot regrowth from other less intensive shoot pruning (pollarding or lopping) could be energetically supported from carbohydrate stores in stems and roots of the pruned tree stump.

Shoot pruning alters the growth and development of trees at different organ levels. This practice changes the leaf area and photosynthetic capacity of a tree. Also, it is thought to affect the metabolic equilibrium between the above- and below-ground organs by reducing the amount of growing shoots that function as sources and sinks for nutrients and hormones. Shoot pruning could cause death of fine roots and nodules under some conditions because of inadequate carbohydrate supply and so temporarily interrupt the nitrogen fixing ability of the tree.

3.2.1 Effect of shoot pruning on nodules

Shoot pruning affects root nodulation and temporarily interrupts the nitrogen fixing ability of leguminous tree. Fownes & Anderson (1991) reported nodule loss after cutting *S. sesban* and *L. leucocephala* in a pot study, which was relatively greater that root loss, but recovery to uncut equilibrium occurred within two weeks of shoot pruning. They suggested that a complete turnover of nodules would liberate about 5 kg N ha^{-1} assuming living nodules are approximately 10% N, there is no reabsorption of nitrogen out of senescing nodules and that nodule decomposition is rapid. Chesney & Nygren (2002) reported that nodules of *E. poeppigiana* may be more sensitive than fine roots to aboveground disturbance, which may be more pronounced in older trees (8-year-old) compared to younger trees (2-year-old). During the time when nodulation is affected, tree requirements for nitrogen would be met from uptake of mineral nitrogen. New nodules and fine roots of *E. poeppigiana* are initiated from 10-14 weeks after pruning (Chesney & Nygren 2002; Vaast & Snoeck, 1999).

G. sepium nodulates mostly on lateral roots. Parrota & Singh (1992) found first order laterals of 0.9-2.5 m long in the upper 20 cm of soil in Puerto Rico, where most plant available nutrients are found. This would suggest that in addition to shoot pruning, soil tillage in the crop planting rows could manage potential inter-specific competition for growth factors.

The strain of *Rhizobium* has an effect on the nitrogen fixing potential of *G. sepium*. Awonaike et al. (1992) observed that di-nitrogen fixation and general performance could be either low or high depending on inoculum strain. The nitrogen derived from transfer (Ndft) when *G. sepium* was in association with *Bradyrhizobium* and *Rhizobium* was 47% = 20 mg N per plant and 61% = 28 mg N per plant, respectively.

3.2.2 Effect of shoot pruning on fine roots

Above-ground pruning is known to cause death of fine roots under some conditions because of inadequate carbohydrate supply (Fownes & Anderson 1991; Erdmann et al., 1993). Other factors contributing to root death are natural senescence and water stress. Govindarajan et al. (1996) reported that the first pruning of Leucaena in the semi-arid highlands of Kenya did not induce root death because root system was least active towards the end of the dry season. Root growth started with the commencement of rains. As rainfall declined and water stress sets in, root death occurred. Shoot pruning at this time accelerated root death. The researchers found that nutrient contribution through fine root turnover of hedgerows for crop growth to be small compared to aboveground biomass.

Chesney & Nygren (2002) reported that nodule and fine root turnover as a result of shoot pruning was compensated for by new production at 10-14 weeks after pruning thus corroborating earlier observations that *E. poeppigiana* requires 10-16 weeks to renew N_2 fixation (Vaast and Snoeck, 1999). Half yearly (Nygren and Ramirez, 1995) or four (Chesney and Nygren, 2002) shoot prunings per year resulted in complete turnover of nodules and over 50% decrease in fine root mass (Nygren and Campos, 1995; Muñoz and Beer, 2001). The authors concluded that the retention of a branch on the pruned *E. poeppigiana* allow better fine root and nodule survival and enhances tree biomass production.

Further evidence of how aboveground biomass retention influences root behaviour was presented by other researchers. Fownes & Anderson (1991) reported that fine root biomass was correlated with leaf biomass in uncut tress but cutting disrupted this equilibrium. Akinnifessi et al. (1995) working with Leaucaena hedgerows on an alfisol found fewest roots in regularly pruned hedgerows with prunings removed. Fewer structural roots were present in topsoil when continuous pruning and no alley cropping and prunings removed were applied. Regular removal of pruning biomass reduced abundance of fine roots by 61.4% and increased the number of roots by 24%. The abundance of structural roots (>20 mm) was not significantly affected by hedgerow pruning and cultivation and a shift from fine root to coarse root was observed in unpruned trees. Regular pruning and biomass export from the plot significantly depressed fine root growth by 88% compared to unpruned hedgerow. Hedgerow pruning and cultivation (root pruning especially with hoe-weeding) can be used to reduce presence of structural root growth in the plough layer.

Another potential indicator of tree productivity is stem basal diameter as suggested by Parotta & Singh (1992). The researchers worked with *G. sepium* and found stem basal diameter to be a good predictor of both shoot and root biomass, which could in turn could be correlated with tree regrowth potential and contribution of biomass and nutrients to soil. Further work is needed to test the goodness of this indicator in an agroforestry system where trees are managed by periodic shoot pruning.

3.2.3 Resprouting of pruned trees

Shoot pruning affects the physiological processes of photosynthesis and non-structural carbohydrate synthesis. Non-structural carbohydrate reserves, mainly starch provide the energy to drive regrowth of pruned trees. Starch provides energy for respiration of active buds and synthesis of chlorophyll, proteins and structural compounds during early stages of leaf growth, processes that influence the rate of resprouting and biomass output of pruned trees. Other factors that affect the regrowth of pruned trees include the severity of disruption to the photosynthetic capacity and the resprouting rate.

Chesney and Vasquez (2007) found that the critical tree regrowth stage for starch mobilisation was that of vigorous sprout development at six or four weeks (depending on wet or dry season) after pruning, particularly in completely pruned trees. The authors reported that there was an important species difference with respect to starch replenishment in trees regrowing from pruning. For *G. sepium*, starch accumulation in roots recommenced at 12 weeks after pruning compared to *E. poeppigiana* roots where starch accumulation recommenced later than 12 weeks. At that time, new nodules and fine roots are produced in these species.

In a study with *E. fusca* Lour. and *G. sepium* in the humid Atlantic lowlands of Costa Rica, Muschler et al. (1993) found that of these trees pollarded twice per year, *G. sepium* was the first to resprout. Its crown base after four months shifted upward at maximum diameter in a form which allows for good light transmission to the associated crop while *E. fusca* continued to expand and achieved crown closure at six months of regrowth thus not permitting penetration of photosynthetically active radiation into the stand. Since the main consideration is on labour saving in pruning but with reduced competition, the authors concluded that *G. sepium* appears best for this role.

The implications for associated crop management are several. Since shoot pruning removes competition for light between the tree and associated crop, it also provides a time window of almost one month when no competition in the soil can be expected between tree and crop roots for plant available nutrients. Transplanting of crop seedlings can then be made at shoot pruning to aid the early growth of seedlings. Depending on the needs of the crop, another shoot pruning of the agroforestry trees may be needed during the life of the crop, preferably before the onset of the reproductive phase of crop development.

4. Tree pruning and contribution to ecosystems

4.1 Biomass and carbon pools

The management of both tree and crop for the benefit of the crop and at the same time for maintenance of soil fertility and reduced environmental contamination is the main challenge to farmers and researchers alike. The nature of the interaction depends mainly on species selection, pruning management of the trees and time of association.

Erythrina spp. produce more above-ground biomass than *G. sepium* when similarly pruned (Table 1). These data are site specific but serve as a useful guide to biomass yield from trees managed by periodic shoot pruning in agroforestry systems. Increasing tree density and pruning frequency did not increase the biomass output of *G. sepium*. Chesney (2008) reported that increasing pruning frequency increased biomass yield and available nitrogen, a finding that depends on species and ecosystem type.

Tree species	Tree density (plants/ha)	Pruning frequency	Tree biomass (Mg DM/ha/yr)	Available N (kg/ha)	Source
E. berteroana Urb.	1,600	Twice/year	3.8	146	Muschler et al., 1993
E. poeppigiana	1,666	Four/year	4.9-8	141-221	Chesney, 2008
E. fusca			3.4	124	
G. sepium			2.3	90	
			2-7		Otu & Agboola, 1994
G. sepium	2,500	Thrice/year	2.1		
				109	Brook, 1992

Table 1. Biomass production of N-fixing trees used in simultaneous agroforestry systems

Effect of pruning on performance of tree species varies. Siriri et al., (2010) reported that pruning increased survival in *Calliandra* spp., reduced survival in *Sesbania* spp. while *Alnus* spp. was unaffected by pruning.

In some cases, continual pruning can reduce dry matter yield over time. Keerthisena (1995) reported that annual shoot dry matter yield decreased from a maximum of 9 t ha^{-1} in year 2, to 4.3 t ha^{-1} by year 5, which would still be adequate to maintain soil fertility at a desirable level in the sub-humid tropics (Young, 1981). Increasing lopping height increased shoot dry matter yield meaning more food reserves available for vigorous regrowth. Difference in dry matter yield between short and tall trees will increase in time showing a decreasing trend in annual shoot dry matter yields at high levels. According to Karim & Savill (1991), 2 m wide alleys produced 2.8 times more biomass than 4 m wide alleys at first harvest one year after tree establishment. However, short term yield of tree biomass in hedgerows was not found to be a useful predictor of long-term yield (Keerthisena, 1995).

Kang (1993) proposed that there is functional similarity of trees in alley cropping and bush fallows which include the provision of nitrogen from atmospheric fixation, recycling of nutrients, suppression of weeds and increasing organic matter content. During the cropping phase, which alternates with a bush fallow, the stumps of the trees help to re-establish woody vegetation, which can partially restore soil fertility during the fallow period. In alley cropping, trees and crops grow together, not necessarily at the same rate but do present opportunity for interaction. In some species, woodiness appears from week 4 onwards, and as long as the interval of successive shoot pruning is greater than four weeks, biomass yield will be greater.

4.2 Pruning and nitrogen dynamics

Research has shown that partial shoot pruning is preferred to complete shoot pruning to preserve the service attributes of trees, including biomass production, nutrient availability and faster tree recovery.

Before a managed tree can be of use to the agroforestry system to which it is a part, it must fulfil its own needs. In terms of fulfilling its nitrogen and phosphorous requirements, *G. sepium* seems a very efficient tree. Liyanage et al. (1994) reported that Gliricidia could obtain some 64% of its nitrogen from the atmosphere under field conditions. Duhoux & Dommergues (1984) quantified N-fixation in *G. sepium* to be about 13 kgN ha^{-1} yr^{-1}. The requirement of this species for phosphorous seems to have been met by mycorrhizal association. Mulongoy (1983) reported an infection of 25 to 82% suggesting that Gliricidia can thrive well in soils low in available phosphorous.

It has been reported that some 40kg N could be available to associated crops from the biomass of *G. sepium* (Kang & Mulongoy, 1987). van Noordwijk and colleagues (1997) calculated that the nitrogen yield of prunings from trees pruned twice is usually not more that the equivalence of 60 kg N as urea per crop. Taking a conservative estimate of labour costs of pruning as 20 man-days ha^{-1} cycle^{-1}, these authors made the interesting observation that the rewards for this labour are 1.5 kg urea day^{-1} or US$0.38 day^{-1}. They concluded that although trees can be successful in a supportive role from a biophysical point of view, farmer acceptance of such technology is more likely if the trees have a productive role as well.

Shoot pruning or shading can reduce the rate at which legume plants fix nitrogen. Ryle et al. (1985) found that defoliation reduced the rate of N-fixation, photosynthesis and respiration by >70, 83-96 and 30-40 %, respectively. The original rates of N-fixation were attained after one week's growth. Siddique & Bal (1990) reported that the rate of N_2 fixation decreased at night and under shady conditions during the day. Thus, any shading and/or defoliation which diminish photosynthate supply can also limit the fixation of nitrogen.

Several authors have shown the high contribution of nitrogen in aboveground biomass of *E. poeppigiana*. Both Beer (1988) and Kass et al., 1993) have reported N-yield in excess of 250 kg N ha yr^{-1} of trees managed by twice-yearly complete pruning. Chesney (2008) reported the amount of N cycled in aboveground biomass was 123 or 187 kg ha^{-1} (2 year old trees) and 160 or 256 kg ha^{-1} (8 year old trees) when managed by complete or partial pruning, respectively.

Using the nutrient requirements of certain 'stakeable' vegetables that could be included in simultaneous agroforestry systems, it is clear how their major nutrient needs could be met from nutrient content of pruned biomass (Table 2). However, continuous cultivation of annual crops on many humid tropical soils leads to a decline in nitrogen availability and total soil nitrogen (Sanchez et al., 1983). Palm (1995) reported that legume mulches applied at the realistic rate of 4 t ha^{-1} yielded 8-12 kg P ha^{-1}. Sanginga and colleagues (1994) reported that irrespective of pruning treatments in *G. sepium* more total P was allocated to stems than to leaves and branches suggesting a possible role in tree regrowth and consequently, less availability for turnover.

Crop	Yield (kg/ha)	Nutrient requirement (kg/ha)			Source
		N	P	K	
Tomato	14,500	98	11.88	118.69	IICA 1989
Cucumber	10,900	45	15.84	58.93	IICA 1989
Black pepper	350	75	49.5	46.5	De Geus 1973

Table 2. Nutrient needs (based on extractive potential) for selected vegetables.

4.3 Quality of biomass and nutrient release

Myers and colleagues (1994) stated that the synchronisation of nutrient release from plant residues and uptake by plants is a central paradigm in applied soil biological research. This concept was earlier developed by Swift (1985) and elaborated by Haggar et al. (1993).

The rate of decomposition and the amount of nitrogen mineralised from plant residues determine the short-term benefits of tree pruning to crop nitrogen uptake. Efficiency of use of nitrogen in plant residue depends on the rate of decomposition affected by the ratio of nitrogen:polyphenol:lignin (Palm & Sanchez, 1991), mineralisation as affected by the C:N ratio (Weeraratna, 1979), and protein binding (Handarayan et al., 1997). Gliricidia has a C:N ration of 10, low lignin content of 3.9% and could lose 50% of initial P after 20 days of decomposition (Mulongoy, 1983). Wilson et al., (1986) reported that rate and extent of dry matter loss from Gliricidia leaves is much faster under high rainfall conditions. Budelman (1986) reported that leaf mulch decompose rapidly with a half-life of 20 days.

Handarayan et al. (1997) suggested that the nitrogen mineralisation rate of prunings may be manipulated by mixing different quality materials such as high quality tree prunings of *G. sepium* and low-quality legume tree prunings such as *Peltophorum dasyrachis* (Miq.) Kurz. Pruning two weeks before transplanting vegetable seedlings and mulching with pruning may confer more efficient nutrient use on the agro-ecosystem.

5. Correlative processes in a pruned tree

5.1 Pruning and the physiology of tree regrowth

Pruning alters the growth and development of trees at different organ levels (Genard et al., 1998). This practice changes the leaf area and photosynthetic capacity of a tree. Also, it appears to affect the metabolic equilibrium between the root system and the aerial part of the tree by reducing the amount of growing shoots that function as sources and sinks for nutrients and hormones (Grochowska et al., 1984). Pruning height at or above 1.5 m seems to be best for tree survival and regrowth owing to a higher number of resprouting buds that may occur on a taller pruned stem (van Noordwijk & Purnomosidhi, 1995).

Like fruit load in horticultural species, biomass may also affect starch dynamics. Root starch levels drop for trees when fruit is removed and this mobilised starch is used for vegetative flushing in mango (Davie & Stassen, 1997). Lowering of root starch level in support of regrowth may lead to a decrease in total wood starch. Removal of canopy by shoot pruning reduced starch content as well. Erdmann and colleagues (1993) reported that *G. sepium* use stem starch to support initial coppice shoot regrowth after cutting and this carbohydrate was present in sufficient concentration to preclude use of root reserve carbohydrate.

Fownes & Anderson (1991) indicated that apparent equilibrium between leaf biomass and roots and nodules and similarly of stem growth efficiency between cut and uncut treatments suggest that coppice shoots behave physiologically much the same as original shoots.

5.1.1 Role of starch

According to Chesney & Vasquez (2007), shoot pruning affects the processes of photosynthesis and synthesis of non-structural carbohydrates. This means that energy for tree regrowth comes from reserves of non-structural carbohydrates, mainly starch (Loescher et al, 1990) stored in the pruned tree. Starch provides energy for respiration of active buds and synthesis of chlorophyll, proteins and structural compounds during early stages of leaf growth. These are processes that influence the rate of resprouting and biomass accumulation in pruned trees. The organ donor of starch during tree regrowth may be species specific. In some species, stem starch is more depleted than root starch (Chesney & Vasquez, 2007; Erdmann et al., 1993).

von Fircks & Sennerby-Forsse (1998) in a pot study with *Salix viminalis* L., usually used for biomass production in short rotation coppice plantations (Sennerby-Forsse & Christersson 1994), found that this species had a high capacity for resprouting. After pruning, regenerating stems rely on internal carbon and nutrient reserves (Dickman & Pregitzer 1992) mainly comprising carbohydrates, lipids and proteins (Dickson, 1991). Carbohydrate reserves in roots and stumps are important in resprouting of coppiced trees but starch is more important as a sensitive indicator of sprouting ability than other carbohydrates.

In their study with *E. poeppigiana* and *G. sepium*, Chesney & Vasquez (2007) found that starch reserves were higher in roots than in stems, a finding consistent with that reported by Loescher et al. (1990). Depletion in starch levels starts in stems than in roots owing to a higher correlation with developing stem sprouts. This is related to the sink strength being greater at the utilisation site in meeting the respiratory energy demand of regrowing shoots. Typically, starch reserves closest to sites of greatest sink activity, e.g. developing stem sprouts, are depleted first (Kozlowski, 1992). Therefore, shoot pruning creates a demand for starch to support stem bud development into sprouts. This effect is stronger during the dry season compared to the wet season (Chesney & Vasquez, 2007). Rapid biomass accumulation and rapid replenishment of tree reserves (Chesney, 2008; Loescher et al., 1990) increase the tolerance of woody perennials to pruning which helps to explain the findings of Duguma et al., 1988, and are critical to the sustainability of low input agroforestry systems as observed by Beer et al. (1990).

5.1.2 Role of nitrogen

Greater nitrogen availability increases shoot growth. There is increased utilisation of photosynthates and lower carbohydrate availability for storage in high nitrogen containing plants. During pre-dormancy, roots of lower nitrogen plants contained significantly more starch than roots of higher nitrogen plants thus roots play an important role in starch storage under low nitrogen conditions. From dormancy to regrowth, starch continues to decrease particularly in root phloem and cortical cells. This decrease may be attributed to the conversion of starch to sugars and the translocation of sugars to expanding buds for use in regrowth. Tschaplinski & Blake (1994) investigated the influence of decapitation of actively growing hybrid poplars and found that 10 days after, stem starch concentration declined to 50% that of intact plants as a result or resprouting.

Greater fine root length increases the capacity of trees to absorb available nitrogen. Partially pruned trees maintain fine roots and nodules for nutrient uptake and transport, and nitrogen fixation, respectively (Chesney and Nygren 2002). The retention of the branch on the pruned stump conserves more fine roots compared to complete pruning. Chesney (2008) found that the respective mean root length was 489 or 821 m (2 year old trees) and 184 or 364 m (8 year old trees) for trees pruned completely or partially. Corresponding nitrogen accumulation in aboveground biomass was 123 or 187 kg ha^{-1} and 160 or 256 kg ha^{-1}.

In addition, there appears to be a role for nitrogen in the growth of resprouting shoots (Chesney & Vasquez, 2007; Kabeya & Sakai, 2005). The level of nitrogen storage whether in roots or stems is important for the growth of resprouting shoots since shoot pruning causes death of fine roots and nodules. In species that show good potential for rapid regrowth after shoot pruning, there is higher concentration of nitrogen in roots than shoots.

5.2 Evidence from other ecological interactions

5.2.1 Perennial legume covercrops

Perennial legumes, which thrive under shade, could be good candidates for inclusion in agroforestry systems with an emphasis on soil conservation. The results from studies with peanut (*Arachis hypogaea* L.) could be validated for a perennial legume such as *Arachis pintoi* Krapov & W.C. Gregory. Siddique & Bal (1990) found that peanut, unlike other known grain legumes, can sustain N-fixation when prolonged periods of darkness or de-topping curtail supply of photosynthate to the nodule. This ability to withstand photosynthate stress is attributed to the presence of lipid bodies in infected nodule cells. Apparently, the N_2 fixation is not limited to photosynthate but rather by utilisation of carbon within the nodule (Vance & Heichel, 1991). Interestingly, the inclusion of legume cover in a crop rotation for 3-6 months could benefit soil fertility via its organic matter input (2-3 Mg ha^{-1}) aboveground and N input (60-90 ka ha^{-1}) (Hairiah et al., 1992). This can lead to yield advantage in subsequent crops (van Noordwijk et al., 1995).

The use of legume covercrop in a simultaneous agroforestry system may have similar benefits to the use of fast growing nitrogen fixing trees but may also require management like shoot pruning of trees to remove competition, not for light, but for nutrients with the crop. Together, shoot pruning of trees and covercrop may yield substantial benefits to the crop and agro-ecosystem.

5.2.2 Nitrogen derived from transfer

Exactly what will happen to the nitrogen dynamics if a leguminous covercrop is included in an agroforestry system with leguminous N-fixing trees is not altogether clear. It has been found that grasses growing in association with Gliricidia or Leucaena could derive up to 21% of N as N derived from transfer (Ndft) (Jayasundara et al., 1997). The authors were however cautious to note that Ndft is apparent nitrogen transfer since additions of nitrogen rich plant residue from N_2 fixing legumes in mixture could stimulate mineralisation of native N from soil organic matter (Birch & Dougall 1967). Catchpoole & Blair (1990) and Rao & Giller (1993) found 7-32 Ndft for grass growing with Gliricidia and Leucaena under controlled environmental conditions.

The transfer of nitrogen from legumes to associated grass is believed to occur through senescence and decomposition of leaf litter, fine root and nodule turnover, root exudation and direct transfer through interconnected mycorrhizal hyphae (Giller et al., 1991). Relative importance of each mechanism depends on duration of cropping system, intimacy of component crops and nature of management. There is recognition that N_2 fixing legumes must be in some form of stress for significant nitrogen transfer to occur. Perhaps, in the presence of a perennial leguminous covercrop, N-fixing trees may subserve its N-fixing role. Pruning both legume components before crop establishment may be beneficial to the system in two ways. Firstly, more biomass and nitrogen available for the crop, and secondly, Arachis may be able to continue N-fixation without diminishing soil nitrogen, something that completely pruned trees are not able to carry out. On the other hand, partially pruned trees could maintain system nitrogen absorptive capacity.

Complete shoot pruning may lead to more available nitrogen present in soil solution through residue decomposition. The death of fine roots could reduce the ability of tree to absorb nitrogen leached beyond the crop-rooting zone especially in a humid environment. This occurrence is more important for the first pruning, when no crop is present or is mature enough, to absorb a lot of available nitrogen and thus may lead to high nitrogen losses. Moreover, before first pruning a high amount of surface litter (accumulation through leaf dropping during dry season) is already present (Vanlauwe & Sanginga 1995). Partial pruning (i.e. thinning trees to one or more apical branches) increases percent nitrogen in crop since there is a reduction in crop/tree competition for light and part of the canopy to maintain ability of trees to absorb nitrogen.

Cutting of legume trees does not always result in negative effects of the trees. Miquilena et al. (1995) in applying a cutting regime of 6, 9 and 12 weeks and planting density of 2 x 1 m or 2 x 2 m found high total nitrogen in Gliricida and this was not affected by density or cutting frequency

6. Models and pruning management

Mathematical modelling could provide useful stopgap information on pruning effects generation utilising existing information garnered through alley cropping other annuals. This approach seems even more attractive given the need to reflect social, economic and environmental relevance.

Carbon based ecophysiological models, which integrate photosynthesis and respiration functions, exist. Some of these models consider interactions between tree root systems and aerial parts to provide a sound conceptual frame for studying these models. They do not consider the structure of the tree to be pruned. According to Génard et al. (1988), some models integrate morphological development and physiological processes. Using a carbon balance model of growth and development to study the pruning response, these researchers found that the rhythmicity of growth was enhanced by pruning and might result from variations induced in the root:shoot ratio. Variation in pruning severity has a greater effect that variation in pruning date and that tree growth was mainly dependent on assimilate availability.

The model of Barteling (1998) could be modified to study conditions for dynamic distribution of dry matter using mechanistic and allometric relationships between tree components. This could allow for a quantification of competition for resources on growth and development of crops. Using another important function, McIntyre et al. (1996) argued that evapo-transpiration can be predicted for a variety of canopy systems when light interception measurements are used in conjunction with a simple model of plant water uptake. The delay of hedge pruning until after the annual crop is established could result in greater water utilisation by the hedges and consequently, reduced evaporation. The roots of adult fruiting trees are more susceptible to prolonged soil drying that rots of seedlings, irrespective of form similarity (Espeleta & Eissenstat, 1998). For forest ecosystems, the most frequently suggested cause of root death is water deficit (Persson, 1979).

Chesney & Nygren (2002) applied the compartment flow model to fine root and nodule biomass and necromass measured in sequentially taken core samples in an alley cropping system with *E. poeppigiana* in Costa Rica. They found that the model provided more reasonable estimate of nodule dynamics than for fine root data. Nodulation was not interrupted in partially pruned trees as it did in completely pruned trees.

Oelbermann & Voroney (2010) reported on the usefulness of the Century Model to predict soil organic carbon stocks in a Costa Rican soil amended with organic residues from periodic pruning.

7. System-wide benefits of shoot pruning

Shoot pruning as a management practice, can determine the contribution of woody perennials to food and agricultural productivity as well as environmental issues such as carbon sequestration at the farm and landscape levels.

At the farm level, (ecological) sustainability of production is more limited by biophysical rather than socio-economic or institutional factors (Poudel et al., 1998; Kass et al., 1997). Management strategies of soil conservation, appropriate cropping sequence and plant protection, packaged in agroforestry practices may have even greater relevance at the watershed level (Lindarte & Benitez, 1993). For example, use of biomass of *G. sepium* could be the most appropriate way to recuperate degraded soils in the watershed areas in Central America (Jiménez et al., 1998). Thus, shoot pruning as a management practice to avoid competition for light between the fast growing, N-fixing tree and crop also contributes high quality tree biomass to the ecosystem for its restoration and maintenance of health. Partial shoot pruning can help keep nitrogen from being leached into waterways or volatilised into the atmosphere by maintaining a nitrogen absorptive capacity in the retained shoots, a phenomenon emphasised by the branch autonomy for carbon.

Biomass accumulation is critical to the sustainability of low-input agroforestry systems. Biomass accumulation and rapid replenishment of tree reserves increase the tolerance of woody perennials to shoot pruning. In agroforestry systems, managed trees can sequester between 39-102 t C ha^{-1} yr^{-1}. Albrecht & Kandji (2003) estimated the carbon sequestration potential of agroforestry systems to be between 12 and 228 Mg ha^{-1}.

Given that worldwide some 630 million hectares of unproductive cropland and grassland are available for agroforestry land use, the potential for carbon sequestration using an average value of 50 t C ha^{-1} is 45 billion t C †. In some agroforestry systems, the woody component can cycle in the aboveground biomass some 250 kg N ha^{-1} $year^{-1}$, as well as other plant nutrients such as phosphorous and potassium.

8. Conclusions

Shoot pruning, as a management practice in simultaneous agroforestry systems with annual crops, has the high potential to assist farmers and agroforestry practitioners avoid negative ecological interaction between the service trees and associated food crops. Most of the service trees are fast growing, nitrogen fixing leguminous trees that have certain attributes that allow them to withstand periodic pruning, recover rapidly and contribute biomass and nutrients to the agroforestry system.

Physiologically, the storage of high amount of non-structural carbohydrates play an important role in tree recovery after pruning and the organ source of non-structural carbohydrates is an important determinant of how much to prune and when to prune.

Shoot pruning that retains some photosynthetic capacity on the pruned stump is preferable to complete removal of all shoots as it enables the trees to continue to function and contribute inputs to the ecosystem.

Of the tree species evaluated in the humid tropics, *G. sepium* seems to be best suited tree species for use in agroforestry with annual crops. Its principal advantages over the others are its small canopy, its tolerance to frequent pruning, and rapid recovery from shoot pruning. However, it contributes less biomass and nutrients compared to *E. poeppigiana*.

Selection of the appropriate shoot pruning method depends on a number of factors including, purpose of the agroforestry practice, species of woody component, arrangement of the woody component relative to the food crops, and resources available, especially labour. Coppicing is the most severe pruning method and will require a recovering tree to utilise root starch to meet energy needs for regrowth. Some species like *G. sepium* would be suitable candidates for this method because they have more carbon stored in below ground parts. Pollarding and lopping have a lesser impact on the woody component compared to coppicing and those woody components with small root stores of carbon are better managed using these pruning methods. Coppicing appears more feasible for woodlots where firewood is the main purpose of the agroforestry practice. Lopping appears a more suitable pruning method for shaded cacao (*Theobroma cacao* L.) and coffee systems, while pollarding appears more suitable for alley cropping systems.

† UNFCCC Special Report, 2000.

The material cost of pruning is low since only a cutlass (machete) and a sharpening file are all that are needed by one operator to prune trees. Labour costs depend on number of trees to be pruned and method of pruning. Data are not available to allow a comparison of pruning methods in terms of costs.

Modelling presents a unique option to assist in refining the timing of shoot pruning and other operations to assist decision making and resource use. It would appear that available information is adequate to facilitate this, thereby improving the utility of shoot pruning as an important management tool.

Judicious pruning of the shoots of fast growing nitrogen fixing trees is a beneficial way to obtain tree products of use to mankind whilst reducing negative tree-crop interactions and making available to the agroforestry system nutrient rich biomass for soil amelioration and moisture conservation, and plant available nutrients for the associated crops. Adding legume covercrops to such an agro-ecosystem may increase its biological value.

9. References

Akinnifesi, F.K., Kang, B.T., Tijani-Eniola, H. (1995). Root size distribution of a *Leucaena leucocephala* hedgerow as affected by pruning and alley cropping. *NFT Research Reports* 13:65-69.

Akunda, E. & Huxley, P.A. (1990). *The Application of Phenology to Agroforestry Research.* ICRAF Working Paper No. 63. ICRAF, Nairobi. 50pp.

Albrecht, A. & Kandji, S.T. (2003). Carbon sequestration in tropical agroforestry systems. *Agriculture, Ecosystems and Environment* 99:15-27.

Anderson, L.S. & Sinclair, F. (1993). Ecological interactions in agroforestry systems. *Agroforestry Abstracts* 6:57-91

Bartelink, H.H. (1998), A model of dry matter partitioning in trees. *Tree Physiology* 18:91-101, ISSN 0829-318X

Bayala, J., Ouedraogo, S.J. & Teklehaimanot, Z. (2008). Rejuvenating trees in agroforestry systems for better fruit production using crown pruning. *Agroforestry Systems* 72:187-194, ISSN 0167-4366

Beer, J. (1988). Litter production and nutrient cycling in coffee (*Coffea arabica*) or cacao (*Theobroma cacao*) plantations with shade trees. *Agroforestry Systems* 7:103-114, ISSN 0167-4366

Beer, J., Bonnemann, A., Chavez, W., Fassbender, H.W., Imbach, A.C. & Martel, I. (1990). Modelling agroforestry systems of cacao (*Theobroma cacao*) with laurel (*Cordia alliodora*) or poro (*Erythrina poeppigiana*) in Costa Rica. *Agroforestry Systems* 12:229-249, ISSN 0167-4366

Beer, J., Muschler, R., Kass, D. & Somarriba, E. (1998). Shade management in coffee and cacao plantations. *Agroforestry Systems* 38:139-164, ISSN 0167-4366

Birch, H.F. & Dougall, H.W. (1967) Effect of a legume on nitrogen mineralisation and percentage N in grass. *Plant and Soil* 27:292-296, ISSN 0032-079X

Brook, R.M. (1992). Early results from an alley cropping experiment in the humid lowlands of Papua New Guinea. *NFTResearch Reports* 10:73-76

Brouwer, R. (1962). Distribution of dry matter in the plant. *Netherlands Journal of Agriculture Science* 10:361-376, ISSN 0028-2928

Brouwer, R. (1983). Functional equilibrium: sense or nonsense? *Netherlands Journal of Agriculture Science* 31:335-348, ISSN 0028-2928

Budelman, A. (1990). Woody legumes as live support systems in yam cultivation II. The yam-*Gliricidia sepium* association. *Agroforestry Systems* 10:61-69, ISSN 0167-4366

Catchpoole, D.H. & Blair, G.J. (1990). Forage tree legumes. II Investigation of N transfer to an associated grass using a split root technique. *Australian Journal of Agricultural Research* 41: 531-537, ISSN 1836-0947

Chadhokar, P.A. (1982). *Gliricidia maculata* a promising legume fodder plant. *World Animal Review* 44: 36-43, ISSN 1014-6954

Chandrashekara, U.M. (2007). Effects of pruning on radial growth and biomass increment of trees growing in homegardens of Kerala, India. *Agroforestry Systems* 69:231-237, ISSN 0167-4366

Chesney, P. & Nygren, P. (2002). Fine root and nodule dynamics of *Erythrina poeppigiana* in an alley cropping system in Costa Rica. *Agroforestry Systems* 56:259-269, ISSN 0167-4366

Chesney, P. & Vasquez, N. (2007). Dynamics of non-structural carbohydrate reserves in pruned *Erythrina poeppigiana* and *Gliricidia sepium* trees. *Agroforestry Systems* 69:89-105, ISSN 0167-4366

Chesney, P. (2008). Nitrogen and fine root length dynamics in a tropical agroforestry system with periodically pruned *Erythrina poeppigiana*. *Agroforestry Systems* 72:149-159, ISSN 0167-4366

Chesney, P.E., Schlönvoigt, A. & Kass, D. (2000). Producción de tomate con soportes vivos en Turrialba Costa Rica. *Agroforesteria en las Américas* 7:57-60

Current, D., Lutz, E. & Scherr, S.J. (1995). Costs, benefits and farmer adoption of agroforestry. In: *Costs, Benefits and Farmer Adoption of Agroforestry: Project experience in Central America and the Caribbean,* D. Current, E. Lutz, & S. Scherr, (Eds.), 1-27, The World Bank, Washington, D.C., ISBN 0-8213-3428-X

Davie, S.J. & Stassen, P.J.C. (1997). The effect of fruit thinning and tree pruning on tree starch reserved and on fruit retention of "sensation" mango trees. *Acta Horticulturae* 455:160-166, ISSN 0567-7572

Dickman, D. & Pregitzer, K.S. (1992). The structure and dynamics of woody plant root systems. In: *Ecophysiology of Short Rotation Forest Crops,* C.P. Mitchell, J.B. Ford-Robertson, T. Hinckley & L. Sennerby-Forsse, (Eds), 95-123. Elsevier Applied Science, London, ISBN 978-1-85166-848-9

Dickson, R.E. (1991). Assimilate distribution and storage. In: *Physiology of Trees,* A.S. Raghavendra, (Ed.), 51-85. John Wiley and Sons, ISBN 10: 0471501107.

Duguma, B., Kang, B.T., & Okali, D.U.U. (1988). Effect of pruning intensities of three woody leguminous species grown in alley cropping with maize and cowpea on an alfisol. *Agroforestry Systems* 6:19-35, ISSN 0167-4366

Duhoux, E. & Dommergues, Y. (1984). The use of nitrogen fixing trees in forestry and soil restoration in the tropics. In: *Biological Nitrogen Fixation in Africa,* H. Ssali & S. O. Keya, (Eds.), 384-400. MIRCEN, Nairobi, Kenya

Erdmann, T.K., Nair, P.K.R. & Kang, B.T. (1993). Effects of cutting frequency and cutting height on reserve carbohydrates in *Gliricidia sepium* (jacq.) Walp. *Forect Ecology and Management* 57:45-60, ISSN 0378-1127

Espeleta, J.F. & Eissenstat, D.M. (1998). Responses of citrus fine roots to localised soil drying: a comparison of seedlings and adult fruiting trees. *Tree Physiology* 18:113-119 ISSN 0829-318X

Fownes, J.H. & Anderson, D.G. (1991). Changes in nodule and root biomass of *Sesbania sesban* and *Leucaena leucocephala* following coppicing. *Plant and Soil* 138:9-16, ISSN 0032-079X

Génard, M., Pages, L. & Kervella, J. (1998). A carbon balance model of peach tree growth and development for studying the pruning response. *Tree Physiology* 18:351-362, ISSN 0829-318X

Giller, K.E., Ormesher, J. & Awah, F.M. (1991). Nitrogen transfer from *Phaseolus* bean to intercropped maize measured with ^{15}N-enrichment and ^{15}N-isotope dilution methods. *Soil Biology and Biochemistry* 23:339-346, ISSN 0038-0717

Govindarajan, M., Rao, M.R., Mathuva, M.N. & Nair, P.K.R. (1996). Soil-water and root dynamics under hedgerow intercropping in semiarid Kenya. *Agronomy Journal* 88:513-520, ISSN 0002-1962

Grochowska, M.J., Karaszewska, A., Jankowska, B., Maksymiuk, J. & Williams, M.W. (1984). Dormant pruning influence on auxin, giberellin, and cytokinin levels in apple trees. *Journal of American Society for Horticultural Science* 109:312-318, ISSN 0003-1062

Haggar, J.P., Tanner, E.V.J., Beer, J.W. & Kass, D.C.L. (1993). Nitrogen dynamics of tropical agroforestry and annual cropping systems. *Soil Biology and Biochemistry* 25(10):1363-1378, ISSN 0038-0717

Hairiah, K. Utomo, W.H. & van der Heide, J. (1992). Biomass production and performance of leguminous cover crops on an Ultisol in Lampung. *Agrivita* 15:39-44, ISSN 0126-0537

Handarayan, E., Giller, K.E. & Cadisch, G. (1997). Regulating N release from legume tree pruning by mixing residues of different quality. *Soil Biology and Biochemistry* 29(9/10):1417-1426, ISSN 0038-0717

ICRAF (1996). *Annual Report for 1995*, ICRAF, Nairobi

Islam, M.S., Hossain, M.A. & Mondol, M.A. (2008). Effect of pruning and pollarding on shoot development in bakphul (*Sesbania grandiflora* L.). *Journal of Bangladesh Agricultural University* 6(2):285-298, ISSN 1810-3030

Jayasundara, H.P.S., Dennet, M.D. & Sangakkara, U.R. (1997). Biological nitrogen fixation in *Gliricidia sepium* and *Leucaena leucocephala* and transfer of fixed nitrogen to an associated grass. *Tropical Grasslands* 31:529-537, ISSN 0049-4763

Jimenez, J.M., Collinet, J. & Mazariego, M. (1998). Recuperación de suelos degradados con *Gliricidia sepium* o gallinaza en la micro cuenca rio Las Cañas, El Salvador. *Agroforestería en las Américas* 5(20):10-16

Kabeya, D. & Sakai, S. (2005). The relative importance of carbohydrate and nitrogen for the resprouting ability of *Quercus crispula* seedlings. *Annals of Botany* 96(3):479-488, ISSN 0305-7364

Kandiah, S., Wettasinghe, D.T. & Wadasinghe, G. (1984). Root influence on shoot development in tea (*Camellia sinensis* (L.) O. Kuntze) following shoot pruning. *Journal of Horticultural Science* 59:581-587, ISSN 1462-0316

Kang, B.T. & Mulongoy, K. (1987). *Gliricidia sepium* as a source of green manure in an alley cropping system. *Proceedings of a Workshop Gliricidia sepium (Jacq.) Walp. Management and Improvement,* CATIE, Turrialba, Costa Rica, June 1987. NFTA Special Publication 87-01:44-49

Kang, B.T. (1993). Alley cropping: past achievements and future directions. *Agroforestry Systems* 23:141-155, ISSN 0167-4366

Kang, H., Shannon, D.A., Prior, S.A. & Arriaga, F.J. (2008). Hedgerow pruning effects on light interception, water relations and yield in alley-cropped maize. *Journal of Sustainable Agriculture* 31(4):115-137, ISSN 1044-0046

Karim, A.B. & Savill, P.S. (1991). Effect of spacing on growth and biomass production of *Gliricidia sepium* (Jacq.) Walp. in an alley cropping system in Sierra Leone. *Agroforestry Systems* 16:213-222, ISSN 0167-4366

Kass, D., Jiménez, J. & Schlönvoigt, A. (1997). Como hacer el cultivo en callejones más productivo, sostenible y aceptable a pequeños productores. *Agroforestería en las Américas* 4(14):21-23

Kass, DC.L., Jiménez, J., Sánchez, J., Soto, M.L. & Garzón, H. (1993). *Erythrina* in alley farming: In *Erythrina in the new and old worlds: nitrogen fixing tree res report Special Issue,* S.B. Westley & M.H. Powell (Eds.), 129-137

Keerthisena, R.S.K. (1995). *Gliricidia sepium* biomass production varies with plant row spacing and cutting height. *NFT Research Reports* 13:60-63

Kozlowski, T.T. (1992). Carbohydrate sources and sinks in woody plants. *Botanical Review.* 58(2):107-223, ISSN 0006-8101

Lindarte, E. & Benítez, C. (1993). Sostenibilidad y agricultura de laderas en América Central, *Serie Documentos de Programa* 33, IICA, San José, Costa Rica

Loescher, W.H., McCamant, T. & Keller, J.D. (1990). Carbohydrate reserves, translocation and storage in woody plant roots. *HortScience* 25:274-281, ISSN 0018-5345

McIntyre, B.D., Riha, S.J. & Ong, C.K. (1996). Light interception and evapotranspiration in hedgerow agroforestry systems. *Agricultural and Forest Meteorology* 81:31-40, ISSN 0168-1923

Mulongoy, K. (1983). Field decomposition of leaves of *Psophocarpus palustris* and *Gliricidia sepium* on an Alfisol as affected by thidan and benomyl. In: *Transactions of Joint Meeting of the British Society of Soil science and Commissions III and IV of the International Society of Soil Science on biological processes and soil fertility,* 91. Reading University, England.

Muñoz, F. & Beer, J. (2001). Fine root dynamics of shaded cocoa plantations in Costa Rica. *Agroforestry Systems* 51:119-130, ISSN 0167-4366

Muschler, R.G., Nair, P.K.R. & Melendez, L. (1993). Crown development and biomass production of pollarded *Erythrina berteroana, E. fusca* and *Gliricidia sepium* in the humid tropical lowlands of Costa Rica. *Agroforestry Systems* 24:123-143, ISSN 0167-4366

Myers, R.J.K., Palm, C.A., Cuevas, E., Gunatilleke, I.U.N. & Brossard, M. (1994). The synchronization of nutrient mineralization and plant nutrient demand. In: *Biological*

Management of Tropical Soil Fertility, P.L. Woomer & M. J. Swift (Eds.), 81-116. Wiley, United Kingdom, ISSN

Nygren, P. & Campos, A. (1995). Effect of foliage pruning on fine root biomass of *Erythrina poeppigiana* (Fabaceae). In: *Ecophysiology of Tropical Intercropping*, H. Sinoquet & P. Cruz, (Eds.), 295-302, ISBN 27380006035.

Nygren, P. & Ramirez, C. (1993). Production and turnover of N_2 fixing nodules in relation to foliage development in periodically pruned *Erythrina poeppigiana* (Leguminosae) trees. *Forest Ecology and Management* 73:59-73, ISSN 0378-1127

Oelbermann, M. & Voroney, R.P. (2010). An evaluation of the century model to predict soil organic carbon: examples from Costa Rica and Canada. *Agroforestry Systems* 82(1):37-50, ISSN 0167-4366

Ong., C.K., Black, C.R., Marshall, F.M. & Corlett, J.E. (1996). Principles of resource capture and utilization of light and water. In: *Tree-Crop Interactions: A physiological approach*, C.K. Ong & P. Huxley (Eds.), 73-158, CAB International, ISBN 0 85198 987 X

Otu, O.I. & Agboola, A.A. (1994). The suitability of *Gliricidia sepium* in in-situ live stake on the yield and performance of white yam (*Dioscorea rotundata*). *Acta Horticulturae* 380:360-366, ISSN 0567-7572

Palm, C.A. (1995). Contribution of agroforestry trees to nutrient requirements of intercropped plants. *Agroforestry Systems* 30:105-124, ISSN 0167-4366

Parrota, J.A. & Singh, I.P. (1992). *Gliricidia sepium* root system morphology and biomass allocation. *NFT Research Reports* 10:169-172

Persson, H. (1979). Fine root production, mortality and decomposition in forest ecosystems. *Vegetatio* 41:101-109, ISSN 1385-0237

Poudel, D.D., Midmore, D.J. & Hargrove, W.L. (1998). An analysis of commercial vegetable farms in relation to sustainability to the uplands of Southeast Asia. *Agricultural Systems* 58(1):107-128, ISSN 0308 521X

Raintree, J.B. (1987). *D&D User's Manual: An Introduction to Agroforestry Design and Diagnosis*. ICRAF, Nairobi, Kenya

Rao, A.V. & Giller, K.E. (1993). Nitrogen fixation and its transfer from Leucaena to grass using ^{15}N. *Forest Ecology and Management* 61:221-227, ISSN 0378-1127

Ryle, G.J.A., Powell, C.E. & Gordon, A.J. (1985). Defoliation in white clover: regrowth, photosynthesis and N_2 fixation. *Annals of Botany* 56:9-18, ISSN 0305-7364

Sanchez, P.A. (1995). Science in agroforestry. *Agroforestry Systems* 30:5-55, ISSN 0167-4366

Sanchez, P.A., Villachica, J.H. & Brady, D.E. (1983). Soil fertility dynamics after clearing a tropical rainforest in Peru. *Soil Science Society of America Journal* 47:1171-1178, ISSN 0361-5995

Sanginga, N., Danso, S.K.A., Zapata, F. & Bowen, G.D. (1994). Influence of pruning management on P and N distribution and use efficiency by N_2 fixing and non-N_2 fixing trees used in alley cropping systems. *Plant and Soil* 167:219-226, ISSN 0032-079X

Shigo, A.L. (1990). Tree branch attachment to trunks and branch pruning. *HortScience* 25(1):54-59, ISSN 0018-5345

Siddique, A.M. & Bal, A.K. (1990). Nitrogen fixation in peanut nodules during dark periods and detopped conditions with special reference to lipid bodies. *Plant Physiology* 95:896-899, ISSN 0032-0889

Siriri, D., Ong, C.K., Wilson, J., Boffa, J.M. & Black, C.R. (2010). Tree species and pruning regime affect crop yield on bench terraces in SW Uganda. *Agroforestry Systems* 78:65-77, ISSN 0167-4366

Somarriba, E., Beer, J. & Bonnemann, A. (1996). Arboles leguminosas maderables como sombra para cacao. Serie Técnico No. 18, CATIE, Turrialba, Costa Rica

Soule, J. (1985). *Glossary for Horticultural Crops*. John Wiley & Sons, ISBN 10: 0471884995

Sprugel, D.G., Hinckley, T.M. & Schaap, W. (1991). The theory and practice of branch autonomy. *Annual Review of Ecology and Systematics* 22:309-334

Swift, M.J. (1985). *Tropical Soil Biology and Fertility (TSBF)*: Planning and Research. Biology International Special Issue 9, International Union of Biological Sciences, Paris

Timmer, L.A., Kessler, J.J. & Slingerland, M. (1996). Pruning of nere trees (*Parkia biglobosa* (Jacq.) Benth.) on the farmlands of Burkina Faso, West Africa. *Agroforestry Systems* 33:87-98, ISSN 0167-4366

Tipu, S.U., Hossain, K.L., Islam, M.O. & Hussain, M.A. (2006). Effect of pruning height on shoot biomass yield of *Leucaena leucocephala*. *Asian Journal of Plant Sciences* 5(6):1043-1046, ISSN 1682-3974

Tschaplinski, T.L. & Blake, T.J. (1994). Carbohydrate mobilization following shoot defoliation and decapitation in hybrid poplar. *Tree Physiology* 14:141-151, ISSN 0829-318X

Vaast, P. & Snoeck, D. (1999). Hacia un manejo sostenible de la material orgánica de la fertilidad biológica de los suelos cafetaleros. In: *Desafíos de la Caficultura en Centroamérica*. B. Bertrand & B. Rapidel, (Eds.), 139-169 CIRAD, France.

van Noordwijk, M. & Purnomosidhi, P. (1995). Root architecture in relation to tree-soil-crop interactions and shoot pruning in agroforestry. *Agroforestry Systems* 30:161-173, ISSN 0167-4366

van Noordwijk, M., Tomich, T.P., Winahayu, R., Murdiyarso, R., Suyanto, D., Partoharjono, S. & Fagi, A.M. (Eds.). (1995). *Alternatives to Slash and Burn in Indonesia*. Summary Report Phase 1. ABS-Indonesia Report No. 4. Bogor, Indonesia. 154p.

Vance, C.P. &Heichel, G.H. (1991). Carbon in N_2 fixation: limitation of exquisite adaptation. *Annual Review of Plant Physiology and Plant Molecular Biology* 42.373-392

Vanlauwe, B. & Sanginga, N. (1995). Efficiency of the use of nitrogen from pruning and soil organic matter dynamics in *Leucaena leucocephala* alley cropping in South-western Nigeria. *FAO Fertilizer and Plant Nutrient Bulletin* 12:279-292

Vasquez, P.C. & Quintero, F. (1995). Efecto del diámetro de las estacas de mata ratón (*Gliricidia sepium*) sobre crecimiento de ramas laterals. *Zootecnia Tropical* 13(1):113-123, ISSN 0798-7269

von Fircks, Y. & Sennerby-Forsse, L. (1998). Seasonal fluctuations in starch in root and stem tissues of coppiced *Salix viminalis* plants grown under two nitrogen regimes. *Tree Physiology* 18:243-249, ISSN 0829-318X

Weeraratna, C.S. (1979). Pattern of nitrogen release during decomposition of some green manures in a tropical alluvial soil. *Plant and Soil* 53:288-294, ISSN 0032-079X

Wilson, B.F. (1990). The development of tree form. *HortScience* 25(1):52-54, ISSN 0018-5345

Wilson, G.F., Kang, B.T. & Mulongoy, K. (1986). Alley cropping: trees as sources of green manure and mulch in the tropics. *Biological Agriculture and Horticulture* 3:251-267, ISSN 0144-8765

Young, A. (1981). *The potential of agroforestry for soil conservation*: Part II Maintenance of soil fertility. Working Paper No. 43. ICRAF, Nairobi

Improved Policies for Facilitating the Adoption of Agroforestry

Frank Place[1], Oluyede C. Ajayi[1], Emmanuel Torquebiau[2,3], Guillermo Detlefsen[4], Michelle Gauthier[5] and Gérard Buttoud[6]
[1]World Agroforestry Centre, Nairobi
[2]Centre de Coopération Internationale en Recherche Agronomique pour le Développement (CIRAD), UR 105, Montpellier
[3]Centre for Environmental Studies (CFES), University of Pretoria, Pretoria,
[4]Centro Agronómico Tropical de Investigación y Enseñanza, Turrialba,
[5]Food and Agriculture Organization of the United Nations (FAO)
[6]University of Tuscia and FAO
[1]Kenya
[2]France
[3]South Africa
[4]Costa Rica
[5,6]Italia

1. Introduction

1.1 The increasing importance of agroforestry as a major land use practice

There is now general agreement about the magnitude and scale of the integration of trees into agricultural lands and their active management by farmers and pastoralists. Zomer et al. (2009) conducted a global assessment of tree cover on agricultural land and found that 48% of all agricultural land had at least 10% tree cover. A high percentage of tree cover is found in nearly all continents of the world, highest being in Central America and southeast Asia. Although Africa shows a smaller percentage of tree cover at continental level, the most widespread farming system in Africa is the so-called agroforestry parkland (scattered trees in cropland), making Africa a typically "treed continent" in agricultural areas (Boffa, 1999). The FAO Forest Resources Assessment Report has integrated since 2000 the assessment of trees outside forests, which consist mainly in agroforestry systems as well as tree systems in urban areas. More countries are now measuring and reporting trees outside of forests and country provided data indicate that such areas are significant. For example such area is greater than forest area in countries such as Kenya, Tunisia, and Niger and is a high percent in many others including temperate countries (FAO, 2011a). Evidence on the significance of specific agroforestry systems (e.g. agroforests in Indonesia, farmer managed parklands in Africa, treed rangelands, scattered trees on pastures and shade trees with plantation crops such as coffee and cocoa in Central America, Brazil or Cameroon) or practices (e.g. widespread fodder shrubs and trees in semi-arid and sub-humid Africa or in East Asia, fruit growing in Kenya) is also available in a large base of literature.

The economic importance of agroforestry can be partly understood by examining data on the export value of major tree products. Drawing upon data from FAOSTAT (2011), Table 1 shows that conservative estimates of international trade of this list of tree products was valued at a whopping US$140 billion in 2009. The actual production levels are much higher, considering that the list includes only well known and common tree products and that many tree products in developing countries are not marketed internationally (e.g. firewood, fodder, medicinal uses) and for products such as fruit, as much as 90% of production is consumed domestically. In addition, the positive externalities (or ecosystem services) represented by trees (e.g. carbon sequestration, nutrient cycling, provision of shade, etc.) are not counted.

Commodity	2001	2003	2005	2007	2008
Coffee	8661842	9769085	15637891	22061510	26800406
Citrus	7709475	10217484	11597821	15869879	17689609
Cocoa	2208064	4200355	4954083	5708236	7246038
Tea	2820992	2942887	3582778	4042636	5520560
Coconut	895924	1210337	1876246	1996676	2895301
Cashew	947931	1118091	1850100	2025783	2735722
Natural rubber	428511	808637	1055177	1910370	2052320
Avocado	320124	545553	844884	1281887	1279566
Mango	428299	578874	646821	918524	1001681
Oil of Castor Beans	162196	158904	254711	363456	566613
Cinnamon	107135	109066	139606	185115	199092
Papaya	124014	161481	185248	186153	188050
Fig	23073	38283	44751	57030	83125
Shea kernel	10452	22807	7167	30399	42410
Plant-based Gums	6628	11656	8311	6747	6513
Kolanut	6932	1668	477	1916	1904

Table 1. The global export value of some major tree products (in US $1000's)
Source: Compiled from FAOSTAT (2011)

In another testament to the importance of agroforestry, FAO (2003) observed that forest cover in Africa continues to decrease while tree cover on farms is increasing. Indeed, it is reasonable to expect the demand for tree products including export values as shown in Table 1 to continue to increase. The importance of smallholder agroforestry is only likely to be reinforced with increased attention and resources to climate change adaptation and mitigation whereby more efforts are being made to protect forests while simultaneously expanding tree growing on farms. In some parts of the world (e.g. Southern Africa), an upward trend in tree density in savanna landscapes has been observed in recent years (possibly linked to climatic variables such as rainfall and CO2 levels) and may further reinforce the importance of trees in the livelihoods of local people (Bond et al., 2003; Kgope et al., 2010; Midgley and Thuillier, 2011).

The data presented above paints a very positive picture of the spread of agroforestry. Yet the general trend masks some important caveats, areas where agroforestry has not developed or spread with much vigor. Many locations are in desperate need of more trees for fuelwood (e.g. much of Ethiopia or Bangladesh) and for improved catchment protection (e.g. wide areas of India). While some areas have thriving fruit growing systems (e.g. South Africa, Kenya, India), others still exhibit poor production figures and very low consumption (e.g in Southern Africa). Tree growth and productivity is often low and variable due to lack of access to better quality germplasm. Furthermore there are many missed opportunities for reducing the period to full production by disseminating advanced propagation methods. Some more innovative and new ways of managing trees on farms (e.g. intercrop systems for soil health) are yet to be known by the vast majority of farmers. Lastly, and most importantly, while some countries have found tree growing to be enormously profitable others do not even consider it as a potential livelihood. In fact, the study by Zomer et al. (2009) shows that there exist many landscapes across the globe where tree cover is less than expected given the rainfall characteristics of the landscapes.

The evidence suggests that policy plays an important role in distinguishing countries and regions which have benefited greatly from agroforestry from those who have not. Three policy areas appear to be most important. The first concerns essential long term private property rights over land and trees. Where these have been absent or contested, tree planting and management by farmers has been limited. Second, policies related to tree germplasm multiplication and dissemination are important in facilitating expansion of agroforestry. Finally, the recognition of agroforestry as an attractive investment area within agricultural institutions and programmes is also important. The remainder of this chapter explores this role in more detail. To set the context, section 2 reviews recent experiences in expanding agroforestry in order to understand some of the challenges involved in scaling up agroforestry systems. Based on these case studies and other literature, section 3 then discusses in detail key policy areas that hinder or promote the impact and adoption of agroforestry. Section 4 then presents examples of recent policy reforms that have been favorable for agroforestry and the final section concludes with key messages.

2. Lessons learnt from previous efforts to promote agroforestry in different countries

Although some agroforestry systems have been practiced for generations, others, have been designed or adopted more recently. This section analyses the factors behind some of these recently adopted systems. In particular, how was awareness created, knowledge disseminated, and germplasm made available? What were the key success factors and roles of private sector, NGOs, government and other actors? It is useful to begin by describing in more detail some of the characteristics of agroforestry systems that have recently been upscaled. Some could be characterized as having some foundation in the farming traditions. For example, it could be a modification of an existing practice - e.g. different species but managed in a familiar way. Others could be much more novel to farmers - e.g. the introduction of improved fallows is a completely new way of farming in most areas. This distinction is important in terms of the requirements placed on activities such as awareness creation and dissemination of technical management information and skills. The introduction of a new fruit cultivar may require awareness raising, but little technical training if farmers are already managing fruit trees. So this key distinction should be kept in mind in the following discussion.

In the majority of cases reported below, the main objective of the promotion of agroforestry was to increase private benefits for smallholder farmers. Thus, the particular agroforestry systems and species were expected to provide benefits such as wood products, fruits, fodder, and improved soil fertility which would benefit farmers directly. Where farmers do perceive private benefits the demand for agroforestry knowledge and germplasm will be higher than in the absence of such benefits. However, there is increasingly more promotion of agroforestry for other benefits as well, such as for environmental services that may accrue to broader society. These include watershed protection, biodiversity and carbon sequestration. Dissemination of agroforestry systems and species to meet these needs will face similar challenges to those aimed more towards private benefits (and many agroforestry can simultaneously provide both, as noted in the introduction). However, there are additional challenges in that incentive systems for farmers to produce societal level benefits need to be established and clarified to farmers (Leimona, 2011)

2.1 Awareness creation

As may be expected, awareness creation for agroforestry has involved a variety of actors. In the case of the farmer-managed natural regeneration agroforestry practice in Niger, the NGO (Serving in Mission) who pioneered the approach in the Maradi region was also instrumental in creating awareness beyond the initial locality (Reij et al., 2009) and was soon joined by CARE in the promotion of these practices. The World Agroforestry Centre (ICRAF) played a significant role in the development of fertilizer tree and fodder shrub options for the Sahel (Torquebiau and Moussa, 1990, 1991) and then later became a key driver for the same in East and Southern Africa (Ajayi et al., 2007a). Likewise, ICRAF and national partners in Tanzania helped to scale up a local practice of regeneration called *ngitili* modified partly by purposeful selection and planting of valuable trees (Pye-Smith, 2010). In all these cases, projects were an important vehicle in awareness creation (and also for training on technical knowledge). The case of the wide scale dissemination of *Faidherbia albida* and conservation agriculture in Zambia had strong participation by the private sector (Donavant cotton), the government (Conservation Farming Unit in the Ministry Agriculture), and the national farmers' association (Garrity et al., 2010; Haggblade and Tembo, 2003;). The private sector seems to have played a more significant role in the awareness creation for agroforestry practices that produce relatively higher value product. This can be seen in the case of the rapid expansion of poplar growing by smallholders in India, where wood processors in Haryana State were critical in awareness creation and eventually also in supplying seedlings (Zomer et al., 2007). Unilever is investing significantly in the more recent upscaling of Allanblackia, which produces an oil with properties that are attractive for a range of food products (Pye-Smith, 2009). The more gradual expansion in the number of fruit growers and fruit varieties grown in Kenya was also influenced considerably by the private sector, including companies and trade associations. A strong parastatal agency for horticulture also played a key role.

So there is clearly no single pathway to creating awareness. Governments have not often been involved in these examples, most likely due to the problems of agroforestry being neglected or not championed by a single government ministry (see below). However, this appears to be changing particularly with the increased importance of climate change and the embracing of agroforestry as a key climate smart practice. It is positive that the private sector has been involved in creating awareness of agroforestry opportunities. Their involvement is accompanied by value chain development which is critically needed for many agroforestry products. Recent announcements by Coca-cola, Pepsi, and Del Monte, that they were all interested to invest in developing smallholder fruit market chains in East Africa are a further sign of potential upscaling in the region. Chocolate companies aiming to purchase certified cocoa have played a similar role for the development of tree shaded cocoa cultivation.

2.2 Dissemination of technical knowledge and skills

Many recently developed agroforestry systems are novel in terms of management compared with conventional practices which farmers are more familiar with and which they have received training for a longer period. Human capacity, infrastructure and institutional supports for agroforestry systems are low in most national extension programs (Ajayi et al., 2009). As a result, the same actors involved in awareness creation are often also involved in the greater efforts to build knowledge and skills capacities to manage the agroforestry systems. A major effort was undertaken in Central America to improve the technical skills of extension agents in agroforestry. A Central American Tree Manual was produced to provide information on both important agroforestry practices and nearly 200 indigenous species (Cordero and Boshier, 2004). To ensure uptake, the manual was distributed through a programme of free courses. More than 1000 extensionists of the seven countries of region were trained from 2003 - 2005 under a multiplier effect, covering a mix of foresters, agroforesters, agronomists and extensionists from rural development agencies (Boshier et al., 2009).

In the African examples, much more attention to dissemination of knowledge needed to be given to new practices such as fodder and fertilizer tree systems. A number of different approaches were tried in the various African sites where these were disseminated. Given the limited number of government extension staff, upscaling has tended to emphasize models that rely on farmers and farmer groups to help disseminate information. The farmers are in turn trained and supported by resource persons that are normally paid by a project or programme. This approach is very cost effective, as farmer trainers often train many other farmers (Franzel and Wambugu, 2007). Moreover, those who have been trained, often pass on information. The concern with such an approach is that the farmer trainers are not remunerated well (or at all) and therefore their commitment may be expected to wane over time. In Zambia, where there is a committed support structure and financing for conservation agriculture with trees, there has been impressive scaling up to more than 100,000 farmers. A similar model was first tested by ICRAF for fodder shrubs in East Africa and the approach has been incorporated into a larger development project running for the past 4 years. The effectiveness of such approaches contrasts with the Farmer Field School approach, which is recognized as effectively training farmers, but not reaching many for a given amount of funds (Feder et al., 2003). The farmer trainer method is new and is only being evaluated now. Therefore, while such an approach has clearly facilitated the wide spread of agroforestry, it remains to be seen whether it has provided sufficient depth in the dissemination to result in large benefits for adopting farmers.

2.3 Germplasm inputs

In all cases, these recent scaling up efforts have tried to use the private sector, including farmers themselves, in the collection of seed and production of tree seedlings. In the case of India, the private sector invested in production of high quality seedlings that were given on credit to farmers. This had multiple benefits - to quicken the pace of adoption and supply of wood, to ensure that quality of the wood was sufficient, and therefore to increase the profit potential for the farmers so as to create a sustainable sector. Similarly, timber and fruit seedlings are being produced and sold by private sector nurseries in many countries in the world. For new agroforestry systems such as fertilizer trees and fodder shrubs, a demand needed to be created before private sector supply could be expected to respond. So in initial phases, seeds were supplied freely by projects for demonstration purposes. As local demand grew, ICRAF and other NGOs withdrew from bringing in seeds externally but rather encouraged local seed collection and later local seedling production, by playing middlemen and then broker roles. Demand for fodder shrubs in Kenya became so high that stakeholders agreed to form an agroforestry tree seed association which would facilitate the bringing together of suppliers and demanders of fodder shrub seed. Seed and seedling systems for fertilizer tree systems are still not well privatized. The densities of trees required (up to 10,000 per hectare), the reduced importance of quality seed (as compared to the quality of a fruit or timber tree), and the fact that they provide an input service role rather than a valued product of their own, means that farmers' interest in paying for seed is rather low. So NGOs or other intermediaries still play a significant role in fertilizer tree seed supply.

While there are strong movements towards privatization in seed supply globally, there remains heavy involvement by governments in some instances. In Ethiopia, the government has played an active role in all facets of upscaling tree planting including the establishment of government nurseries and sales at subsidized rates. In many, if not most countries, governments become directly involved in providing seed and seedlings for tree planting efforts in non-agricultural areas, for example on hillsides to provide watershed protection services. The Kenya government is considering various options related to agroforestry tree seed and seedling supply to meet the newly enacted regulation that all farms must have 10% tree cover.

3. The importance of policy for agroforestry

The adoption or lack of adoption of agroforestry is influenced by a variety of factors. Some have relatively little to do with policy -- including climate conditions (e.g. rainfall), household and farm characteristics (e.g. resource endowment, size of household), and attributes of the particular agroforestry technology (e.g. time lag between costs and benefits) (Ajayi et al., 2007b). However, a number of important factors are directly linked to policy. In some cases, these policy 'failures' can be over-riding of others and their alleviation critical to wider adoption. This is the first justification for why adoption of agroforestry is a policy issue. The second reason why the adoption of agroforestry is a policy issue is that agroforestry generates significant public environmental services such as watershed protection, biodiversity, and carbon sequestration for which market failures exist. The result is that without government involvement in providing greater incentives, the level of private investment in agroforestry will be less than socially optimal.

In the following paragraphs, the key policy-related constraints to agroforestry adoption are discussed, in no particular order of importance.

3.1 Property rights – Land tenure

Due to the longer period (relative to annual crops) through which farmer testing, adaptation and eventual "adoption" of agroforestry technologies takes place (Mercer, 2004; Scherr and

Müller, 1991), the importance of property rights is greater than for many other types of agricultural enterprises or practices (Place and Swallow, 2002; Ajayi and Kwesiga, 2003). In some places, long term rights to land are insufficient to motivate long term investments such as agroforestry. This can manifest itself as conflicts between the state and land users, such as is the case in smallholder communities within de jure forest land of Indonesia and the Philippines. State ownership of land and reallocation programmes have also been found to inhibit long term land investments in places such as Ethiopia prior to more recent land tenure reforms there. Recent attempts by governments to attract large scale foreign investors have heightened insecurity of rural communities in many countries. Lack of long term rights may also emerge from conflicts between ethnic groups, between indigenes and settlers, families or members of families. Generally, land rights on farm land become more privatized as population pressure increases or commercial opportunities increase. This mainly has a positive effect on incentives for long term investment, but limited rights can arise in such cases if short term land transactions such as land renting become common. While historically the planting of trees was used by farmers to increase tenure security where it was low, this phenomenon is decreasing as inheritance and purchase of land become much more common than allocation by a traditional chief.

Regardless of the overall land security of farming households, in general, women's rights to land and trees are almost always inferior to those of males. This was found to be the case in studies of Uganda, Burundi, and Zambia (Place, 1995). Even in matrilineal societies, the decision making power of women viz tree planting is not guaranteed, such as in Malawi (Hansen et al., 2005; Place and Otsuka, 2001).

Moving from the farm to the other patches of land in and around communities, Elinor Ostrom has shown that the tragedy of the commons is not a universal rule and that that privatizing natural resources is not the route to halting environmental degradation and providing equitable access to resources (Ostrom, 1990). Under certain conditions, when communities are given the right to self-organize they can democratically govern themselves to preserve the environment. Where common property resources provide products such as firewood, fodder and thatch, there are many examples of sustainable management (Otsuka and Place, 2001).

3.2 Tree tenure

Forest policies inhibit tree growing on farms by regulating harvesting, cutting or sale of tree products and certain tree species. Although sometimes well intentioned, such protective policies, when applied to agricultural landscapes, discourages farmers from planting and protecting new seedlings that emerge. Such policies are found in all tropical continents and were perhaps most critically noted in their inhibiting role in Niger and generally in the Forest Codes of West African countries (Elbow and Rochegude, 1990). Restrictions against the felling of trees on farmers' lands are common under forest regulations ranging from India (national and state levels) to Reserved Species in Uganda (Government of Uganda, 2001). Honduras, Nicaragua and Panama have very strict regulations for timber harvesting in agroforestry system and one result is the loss of interest of farmers to associate trees with crops and / or pastures (Detlefsen and Scheelje, 2011).

It is ironic that this important direct source of funds for foresters should result from tree cutting rather than tree growing or tree cover, as transpires in Mali, India and in the Central

American region. Further, when rigid enforcement of such restrictive policies are relaxed, as in the case of Niger, there can be a swift and vast response, resulting in millions of hectares of parklands with young trees. Also, poor regulation of state managed woodlands and forests have led to undervaluing of concessions or stumpage charges resulting over supply from these sources and under supply from farms. Charcoal is a good case in point. The sector, which is largely unregulated in Africa, is characterized by mobile charcoal burners, seeking the cheapest sources of wood as possible, and who have no long term interest in the sustainable use of any particular piece of land. If charcoal producers paid a fair price for their wood sources in woodlands/forests, this would increase opportunities for farmers to supply trees for charcoal makers. This shows how tenure rules on non-farm areas have an implication for agroforestry on farms.

3.3 Agroforestry tree germplasm systems

The problems observed in the agroforestry tree germplasm sector are numerous: narrow base of tree germplasm which is available in areas outside of growing areas, little multiplication of this narrow base so that quantities available for all species are low, the quality of the germplasm is low on average and variable, with little investment in germplasm improvement, and retail level systems - interfaces with farmers are not well developed and are challenged by competition between private and public sector involvement. Seed collection, propagation and multiplication methods are also poorly known and farmers often have no other option but to protect or transplant trees which have germinated spontaneously.

Part of the neglect of the sector has to do with the fact that in most developing countries forest departments have the mandate for all tree seed supply. This is sensible for forests and plantations, but has serious drawbacks for agroforestry species because resident forestry staff are few in the field and are not highly aware of needs of farmers. Agricultural extension staff have a much better understanding of farming systems and potential utility of integrating trees on farms. So this is a critical structural gap which remains problematic in many countries despite efforts of some programmes and projects to better involve the agriculture sector in agroforestry. Another challenge is that governments and NGOs often give away free or subsidized seed and seedlings which competes against entrepreneurs.

Although most agroforestry stakeholders would agree on the need for more private sector involvement in seed/germplasm supply systems, there are numerous constraints. One is related to the business nature of tree demand. Unlike annual crops, farmers may purchase tree seed or seedlings just a few times in their lives. Second, where seedlings are used, the market area is limited by ability to transport seedlings within a reasonable time period (to avoid damage to the seedling) and at an affordable cost. So demand limitations can reduce the interest in retail germplasm supply as a profession. There are also information problems concerning the quality and source of germplasm. It is not easy to discern different varietial type or other quality features of seed or young seedlings and this hampers the ability of suppliers to charge prices commensurate with quality. There are some exceptions, such as with the development of market chains for eucalyptus seedlings and some fruit cultivars. But generally, the sector is beset by market failure problems that require attention by policy makers.

However, a lot remains to be done in terms of germplasm diversification. There is no consolidated global picture on the status and trends of tree genetic resources, and a lack of estimators of the rate of genetic diversity loss. This limits the capacity of countries and the international community to integrate tree genetic resources management into overall cross-cutting policies. The State of the World's Forest Genetic Resources, in preparation by FAO will publish specific information on the status and trends in forest genetic resources (FAO, 2009). Despite limitations on understanding of genetic diversity, multipurpose trees have now been identified for most regions of the world, though many of these trees are actually never brought into cultivation. They are protected when they germinate naturally in fields (as typically in the African agroforestry parkland), or they are simply used from the wild. The seed technology of many species is simply not known and there are few nurseries providing a range of native multipurpose trees. Out of the more or less 40,000 tree species which make the tropical tree flora, it is probable that a few hundred, at most, are cultivated. The policy context to support a wider use of multipurpose tree germplasm has to be invented from scratch. Depending on the location, policy options could be subsidies to nurseries, germplasm collection campaigns funded by the private sector or validation of local ecological knowledge.

3.4 Subsidies or support for other land use practices

There are many governments that have put in place price floors for food products, subsidies for specific inputs like fertilizer, or favorable credit terms for certain agricultural activities. These almost always exclude agroforestry and therefore discourage its practice. In the case of fertilizer, for example, such government policies induce higher use of fertilizer and less interest in using more sustainable practices like agroforestry. Several years ago, fertilizer tree technology was considered impractical or less economically rational to use in Nigeria because nitrogen fertilizers were a cheaper option at that time (Sanchez, 1999). Fertilizer subsidies have been present for decades in Asia and are making a comeback in Africa (e.g. Malawi, Zambia, Tanzania, Kenya and more recently Nigeria). There is little argument that fertilizers are needed in agriculture, but by subsidizing them without commensurate support for other soil fertility measures such as agroforestry-based fertilizer trees, governments risk promoting a narrow technological package that is not compatible with long term soil health. Many governments support agriculture in some ways, but agroforestry is not often included as an agricultural enterprise for support. For example, in India, credit at low rates is available for agriculture, but agroforestry falls under 'forestry' and faces a much higher interest rate. The same situation was observed in France as far as CAP subsidies are concerned until the development of a very innovative new policy for the country where agroforestry trees are considered as inputs into farming practices, making agroforestry fields eligible for CAP subsidies while they were considered as "forests" under the earlier regulation, and consequently not eligible. Many governments have now improved market information systems for agricultural commodities but again, tree products are usually neglected.

Through economic policies, governments also can significantly influence resulting land use patterns. For example, the Indonesia government provided tax and land tenure benefits for large scale farmers to convert forest land into oil palm. The further development of this sector then led to conversion of traditional agroforests to oil palm. In India (Kerala), specific agroforestry policies do not exist to guide planning and the consequence is that existing land tenure, agriculture and forestry policies favor monospecific plantation crops (Guillerme et al., 2011). Mono-specific tree crop systems are further promoted by the development and testing of tree crop varieties under full sun conditions only, ignoring the potential for improved varieties in more multi-species agroforestry systems. An example is the case of rubber in Indonesia (Williams et al., 2001).

3.5 Extension systems

Studies from several countries in Africa have shown that sustainable land management practices such as agroforestry are not sufficiently known by extension agents and much less likely to be disseminated to farmers (e.g. in Zimbabwe - Chitakira and Torquebiau, 2010; in Nigeria - Banful et al., 2010; in Zambia- Sturmheit, 1990). This creates an information bias towards other types of practices. Indeed, the transmission of new management practices to frontline extension workers has long been acknowledged as a difficulty, especially in Africa. Some agroforestry practices are knowledge intensive and thus do not diffuse as quickly as other technologies. Part of the explanation for this with respect to agroforestry is that silviculture is the domain of forestry officers and agricultural extension messages emphasize conventional crop husbandry methods. Even where extension agents are trained, they often are understaffed and cannot easily meet the time commitments required to fully train farmers on new farming methods like agroforestry.

3.6 National government and programme structure

Agroforestry has a de facto "orphan" status in many national government settings (some Central American countries are exceptions where agroforestry is more widely recognized); agroforestry in principle is important to many ministries but in practice, it belongs to none. Agroforestry was first attached to the forestry sector but forest departments have historically had relatively few resources for programmes, been unfamiliar with agricultural practices, and often played a more policing than advisory role. Agriculture is the natural home for this farmer practice and there is a noticeable shift of agroforestry towards agriculture, especially as the soil fertility benefits of agroforestry have become more well known. Thirty years ago, one would be pressed to find agroforestry articulated in any national policy or strategy document. Now, as it is gaining recognition, it is increasingly mentioned. There are references to agroforestry in forest acts (e.g. Kenya), but often it receives minor attention with natural forests and plantations receiving the most attention. Thus, as noted above, when it comes to tree germplasm, there is inadequate attention paid to the needs of farmers and agroforestry trees. Agroforestry is also appearing more in agricultural strategies, but often merely in a list of options for addressing sustainability. The capacity for agroforestry to generate income is hardly ever recognized in policy documents. Recent review of policies in Malawi shows that agroforestry has a very low profile in most of the sectoral policy documents. In the national Forestry policy document, the word "agroforestry" appears only on 2 out of a total 19 pages; one page out of the 293 pages of the Malawi Growth and Development Strategy document; twice in the 210 pages of the Agricultural Sector Wide Approach (ASWAp) policy document, once only out of the 40 pages of the Livestock Policy document (Pangapanga and Ajayi, 2011). More recently, agroforestry is given strong attention in climate change adaptation and mitigation strategies, which themselves are often managed by ministries of environment. But ministries of environment often do not have capacity to support agroforestry in a meaningful way at the community level and must rely on other ministries, notably agriculture, for implementation. Yet, intersectoral planning and resource sharing is very rare.

Lastly, it is important to note the structural challenges facing agroforestry in managed landscapes that arise from ambiguity and conflict between the mandates or capacities for governance at national and local levels. There has been devolution of control and decision-making authority over natural resources to local governments, but the boundaries of authority are not always clear, local level capacity is often weak, and funding for local level planning and implementation is usually given low priority compared to sectors such as education, health, water, and roads.

3.7 Environmental services

Agroforestry is increasingly being recognized as a key land use for the provision of environmental services, such as carbon sequestration (Smith and Martino, 2007) watershed protection and biodiversity. These externalities are sometimes spatial such as the effects of agroforestry on watershed protection for downstream users, or temporal, such as the effects of agroforestry on long term soil health and land rehabilitation. These services, or positive externalities, are not rewarded by market mechanisms (market failure) and thus the supply of these benefits is less than socially optimal levels. This is a justification for government involvement to establish or catalyze systems and mechanisms that can link consumers (buyers) of the environmental services with suppliers and to increase the efficiency of such markets (e.g. to provide guarantees, to reduce transactions costs).

4. Policy reforms that have been pro-agroforestry

There have been some recent policy reforms that have directly targeted and benefited the expansion of agroforestry. A good number of these are related to revisions in forest policy or its implementation. The first example was already mentioned above, the reforms which occurred in the form of re-interpretation and implementation of the Forest Code in Niger which helped to expand the practice of farmer managed natural regeneration to over 5 million hectares of land (Garrity et al., 2010). The government of Indonesia has altered policies on property rights to grant communities long term rights to forest land in return for environmental stewardship of the land (HKM programme) and have also created a village forest concept (Hutan Desa) which would provide villages rights to benefits of carbon or other environmental services (Pender et al., 2008). Guatemala recognized in the Forest Act in 1996 that procedures for timber harvesting in agroforestry systems should be simplified. Fifteen years later it is observed that farmers produce timber within their farms as another form of diversification of land use, and as another source of income (Detlefsen and Scheelje, 2011). El Salvador has now a similar recognition of agroforestry within their Forest Act (amended in 2004). In Belize, Rosa Cruz (2010) found that timber production in silvopastoral systems has large productive potential because the simplified conditions of the forest law.

Some governments have gone as far as to adopt explicit agroforestry strategies or policies. In France, constraints against agroforestry were mainly economic and linked to taxations of tree products. As long agricultural as subsidies are linked to cultivated area, farmers showed no interest in growing trees in cropland, even if there is a recognized ecological advantage and if long term income can be expected from timber. And if the land is classified as forestry land, taxation is higher. In 2010, the government of France passed an agroforestry policy whose main achievement was to establish agroforestry as a legal agricultural land use qualifying for EC agricultural subsidies in the framework of the common agricultural policy

(CAP). Farmers can receive investment support for the establishment of the agroforestry systems on agricultural lands. Without that, all other agricultural practices were favored (APCA, 2010). Also, a national association on agroforestry was created in France to organize and exchange information, follow up with regulation reforms and increase building capacity of development agents through training programmes. The triggering factor was to stop negotiating with foresters and convince the government that trees in fields were not forestry products but inputs into the farming systems. Within the EU, review processes are underway to examine how agroforestry fits into the two pillars of agricultural support: Pillar I - direct aid and market support, and Pillar II - rural development, as well as within forestry policy schemes for farm woodlands (Organic Research Centre, 2010).

Several countries or regions are developing or refreshing agroforestry strategies. Brazil had earlier developed an agroforestry strategy in 1997 and is currently embarking on a participatory process to refresh the policy. The United States Department of Agriculture (USDA) developed an Agroforestry Strategic Framework 2011-2016 which notes the upcoming release of a policy statement on agroforestry and the establishment of an Agroforestry Steering Committee that will guide the implementation of this strategic framework (USDA, 2011). The report "Portrait of Agroforestry in Québec, Canada, recommends five preliminary strategic components: recognition of agroforestry by government and institutional decision makers; establishment of an intersectoral partnership; adoption of an economic and market development approach; solid technical and economic foundations for agroforestry development; and adequate structural and operational funding (De Baets et al., 2007).

China and India have embarked on ambitious programmes to increase tree cover outside of forests (Grain for Green and Greening India respectively), including some attention to smallholder agroforestry. In 2009, the Government of Kenya, in particular the Ministry of Agriculture, enacted new Farm Forestry rules which require 10% of all farms to be covered with trees. This was in response to recognition of deforestation, the increase in agricultural land area, and the high motivation of farmers to plant trees. The government has also allocated several million dollars to assist farmers in regions where these targets are not already met. The Indian State of Chhattisgarh adopted an agroforestry policy in 2009 which goes as far as to include agroforestry products among several that it establishes a price floor and guaranteed market for, in order to ensure adequate production.

A number of countries have advanced agroforestry in their programmatic development as a result of increased attention to climate change. In order to make agricultural production and income more resilient to climate change and variability, transformations in the management of natural resources (e.g. land, water, soil nutrients, and genetic resources) and higher efficiency in the use of these resources and inputs for production. The key role of agroforestry for climate-smart agriculture is now cited in key publications along with institutional and policy options available to promote the transition to climate-smart agriculture at the smallholder level (e.g. FAO, 2010). The responses of governments are perhaps most explicitly observed through the development of National Adaptation Programmes of Action (NAPAs) and Nationally Appropriate Mitigation Actions (NAMAs). In the agriculture and environment sectors, agroforestry is a priority action in many countries. Support for these processes has come partly from processes at global and regional levels. The UNFCCC recognized agroforestry as a key mitigation method within agriculture (Smith et al., 2008) and methods for quantification of its mitigation potential were accepted. Similarly, African ministers of agriculture endorsed the wide scaling up of agroforestry to address climate change adaptation and mitigation objectives in agriculture in 2009. The Comprehensive African Agricultural Development Programme (CAADP) developed an agriculture climate change adaptation and mitigation framework which was endorsed by the same ministers in 2010 and which also highlights agroforestry.

5. Conclusions and implications for advancing policy reforms at national level for agroforestry

The analysis in this chapter has demonstrated that there are a number of important policy constraints that hinder wider adoption of agroforestry among smallholder farmers in developing countries, both at formulation and implementation levels. Yet, driven by rural development and environmental objectives, there is a greater policy recognition of the importance of agroforestry. This has translated into a few concrete examples of policy reforms that have removed barriers to agroforestry, resulting in positive impacts in cases where studies were conducted. Most, if not all, the policy reforms featured in section 4 were supported by research, development, and other civil society organizations in some way. For example, research played a role in advancement of the recognition of agroforestry at global and regional levels and in providing evidence to support national reforms in some cases (e.g. UNFCCC); non-governmental organizations played important roles in policy reforms as well (e.g. in Niger).

Thus, there is strong reason to believe that a more concerted and collaborative supporting effort among such organizations would lead to even greater policy impacts. The World Agroforestry Centre (ICRAF) proposed the need for an Agroforestry Policy Initiative and embraced it internally in 2009. The FAO is leading an initiative to develop agroforestry guidelines for policy makers, which would support the development of agroforestry through dissemination of good practice in policy and reform processes. The FAO is also supporting the development of a framework for trees outside forests assessment, including agroforestry, at national, regional, eco-regional and global levels, a key instrument for informed decision processes. (FAO, 2011b). A group of organizations have in fact joined forces to support national policy reforms related to agroforestry. The Centro Agronómico Tropical de Investigación y Enseñanza (CATIE) in Costa Rica, Centre de Coopération Internationale en Recherche Agronomique pour le Développement (CIRAD) of France and ICRAF have joined forces with FAO in this endeavor. The three organizations have large agroforestry research programmes spanning all developing regions of the world. This vast experience complements very well the strength of FAO in linking science to policy action through its convening power at global and country levels. It is hoped that the production of the guidelines along with other efforts by countries and institutions will catalyze an even wider partnership and movement towards removing policy barriers that have hitherto constrained agroforestry from reaching its full potential.

6. References

Ajayi, O.C., Akinnifesi, F.K., Sileshi, G., Chakeredza, S. & S. Mgomba. 2009. Integrating Food Security and Agri-environmental Quality in Southern Africa: Implications for Policy. In: Luginaah, I.N. and Yanful, E.K. (Eds.) *Environment and Health in Sub-Saharan Africa: Managing an Emerging Crisis*, Springer Publishers, Netherlands, Pp 39-49.

Ajayi, O.C., Place, F., Kwesiga, F., & P. Mafongoya. 2007a. Impacts of Improved Tree Fallow Technology in Zambia. In: Waibel H. and Zilberman D (eds) *International Research on Natural Resource Management: Advances in Impact Assessment* CABI Wallingford, UK and Science Council/CGIAR, Rome pp.147-168 ISBN: 976-1-84593-283-1.

Ajayi, O.C., Akinnifesi, F.K., Gudeta, S. & S. Chakeredza. 2007b. Adoption of renewable soil fertility replenishment technologies in southern African region: lessons learnt and the way forward *Natural Resource Forum* 31(4): 306-317

Ajayi, O.C. & F. Kwesiga. 2003. Implications of local policies and institutions on the adoption of improved fallows in eastern Zambia *Agroforestry systems* 59 (3): 327-336

APCA. 2010. L'agroforesterie dans les règlementations agricoles. Etat des lieux en juin 2010. *Assemblée Permanente des Chambres d'Agriculture* (APCA), Paris, France, 17 pp.

Banful, A., Nkonya, E. & V. Oboh. 2010. Constraints to Fertilizer Use in Nigeria: Insights from Agricultural Extension Service, IFPRI Discussion Paper 01010, International Food Policy Research Institute, Washington DC.

Boffa, J-M. 1999. Agroforestry parklands in Sub-Saharan Africa. FAO Conservation Guide 34, Food and Agriculture Organization, Rome.

Boshier, D., Cordero, J., Detlefsen, G., & J. Beer. 2009. Indigenous trees for farmers: information transfer for sustainable management in Central America and the Caribbean. In Joseph, P. ed. Écosystèmes forestiers des Caraïbes. Conseil Général de La Martinique, Martinique, Karthala. p. 397 - 410.

Bond, W.J., Midgley, G.F. & F.I. WoodwardI. 2003. The importance of low atmospheric CO_2 and fire in promoting the spread of grasslands and savannas. *Global Change Biology* 9: 973-982.

Chitakira, M. & E. Torquebiau. 2010. Barriers and Coping Mechanisms Relating to Agroforestry Adoption by Smallholder Farmers in Zimbabwe. *Journal of Agricultural Education and Extension* 16 (2): 147-160.

Cordero, J. & D. Boshier. 2003. Árboles de Centroamérica: un manual para extensionistas. Oxford, Inglaterra, OFI - CATIE. 1079 p.

De Baets, N., Gariépy, S. & A. Vézina. 2007. Portrait of agroforestry: Executive summary. Agriculture and Agri-Food Canada, Ottawa.

Detlefsen, G. & M. Scheelje. 2011. Implicaciones de las normativas forestales para el manejo maderable sostenible en sistemas agroforestales de Centroamérica. Turrialba, Costa Rica, CATIE. 41 p.

Elbow, K. & A. Rochegude. 1990. A layperson's guide to the forest codes of Mali, Niger, and Senegal. Land Tenure Center Paper No. 130. Madison, Land Tenure Center, University of Wisconsin-Madison.

FAOSTAT. 2011. Food and Agriculture Organization of the United Nations FAOSTAT Online Database, April-2011, accessed at http://faostat.fao.org

FAO. 2003. Forestry outlook study for Africa: regional report for opportunities and challenges towards 2020. FAO Forestry Paper 141. FAO, Rome.

FAO. 2009. The Commission on Genetic Resources for Food and Agriculture Integrating the potential of forest genetic resources. FAO, Rome.

FAO. 2010. "Climate-Smart" Agriculture. Policies, Practices and Financing for Food Security, Adaptation and Mitigation. FAO, Rome, 41 p.

FAO, 2011a. A Thematic Study prepared in the framework of the Global Forest Resources Assessment 2010. Draft working paper, prepared and edited by H.de Foresta, in collaboration with G. Detlefsen and A. Temu. FAO Forest Assessment, Management and Conservation Division. September 2011. Rome, 210 p.

FAO. 2011b. State of the World's Forests. FAO, Rome. 164 p.
Feder, G., Murgai, R., & J. Quizon. 2003. Sending Farmers Back to School: The Impact of Farmer Field Schools in Indonesia. World Bank Policy Research Working Paper 3022, World Bank, Washington DC.
Franzel S. & C. Wambugu. 2007. The uptake of fodder shrubs among smallholders in East Africa: key elements that facilitate widespread adoption. In: Hare MD, Wongpichet K, eds. *Forages: a pathway to prosperity for smallholder farmers*. Proceedings of an international symposium. Ubon Ratchathani University, Thailand: Faculty of Agriculture. p. 203–222.
Garrity, D.P., Akinnifesi, F.K., Ajayi, O.C., Weldesemayat, S.G., Mowo, J.G., Kalinganire, A., Larwanou, M., & J.Bayala. 2010. Evergreen Agriculture: a robust approach to sustainable food security in Africa. *Food Security* 2:197–214
Government of Uganda. 2001. Uganda Forestry Policy, Uganda Forestry Authority, Government of Uganda, Entebbe.
Guillerme, S., Kumar, B.M., Menon, A., Hinnewinkel, C., Maire, E., & A. Santhoshkumar. 2011. Impacts of Public Policies and Farmer Preferences on Agroforestry Practices in Kerala, India. *Environmental Management* 48: 351-364.
Haggblade, S., & G. Tembo. 2003. Conservation farming in Zambia. EPTD Discussion Paper. Environment and Production Technology Division, International Food Policy Research Institute.
Hansen, J., Luckert, M., Minae, S., & F. Place. 2005. Tree Planting Under Customary Tenure Systems in Malawi: An Investigation into the Importance of Marriage and Inheritance Patters. *Agricultural Systems* 84 (1): 99-118.
Kgope, B.S., Bond, W.J. & G.F. Midgley. 2010. Growth responses of African savanna trees implicate atmospheric [CO2] as a driver of past and current changes in savanna tree cover. *Australian Ecology* 35: 451-463.
Leimona, B. 2011. Fairly Efficient or Efficiently Fair: success factors and constraints of payment and reward schemes for environmental services in Asia. Phd Thesis, Graduate School of Socio-Economic and Natural Sciences of the Environment, Wageningen University, Netherlands.
Midgley, G.F. & W. Thuillier. 2011. Potential responses of terrestrial biodiversity in Southern Africa to anthropogenic climate change. *Regional Environmental Change* 11 (Suppl 1): S127-S135. DOI 10.1007/s10113 010-0191-8
Organic Research Centre. 2010. Agroforestry Policy Review. UK, Elm Farm, 28 p.
Ostrom, E. 1990. *Governing the Commons: the Evolution of Institutions for Collective Action*. Cambridge, U.K.: Cambridge University Press.
Otsuka, K. & F. Place. 2001. Issues and Theoretical Framework, in K. Otsuka and F. Place, *Land Tenure and Natural Resource Management: A comparative study of agrarian communities in Asia and Africa*. Baltimore: Johns Hopkins Press.
Pangapanga, P.I. & O.C. Ajayi. 2011 Review of National Agroforestry Policy: Malawi Case Study Report, Working Paper, World Agroforestry Centre, Malawi 29 pp.
Pender, J., Suyanto, S., & J. Kerr. 2008. Impacts of the Hutan Kamasyarakatan Social Forestry Program in the Sumberjaya Watershed, West Lampung District of Sumatra, Indonesia, IFPRI Discussion Paper 00769, International Food Policy Research Institute, Washington, DC.
Place, F. 1995. The Role of Land and Tree Tenure on the Adoption of Agroforestry Technologies in Uganda, Burundi, Zambia, and Malawi: A Summary and Synthesis, Madison, Wisconsin: Land Tenure Center, University of Wisconsin.

Place, F. & P. Dewees. 1999. Policies and incentives for the adoption of improved fallows. *Agroforestry Systems*, 47(1/3): 323-343.

Place, F. & K. Otsuka. 2001. Tenure, Agricultural Investment, and Productivity in the Customary Tenure Sector of Malawi. *Economic Development and Cultural Change*, 50(1).

Place, F. & B. Swallow. 2002. "Assessing the Relationships between Property Rights and Technology Adoption in Smallholder Agriculture: Issues and Empirical Methods," in Meinzen-Dick, R., Knox, A., Place, F., and B. Swallow. *Innovation in Natural Resource Management: The Role of Property Rights and Collective Action in Developing Countries*, Johns Hopkins University Press, Baltimore, USA.

Pye-Smith C. 2009. Seeds of Hope: A public-private partnership to domesticate a native tree, Allanblackia, is transforming lives in rural Africa.Nairobi: World Agroforestry Centre.

Pye-Smith C. 2010. A Rural Revival in Tanzania: How agroforestry is helping farmers to restore the woodlands in Shinyanga Region. ICRAF Trees for Change no. 7. Nairobi: World Agroforestry Centre.

Reij, C., Tappan, G. & M. Smale. 2009. Agroenvironmental Transformation in the Sahel. Another Kind of Green Revolution. IFPRI Discussion Paper 00914, International Food Policy Research Institute, Washington, DC.

Sanchez, A. P. 1999. Improved fallows come of age in the tropics. *Agroforestry Systems*, 47: 3–12.

Smith, P. & D. Martino. 2007. Agriculture, in Climate Change 2007, Fourth IPCC Assessment Report, IPCC, Geneva, Switzerland

Smith, P., Martino, D., Cai, Z., Gwary, D., Janzen, H., Kumar, P., McCarl, B., Ogle, S., O'mara, F., Rice, C., Scholes, B., Sirotenko, O., Howden, M., McAllister, T., Pan, G., Romanenkov, V., Schneider, S. Towprayoon, U., Wattenbach, M. & J. Smith 2008. Greenhouse-gas mitigation in agriculture. *Philosophical Transactions of the Royal Society*, B., 363: 789-813.

Sturmheit, P. 1990. Agroforestry and soil conservation needs of smallholders in southern Zambia, *Agroforestry systems, 10: 265-289*

Torquebiau, E. & H. Moussa. 1990. Potentialités agroforestières pour la zone semi-aride du Niger. Rapport AFRENA N° 25, ICRAF, Nairobi, 134 pp.

Torquebiau, E. &t H. Moussa. 1991. Propositions de recherches agroforestières pour le système de la vallée du fleuve Niger au Niger. Rapport AFRENA N° 39, ICRAF, Nairobi, 93 pp.

USDA 2011. USDA Agroforestry Strategic Framework, Fiscal Year 2011-2016. United States Department of Agriculture, Washington,.35 p.

Williams,S.E., van Noordwijk, M., Penot, E., Healey, J.R., Sinclair, F.L., & G. Wibawa. 2001. On-farm evaluation of the establishment of clonal rubber in multistrata agroforests in Jambi, Indonesia. *Agroforestry Systems* 53: 227-237.

Zomer, R. J., Bossio, D. A., Trabucco, A., Yuanjie, L., Gupta, D. C., & V.P. Singh. 2007. Trees and water: Smallholder agroforestry on irrigated lands in Northern India. Colombo, Sri Lanka: International Water Management Institute. 47p. (IWMI Research Report 122).

Zomer, R.J., Trabucco, A., Coe, R., & F. Place. 2009. Trees on farm: Analysis of global extent and geographical patterns of agroforestry. ICRAF, Working Paper no. 89. Nairobi, Kenya, ICRAF. 63 pgs.

7

Mainstreaming Agroforestry Policy in Tanzania Legal Framework

Tuli S. Msuya[1] and Jafari R. Kideghesho[2]
[1]*Tanzania Forestry Research Institute (TAFORI),*
[2]*Sokoine University of Agriculture (SUA)*
Tanzania

1. Introduction

Agroforestry has been defined as a dynamic, ecologically-based natural resources management system that, through the integration of trees in agricultural landscapes, diversifies and sustains production for increased social, economic and environmental benefits (Leakey, 1996; ICRAF, 2007). The system is increasingly considered as a solution for limited available resources and is rapidly emerging as a response to global sustainable development goals due to key role it plays in transforming livelihoods and landscapes (ICRAF, 2008). It provides diverse benefits including *inter alia* enhancing biodiversity, climate change adaptation and mitigation, food security, and reducing rural poverty by increasing soil fertility and crop yields.

In Tanzania, agroforestry is potentially important for improving the livelihoods of the majority of people, particularly rural communities, through enhanced food security, primary health care (medicinal plants) and the leading source of fuel energy. Essentially, the system has increasingly become a focal entry point for rural development, environmental stewardship including climate change adaptation and mitigation, and ecosystem sustainability through transformation of livelihoods and landscapes (ICRAF, 2008; Boeckmann and Iolster, 2010; Pye-Smith, 2010). Over time Agroforestry research has developed a wide range of practical and robust technologies for different agroecological zones, which have yielded positive and encouraging results in improving food security, livelihoods and environmental resilience (Mbwambo 2004, Boeckmann and Iolster 2010; Pye-Smith 2010). However, human, infrastructure and institutional capacities for agroforestry development are not well developed (Kitalyi *et al.*, 2011).

Widespread adoption of agroforestry technologies requires appropriate policies at national and local levels (Boeckmann & Iolster 2010). However, there are numerous policy based constraints hindering success of agroforestry in most African countries (Scherr & Franzel, 2002; Place & Prudencio, 2006; Boeckmann & Iolster, 2010) and Tanzania, in particular (Ngatunga and Nshubemuki, 2006; Mmbaga *et al.*, 2007; Otsyina *et al.*, 2010). Among the major constraints are land and tree tenure policies (Lawson *et al.*, 2005; Place and Prodencio, 2006), inadequate legal framework and institutional support and lack of stand alone agroforestry policy besides huge contribution that agroforestry plays in enhancing livelihood improvement and poverty alleviation in the country (Otsyina *et al.*, 2010). Options for developing agroforestry are among the major issues of debate in Tanzania. However, they have received very minimal attention in literature. This chapter, therefore, explores how existing national policies and institutional setups facilitate or constrain development of agroforestry policy and the available options for developing such policy.

2. History of agroforestry in Tanzania and Tanzania legal framework

Tanzania is home to a variety of traditional agroforestry systems that have been in practice since time immemorial (Otsyina *et al.*, 2010). These agroforestry systems are, therefore, part of the history of the Tanzanian rural landscapes. Some have been documented. Examples include the Chagga home-gardens in north eastern Tanzania (Soini, 2005) and the related Kagera and Mara Regions home-gardens in north western Tanzania (Rugalema *et al.*, 1994), the Usambara traditional based domestication agroforestry systems in north eastern Tanzania (Moshi, 1997; Msuya *et al.*, 2008; Reyes, 2008) and the traditional Wasukuma silvopastoral system called "*ngitili*" in Western Tanzania (Otsyina *et al.*, 1993; Kamwenda, 2002; Barrow, 2004; Pye-Smith, 2010). One outstanding aspect of these traditional agroforestry systems is the use of multi-layered systems with a mixture of annual and perennial plants, which imitate natural ecosystems.

Agroforestry evolved as a formal scientific discipline in the mid 1970s, but its promotion through research and development activities started in 1980s (Otsyina *et al.*, 2010). The evolution of agroforestry in the last three decades has seen a major shift from emphasis on land productivity at farm level to systems interactions at landscape level (Kitalyi *et al.*, 2011). Agroforestry systems provide both local and global ecosystem services. They play significant roles in realizing the goals of the three UN conventions on desertification, biodiversity and climate change (Figure 1). The three conventions seek to mobilize the science, economics, social and political will in order to bring about sustainability in the use and management of the Earth's natural resources and enhance the life-support systems. Agroforestry is embedded in these conventions due to its ability to transform landscapes and livelihoods by contributing to poverty reduction, improved productivity and achievement of environmental sustainability (ICRAF, 2007).

The potential of agroforestry practice and science to contribute to sustainable development through transforming landscapes and livelihoods is jeopardized by inadequate policy and legal support along with fragmented policy environment. Tanzania has no stand alone policy to guide agroforestry practices and legislation. The only existing document to support agroforestry in the country is the National Agroforestry Strategy of 2004 designed to support scaling up of agroforestry technologies. However, it is silent on other important aspects of agroforestry, especially those related to policy and legal frameworks. For example, this strategy lacks guidance on how policy and related regulations can be formulated.

The National Agroforestry Strategy envisions that four million rural households will adopt and benefit from agroforestry practices by 2025 (NAS, 2004). Its goal by 2020 is for agroforestry technologies to be adopted and contribute appreciably to improving the livelihoods of 60% of the country's resource-poor households (*ibid*). The goal of the National Agroforestry Strategy complements the Tanzania's Development Vision 2025 and the National Strategy for Growth and Poverty Reduction (MKUKUTA), which aim at increasing household income while conserving the environment. However, formulation of this strategy was not based on reforms of natural resources and agricultural related policies and legislations. It was the Ministry of Agriculture and Food Security (MAFS) and the Ministry of Natural Resources and Tourism (MNRT) that constituted the National Agroforestry Steering Committee (NASCO) in 1993, which in turn formulated the strategy. Although MAFS and MNRT recognize the importance and potential strategy in guiding agroforestry practices and NASCO as the overseer of agroforestry practices in Tanzania, there is little or no structure to institutionalize the Strategy and NASCO into national policy and legal frameworks. Such institutional structures need to be developed, and this can act as important entry point to formulating agroforestry policy.

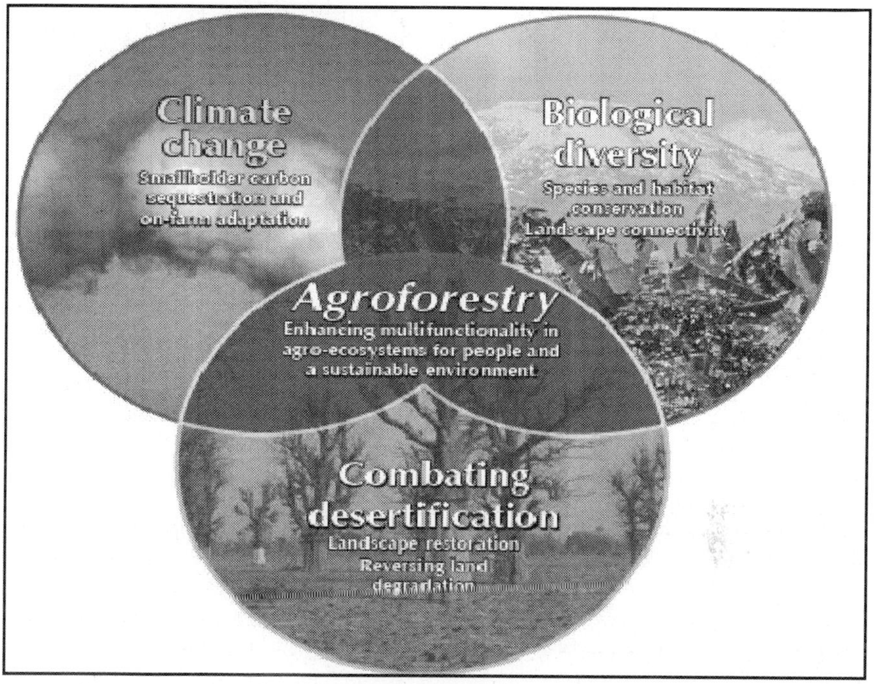

Fig. 1. Agroforestry at the heart of three conventions: combating desertification, biological diversity and climate change (Source: ICRAF, 2007).

Besides the National Agroforestry Strategy, Tanzania has several sectoral policies and legislations. However, they do not systematically address agroforestry issues. The current policies and legislations include:

- The National Forest Policy (1998) and the resultant Forest Act No. 14 of 2002
- The Agricultural and Livestock Policy of Tanzania (1997), Various Legislations
- The National Beekeeping Policy (1998), Beekeeping Act No.15 2002
- The National Fisheries Policy (1998), Act No. 22 of 2003
- The National Environmental Policy (1997), Act No. 20 of 2004

- The Wildlife Policy (1998) and the Wildlife Conservation Act No. 5 of 2009
- National Water Policy of Tanzania (2002), Act No. 11 of 2009
- National Land Policy (1995), Land Act No. 4 of 1999 and Village Land Act No. 5 of 1999

These new policies and legislations resulted from policy reforms, which started in 1980s. These reforms also underpinned the development of various sectoral programmes and strategies such as National Forest and Beekeeping Programmes, the Agricultural Sector Development Programme and the Water Sector Development Programme. Like the policies and legislations, these regulatory institutions, also lack special provisions for agroforestry practices although they can either enable or constrain agroforestry development. The fact that the Forest Policy of 1998 is currently under review gives a hope that important aspects pertaining to agroforestry practices and management will be accorded adequate and deserved priority.

3. Agroforestry in different sectoral policy and legal instruments

Different natural resources policies and legislations (outlined in this section) touch agroforestry issues in various ways.

3.1 The Forest Policy and legislations

The policy and legal documents regulating forest resources in Tanzania are the National Forest Policy of 1998, The National Forest Programme (NFP) of 2001 and the Forest Act of 2002. The Forest Policy encourages agroforestry practices by recognizing contribution of trees outside forests in agricultural productivity and forest conservation. However, many of the statements and directives are specifically focusing on forestry and not specifically on agroforestry practices. For example, maintaining ecosystem stability through conservation of forest biodiversity, water catchments and soil fertility is one of the objectives of Forest Policy but it has indirect provisions for agroforestry practices. In fact, there is scholarly consensus that agroforestry practices are potential for ensuring ecosystem sustainability, biodiversity conservation, watershed conservation and soil fertility improvement (Mbwambo 2004; ICRAF, 2008; Otsyina *et al.*, 2010; Pye-Smith 2010). The only direct reference to agroforestry in National Forest Programme is agroforestry definition. As the Forest Policy requires legal framework to translate its objectives to action, the Programme was launched as an instrument to operationalize the Policy, implemented through the Forest Act of 2002.

Both the Forest Policy and the Forest Act provide a strong foundation and legal basis for community managed and privately managed forests implying indirect provision for agroforestry. It is evident that agroforestry is embedded in community-managed forests (Porter-Bolland *et al.*, 2011). In addition, the Forest Policy, National Forest Programme and Forest Act recognize the potential of trees and forests for rural energy sources, provision of various goods (forest products) and services (climate amelioration, carbon sequestration, watershed protection). However, provisions for payment for services offered by trees and forests are not clearly stipulated in existing forest policy and legal documents. In that vein, the 1998 forest policy is currently under review to capture some issues related to payment for ecosystem services under clean development mechanisms (CDM) and reduced emission from deforestation and degradation (REDD) initiatives. These initiatives are opportunities for agroforestry to flourish.

The Forest Act has some provisions that seem to constrain agroforestry practices. These provisions are related to tree tenure as stipulated in sections 65, 66 and 67 of the Act (URT, 2002). The Act empowers the Minister of Natural Resources to declare any indigenous tree species a "reserved tree" regardless of where they grow, provided it is protected under international agreements due to either importance in biodiversity conservation and genetic resources value or the risk/vulnerability to extinction (URT, 2002). Under these laws, reserved trees or parts of these trees are protected from cutting or removal without permission (*ibid*). On one hand, these provisions can limit investment in agroforestry (tree planting and/or retention), but on the other hand, they can encourage some useful interventions such as domestication and conservation of traditional natural forests in order to capture benefits from CBM and REDD funds.

3.2 The Agricultural Policy and legislations

The agricultural sector in Tanzania is governed by the National Agricultural and Livestock Policy of 1997, the Agricultural Sector Development Strategy (ASDS) of 2001, the Agricultural Sector Development Programme (ASDP) of 2006, and various legislations. The National Agricultural and Livestock Policy of 1997 recognizes the need to utilize the national scientific and technological capacity in the promotion of agricultural production and productivity. The policy underscores the need to harness both science and technology and indigenous knowledge in addressing constraints to agricultural production. While the policy puts more emphasis on technology generation, its emphasis on agroforestry technologies is minimal.

The Agricultural Sector Development Strategy was formulated as an instrument to strategize the Agricultural and Livestock Policy of 1997. The strategy envisages that *by 2025, agriculture becomes modernized, commercial, highly productive and profitable, and utilizes natural resources in a sustainable manner*. This can be achieved by setting up the favorable environment to raise productivity, promotion of public-private partnerships, promotion of private sector production, processing, storage and input supply and decentralization of agricultural planning activities to district level. As the Strategy is the driving force for modernization of agriculture, it puts more emphasis on demand driven and market-led technology development and adaptation, and the role of public sector to be regulatory and supportive to private sector functions. To operationalize the strategy, the Agricultural Sector Development Programme was formulated in 2006. On the other hand, there are a number of legislations governing crops, livestock, pesticides, inputs, market and other related matters pertaining to agricultural and livestock production in agriculture and livestock sectors.

Agriculture and livestock are important components of agroforestry, but agroforestry issues have been hitherto neglected in agricultural development policy and legislation documents. Many of the issues addressed in agriculture and livestock policy and legal documents are not specific to agroforestry technology development and uptake. Mainstreaming agroforestry policy, thus, is essential to bring it to an even playing field.

3.3 The National Environmental Policy and legislations

The policy reform in environmental sector has resulted into the National Environmental Policy (NEP) of 1997 followed by the National Environmental Management Act (NEMA) of

2004, the Environmental Impact Assessment and Audit Regulations of 2005, and the Environmental Management and Soil Quality Standards Regulations of 2007. These policy and legal instruments provide a framework for environmental protection by different sectors in view of ensuring environmental integrity and sustainability. The Environmental Policy and legal documents underscore the need for agricultural sector to contribute to food security and rural poverty alleviation through the promotion of production systems, technologies and practices that are environmentally friendly, with emphasis on strengthening of environmentally sound use. Since agroforestry technologies and practices are environmentally friendly, one would have expected the Environmental Policy to carry provisions on agroforestry, but this is not the case.

3.4 The Land Policy, Land Act and Village Land Act

The Land Policy of 1995 aims at promoting a secure land tenure system. It encourages the optimal use of land resources. The policy states the need for broad-based social and economic development without upsetting or endangering the ecological balance of the environment. The legal basis for land tenure in Tanzania is derived from two basic laws: the Land Act of 1999 and the Village Land Act of 1999. The Acts hold a statement that "all land in Tanzania is public land, which the President holds in trust for all citizens". The President delegates the power to designate, adjudicate, and modify land tenure status to the Commissioner of Land. District councils and village councils play an important role in managing land at the local level. The two legal instruments have the overall objective of formalizing and legalizing what is traditional and customary land tenure systems. In that regards, the Village Land Act has provision for women to own land. This encourages investment in agroforestry for both men and women.

3.5 Water Policy and legislations

Governing policy and legislation instruments in water sector are the National Water Policy of 2002, the Water Sector Development Programme of 2006 and the Water Resources Management Act of 2009. These policy and legal instruments recognize water as a fundamental resource for life and various socio-economic development activities and hence the need to conserve water sources. Though not recognized in water policy and legal instruments, agroforestry plays crucial role in the conservation of water sources and improving water quality through conserving the soils.

3.6 Fisheries Policy and legislations

The major focus of the Fisheries Policy and legal instruments is on the promotion of sustainable exploitation, utilization and marketing of fish resources to realize the intended national socio-economic objectives and achieve effective protection of the aquatic environment for sustainable development. The policy has no direct provisions for agroforestry practices although fish ponds are also found in many farming systems and once the fish feeds on tree biomass the system becomes an agroforestry practice. For example, *Leucaena leucocephala* from alley cropping is known to provide nutritive feed to fish (Sotolu & Faturoti, 2008). The technology involving interaction of trees with fish is generally known as silvopastoral.

3.7 Beekeeping Policy and legislations

The Beekeeping Policy and Act envisage that beekeeping plays a major role in socio-economic development and environmental conservation in Tanzania. The system of agroforestry involving beekeeping is called apiculture. Though not recognized directly in beekeeping policy and legal documents, apiculture is considered to be an agroforestry technology directly once the hives are set up in the trees, or indirectly when the bees gather nectar from tree flowers (Okia *et al.*, 2009).

3.8 Wildlife Policy and legislations

The 1998 Wildlife Policy of Tanzania (revised in 2007) and the Wildlife Conservation Act of 2009, have two important provisions: one encouraging and another one discouraging agroforestry development. On the one hand, the policy and its associated Act recognize the role of trees as habitat and forage for wild animals, thereby encouraging the practice through tree planting and/or retention on farms. On the other hand, the Policy and Act call for protection of wild animals even if they occur on farmlands. This implies that, even in cases where the wild animals raid and destroy crops, farmers are not allowed to kill them. Their action is limited to informing the Game Officers. This can discourage agroforestry as farmers might hesitate to plant trees on their farms because trees provide suitable habitats for wild animals and, therefore, subject agricultural crops to damage.

4. Factors contributing to lack of National Agroforestry Policy

This section highlights the possible factors contributing to lack of Agroforestry Policy in Tanzania's policy and legal framework.

4.1 Scattered/lack of adequate information

Relevant information on agroforestry issues is inadequate and scattered. This, therefore, undermines efforts for formulation of policy. Some important information on agroforestry practices is localized in some areas and not accessible to planners and policy makers. This is compounded by inadequate coordination of agroforestry research and development in Tanzania (Otsyina et al., 2010; Kitalyi et al., 2011).

4.2 Existence of many sectoral policies and legal instruments

Various policies, legal instruments and traditional practices guide agroforestry practices due to their cross-sectoral nature. Several natural resources related policies and legal instruments currently govern Agroforestry practices. There is lack of policy space for coordinating the range of policies, laws and regulations that have impacts on agroforestry. This amplifies potentials for having conflicting and overlapping policy and legal frameworks. Such cases involve examples where agricultural, environmental and forest policies promote tree planting, but the Forest Act protects species and restricts felling; and where agriculture policy promotes small scale stream fed irrigation while the Environmental Act promotes riverbed protection and cropping bans. This situation is attributed to poor institutional coordination.

4.3 Lack of agroforestry sectoral affiliation

There is no single sector in Tanzania where agroforestry is affiliated. As a result different institutions and organizations are undertaking and/or promoting agroforestry activities with little or no coordination. This makes agroforestry information scattered in various sectors.

4.4 Lack of recognition and integration of NASCO in government structure and plans

The coordination of agroforestry research and development activities is vested under the National Agroforestry Steering Committee (NASCO) through its current Secretariat, the Tanzania Forestry Research Institute (TAFORI). However, NASCO is not institutionalized at any level of government structure. As a result, its activities are not properly recognized at national and district levels and, therefore, are not fully supported by the government.

4.5 Lack of financial resources

Since agroforestry has no sectoral affiliation, it scarcely be allocated funds during budgeting session. It is not stipulated in the National Agroforestry Strategy (NAS) how the funds to cater for agroforestry activities can be sourced. As a result, NASCO becomes financially strapped and fail to conduct its scheduled meetings.

4.6 Weak integration of NAS in National Legal Framework

Notwithstanding the role and potential of NAS in contributing to the Tanzania Development Vision 2025 and the Poverty Reduction Strategy, NAS has not been institutionalized in any of the natural resources related policies and legal instruments. The NAS is seen as a stand-alone document, only supported by the World Agroforestry Strategy 2008 - 2015 (ICRAF, 2008).

4.7 Lack of awareness on the importance of Agroforestry Policy

There is inadequate effort devoted to awareness creation on the importance of Agroforestry Policy in Tanzania. The smallholder farmers in Tanzania are the major recipients of agroforestry knowledge and technologies. Unfortunately, majority of farmers and other stakeholders involved in different agroforestry activities have not been sensitized enough on the importance of agroforestry policy in fostering agroforestry development.

5. Need for National Agroforestry Policy in Tanzania

In Tanzania, management challenges are increasingly justifying the need for agroforestry to have its own policy. Some advocacy strategies that can contribute to the formulation of the National Agroforestry Policy include:

- Policy supporting analyses and best practices at different levels
- Establishment of policy dialogue at the national and local levels on agroforestry issues. This should include civil society, private sector, sectoral departments and senior policy-makers

- Capitalizing on the opportunities provided under NAS to influence policy on the need of mainstreaming agroforestry in the policy agenda
- Capitalizing on NASCO as an overseer of agroforestry matters to stir agroforestry policy development
- Involvement of Local Government and its machinery is an essential entry point as a lot of decisions evolve from this important sector
- Institutionalize NAS as part of the official programme in agricultural and natural resources sectors
- Institutionalize and support formation of "science-policy forum" where updates on agroforestry research results and opportunities are presented to policy makers to stir agroforestry policy debate.

6. Key players in Agroforestry Policy development include

- Vice President Office (VPO), Division of Environment
- Local government authorities
- Ministries and their respective agencies
- Development partners and other International Organizations
- Research and academic institutions
- NGOs and other civil society organizations
- Local communities
- Private companies
- World Agroforestry Centre (ICRAF)

7. Some issues that need to be addressed in the National Agroforestry Policy include

- How does agroforestry meet the key social values
- Which costs can agroforestry interventions reduce
- How could agroforestry systems be tailored to respond to local conditions (institutional, cultural, economic, environmental)
- How could agroforestry interventions/practices assist various stakeholders to realize their interests
- Governance and tenure (land and tree tenure): Rights to land and trees for smallholder farmers and rural communities, and women's rights and roles in agroforestry.
- Improved marketing for agroforestry products: Here we consider issues of marketing information; agroforestry products value chains and development of environmental services reward systems for smallholder agroforesters
- Policy coordination: Mechanisms for planning and reviewing agricultural and natural resources policies through agroforestry lens, given that agroforestry is not the domain of a single sector. Space for agroforestry in various inter-sectoral panels/committees such as on climate change and REDD
- Harmonization of different natural resources policy and legal instruments: Since agroforestry means integration of trees on agricultural land to contribute to livelihood strategies and environmental sustainability, all contradictions and conflicting interests and mandates in different policy and legal instruments which touch agroforestry need to be harmonized.

8. Process for enacting Agroforestry Policy

- Stakeholders consultations
- Developing agroforestry draft policy and its implementation plan
- Stakeholders draft policy verifications
- Process approval by Cabinet Secretariat
- Discussion and endorsement of the draft policy at the Inter-Ministerial Committee
- Approval by the Full Cabinet
- Signed by the President

Notwithstanding existence of many uncoordinated policy and legal instruments governing agroforestry, there is still a potential to enact specific policy for agroforestry based on the procedure outlined above. Some African countries have already developed such policy as exemplified by the Agroforestry Policy of Ghana (MOFA, 1986).

9. Conclusions

Agroforestry systems have huge potential to contribute to three pillars of sustainable development: ecological sustainability, economic sustainability and social sustainability through positive transformation of landscapes and the livelihoods of rural Tanzanians. However, the potential of the systems is constrained by lack of supportive regulatory framework and poor coordination of the practices triggered by lack of stand alone agroforestry policy. Since, many agricultural and natural resources related policies and legal instruments touch issues related to agroforestry; it is imperative that these policies are harmonized along with carrying out lobbying and advocacy geared towards the formulation of Agroforestry Policy.

10. Recommendations

The following are the recommendations aimed at facilitating the process of developing Agroforestry Policy in Tanzania:

- Reinforce NASCO to make it more inter-sectoral
- Create public awareness of the importance of Agroforestry Policy
- Set aside agroforestry funds at different levels
- Integrate indigenous and modern technologies in Agroforestry Policy
- Institutionalize NASCO in the government structure and plans, as an overseer of agroforestry activities
- Institutionalize NAS in Tanzania's legal framework
- Forest and Agricultural sectors should take the lead to stir up a process for Agroforestry Policy Development. Therefore, they need to establish effective partnership and collaboration rather than working in isolation.
- Enact National Agroforestry Policy
- Consider redefining agroforestry in the Tanzanian context because the country has already proposed a new forest definition. A Forest, in Tanzania, is defined as *an area of land with at least 0.05 hectares, with a minimum tree crown cover of 10% or with existing tree species planted or natural having the potential of attaining more than 10% crown cover, and with trees which have the potential or have reached a minimum height of 2.0 meters at maturity in situ* (MNRT, 2011).
- Ensure that at least 50% of Agroforestry plot is kept under crop or pasture production.

11. References

Barrow, E. 2004. *Ngitili* for Everything: Woodland Restoration in Shinyanga, Tanzania.

Boeckmann, S.P. & Iolster. 2010. Agroforestry in Africa: Exploring the Lack of Widespread Implementation and the Potential for Expansion. Available from http://www.rmportal.net/library. Accessed on 12 April, 2011

Brochure. Ministry of Natural Resources and Tourism and the Tanzania and Eastern Africa Regional Office of IUCN - The World Conservation Union. Dar es Salaam, Tanzania.

ICRAF (World Agroforestry Centre). 2007. *Tackling Global Challenges through Agroforestry Annual Report for 2006.* World Agroforestry Centre (ICRAF). Nairobi, Kenya. 64pp.

ICRAF (World Agroforestry Centre). 2008. *Transforming lives and landscapes. ICRAF Strategy 2008-2015.* World Agroforestry Centre, Nairobi, Kenya. 48pp.

IUFRO. 2005. Multilingual Pocket Glossary of Forest Terms and Definitions. International Union of Forest Research Organizations, Vienna, Austria. 96 pp.

Kamwenda, G.J. 2002. *Ngitili* agrosilvipastoral systems in the United Republic of Tanzania. *Unasylva* 53: 46-50.

Kitalyi, A.; Nyadzi, G.; Lutkamu, M.; Swai, R.; Gama, B. 2011. New climate, new agriculture: how Agroforestry contributes to meeting the challenges of Agricultural development in Tanzania. *Tanzanian Journal of Agricultural Sciences,* 10 (1): 1 – 7.

Lawson, G.; Dupraz, C.; Liagre, F.; Moreno, G.; Piero Paris, P. and Papanastasis, V. 2005. Options for Agroforestry Policy in the European Union. Silvoarable Agroforestry For Europe (SAFE). Available online at: http://www 1.montpellier.inra.fr/safe/english/results/final-report/D9-3.pdf, Accessed August, 12, 2011.

Leakey, R.R.B. 1996. Definition of agroforestry revisited. *Agroforestry Today* 8: 5-7.

Mbwambo, J.S. and E.E. Chingonikaya. 2004. Adoption of agroforestry practices and their contribution to poverty reduction among rural households: A case study of to maize and woody biomass yields and income in Musoma Rural District, Mara Region Tanzania.

Mmbaga, T. E., C. J. Lyamchai, H.Mansoor, J.Wickama 2007. Practical Approaches for Effective by-laws in Lushoto District. AHI Reports, Lushoto Benchmark MNRT 2011. Proposed National Definition of Forest for Tanzania. Ministry of Natural Resources and Tourism. Dar es Salaam, Tanzania.

MOFA (1986). The National Agroforestry Policy. Ministry of Food and Agriculture Accra, Ghana

Moshi ERF. 1997. Inventory of indigenous agroforestry systems in practice in the West Usambara Mountains. [unpublished MSc thesis]. [Morogoro (Tanzania)]: Sokoine University ofAgriculture.

Msuya TS, Mndolwa MA, Kapinga C. 2008. Domestication: an indigenous method in conserving plant diversity on farmlands in West Usambara Mountains, Tanzania. *African Journal of Ecology*, 46(1):74–78.

NASCO (National Agroforestry Steering Committee). 2004. Popular Version of National Agroforestry Strategy. NASCO Secretariat, Tanzania Forestry Research Institute, Morogoro, Tanzania.

Ngatunga, E.L. and Nshubemuki, L. (2006). Need for policy on agroforestry research and development in Tanzania. In: S.A.O. Chamshama et al. (Eds). Partnerships and

Linkages for Greater Impact in Agroforestry and Environmental Awareness. Proceedings of the Second National Agroforestry and Environment Workshop held in Mbeya 14 - 17 March 2006. Pp 224–229.

Okia, C.A.; Agea, J.G.; Sekatuba, J.; Ongodi, G.; Katumba, B.; Opolot, V.I and Mutabazi, H. 2009. Candidate Agroforestry Technologies and Practices for Uganda. *Agricultural Journal,* 4(5): 208-215.

Otsyina, R., S. Minae, and D. Asenga. 1993. The Potential of *Ngitili* as a Traditional Agroforestry System among the Sukuma of Tanzania. Nairobi, Kenya: World Agroforestry Centre (ICRAF).

Otsyina, R.; Chamshama, S.A.O.; Gama. B.; Kitalyi, A.; Mpanda, M.; Lutkam, M.; Iddi, S. and Mhando, L. 2010. Role of Agroforestry in Improving Livelihoods of Rural Communities and Environmental Sustainability in Tanzania. A Position Paper. National Agroforestry Steering Committee, Morogoro, Tanzania. 19 pp.

Place, F., Prudencio, Y-C., 2006. "Policies for improved Land Management in smallholder Agriculture: The Role of Research in Agroforestry and Natural Resource Management: World Agroforestry into the Future, Garrity, D., Okono, A., Grayson M., Parrot, S., Eds. World Agroforestry Center, 2006. P. 71-78.

Porter-Bolland, L.; Ellis, E.A.; Guariguata, M.R.; Ruiz-Mallén, I.; Negrete-Yankelevich, S.; Reyes-García, V. 2011. Community managed forests and forest protected areas: An assessment of their conservation effectiveness across the tropics. *Article in press. Forest Ecology and Management.*

Pye-Smith C. 2010. A Rural Revival in Tanzania: *How agroforestry is helping farmers to restore the woodlands in Shinyanga Region.* ICRAF Trees for Change no. 7. Nairobi: World Agroforestry Centre. 48 pp.

Reyes, T. 2008. Agroforestry systems for sustainable livelihoods and improved land management in the East Usambara Mountains, Tanzania. PhD Thesis. University of Helsinki, Finland. 166 pp.

Rugalema G. H., A. Okting'ati and F. H. Johnsen. 1994. The homegarden agroforestry system of Bukoba district, North-Western Tanzania. Farming system analysis. *Agroforestry Systems* 26: 53-64, 1994. 9 1994 Kluwer Academic Publishers, The Netherlands.

Scherr, S.J. and Franzel, S. 2002. Promoting New Agroforestry Technology: Policy Lessons from on Farm Research. *In:* Franzel, S. and Scherr, S.J. (Eds). *Trees in the Farm: Assessing the Adoption Potential of Agroforestry Practices in Africa.* Wallingford, Oxon, UK, New York. Pp 145 -168.

Soini, E. 2005. Changing livelihoods on the slopes of Mt. Kilimanjaro, Tanzania: Challenges and opportunities in the Chagga homegarden system. *Agrofeorestry Systems Journal,* 64 (2): 157-167

Sotolu, A.O. and Faturoti, E.O. 2008. Digestibility and nutritional values of Differently Processed *Leucaena leucocephala* (Lam. de Wit) Seed Meals in the Diet of African Catfish (*Clarias gariepinus*). *Middle-East Journal of Scientific Research* 3 (4): 190-199.

URT (United Republic of Tanzania). 1998. National Forest Policy. Government Printer, Dar es Salaam, Tanzania. 59pp.

URT (United Republic of Tanzania). 2002. Forest Act No. 14 of 2002. Government Printer, Dar es Salaam, Tanzania. 93pp.

Effectiveness of Grassroots Organisations in the Dissemination of Agroforestry Innovations

Ann Degrande, Steven Franzel, Yannick Siohdjie Yeptiep, Ebenezer Asaah, Alain Tsobeng and Zac Tchoundjeu
World Agroforestry Centre, West and Central Africa
Cameroon

1. Introduction

Eradicating extreme poverty and hunger is the first Millennium Development Goal (MDG) for a reason: none of the other MDGs can be met without food security and economic development. Because 75 percent of the poor in developing countries live in rural areas, strengthening the agricultural sector can not only improve access to nutritious food, it does more - at least twice as much - to reduce rural poverty than investment in any other sector (FAO, 2011). The role of extension in this battle is clear; there is a great need for information, ideas and organisation in order to develop an agriculture that will meet complex demand patterns, reduce poverty, and preserve or enhance ecological resources.

Therefore in the sixties and seventies, developing-country governments invested heavily in agricultural extension. Nevertheless, as from the 1980s, support for extension declined drastically as governments undertook structural adjustments, leading to public spending cuts and a breakdown in public sector services for agriculture, but also because of disappointing performance (Anderson, 2007). The share of Official Development Assistance (ODA) to agriculture also dropped significantly, falling from a peak of 17 percent in 1979, the height of the Green Revolution, to a low of 3.5 percent in 2004. It also declined in absolute terms: from USD 8 billion in 1984 to USD 3.5 billion in 2005 (FAO, 2011).

After many years of under-investment in agriculture and particularly in extension, the tide has fortunately changed and more funding is becoming available for agricultural extension. The current interest in agricultural advisory services is emerging as part of a broader shift in thinking that focuses on enhancing the role of agriculture for pro-poor development (Birner *et al.*, 2006). For example, twenty-four African countries listed extension as one of the top agricultural priorities in their strategies for poverty reduction. With this renewed interest, there is also growing awareness that farmers get information from many sources and that public extension is one source, but not necessarily the most efficient. In most public systems, extension agents are only indirectly (if at all) accountable to their farmer-clients (Feder *et al.*, 2010). Therefore, over the last decade or so, there have been many reforms to extension and advisory services to make them more pluralistic, demand-driven, cost effective, efficient and sustainable. However, there is limited or conflicting evidence as to their effect on productivity and poverty, as well as on financial sustainability.

While ineffective dissemination methods have contributed to low adoption of agricultural innovations in general, this is particularly true for agroforestry innovations, which are known to be complex and knowledge intensive, involving several components (crops, livestock and trees), requiring the learning of new skills, such as nursery establishment, and often providing benefits only after a long period (Franzel *et al.*, 2001). To face the challenges of inappropriate extension methods for agroforestry, the World Agroforestry Centre (ICRAF) in West and Central Africa has been experimenting with relay organisations and rural resource centres for the dissemination of agroforestry innovations and more particularly participatory tree domestication, for the last 5 years. Relay organisations refer to grassroots, local, or community-based organisations promoting the adoption of innovations. Rural resource centres are venues where new techniques are developed and demonstrated and where farmers can come for information, experimentation and training. Participatory tree domestication is a farmer-driven and market-led process matching the intraspecific diversity of locally important trees to the needs of farmers, product markets, and agricultural environments (Asaah *et al.*, 2011; Simons & Leakey, 2004; Tchoundjeu *et al.*, 2006).

The present paper first gives an overview of major challenges of agricultural extension and institutional innovations that were introduced to overcome some of these problems, with particular focus on community-based extension approaches. The third section presents the methodology including hypotheses, and descriptions of the research area, relay organisations, variables of performance and data collection tools. The results' section describes the approach involving relay organisations and rural resource centres using case studies. Then, the performance of relay organisations in terms of reaching farmers, increasing their knowledge on agroforestry and enhancing adoption of agroforestry innovations in Cameroon is evaluated and factors that affect performance are identified. The concluding section formulates implications for up-scaling of the approach.

2. Institutional innovations in agricultural extension

2.1 Challenges of agricultural extension

Governments employ hundreds of thousands of extension agents in developing countries. About 80 percent of the extension services are publicly funded and delivered by civil servants, justified by the view that many aspects of agricultural knowledge diffusion are 'public goods'. However, there is a general consensus that the performance of extension services has been disappointing (Anderson, 2007; Feder *et al.*, 2010).

According to Feder *et al.* (1999), there are eight generic challenges that make extension services difficult to finance and deliver. First there is the magnitude of the task, which can be understood in terms of numbers, distribution and diversity of staff, farmers and other clients and stakeholders, and in terms of mandate and methodology. Often the top-down managerial style, characteristic of large bureaucracies, tends not to be compatible with participatory, bottom-up approaches and often favours more responsive clients who are typically the better-off. Second, the dependence of agricultural extension on wider policy and other agency functions may also limit the impact of extension on production. Especially the links with research, input supply systems, credit, and marketing organisations are problematic for many extension organisations. Third, inability to identify the cause and effect of extension is leading to other inherent problems, including political support, funding and accountability of extension agents to their clients. Fourth, as the extension service is the most widely distributed representative of government at grassroots level, there is always the temptation to load it with more and more functions, such as collecting statistics and various regulatory functions. This liability for other public service functions is reducing the time that extension workers can spend on the transfer of agricultural knowledge and information. Another generic problem for agricultural extension is the difficulty of cost recovery. Therefore there is a great dependence on direct public funding, making the system very vulnerable to budgetary cuts. Finally, having in mind that the most important element of extension is the quality of its message, insufficient relevant technology to improve productivity is a major constraint. Interaction with knowledge generators is often inadequate because research and extension tend to compete for power and resources and fail to see themselves as part of a broader agricultural technology system.

2.2 Institutional pluralism, empowerment and community-based extension

In an attempt to overcome these challenges, various institutional innovations have been introduced over the last 20 years, some more promising than others. Many of these approaches however stem from the notion that not all extension services need to be organised or executed by government agencies, calling for more decentralisation, institutional pluralism, empowerment and participatory approaches. Furthermore, there is a growing consensus that not all aspects of extension are pure public goods; which explains the move towards privatisation of some of its elements and fee-for-service public provision. However, fully privatised extension is not economically feasible in countries with a large base of small-scale subsistence farmers (Feder *et al.*, 1999). Overreliance on private extension risks neglect of less commercial farmers and lower-value crops. In such circumstances, public sector finance remains essential, mixed with various cost-recovery, co-financing and other transitional institutional arrangements.

Among a series of extension approaches evaluated by Feder *et al.* (1999), three seem to be most relevant for our analysis: institutional pluralism, empowerment and participatory approaches, and interconnecting people using appropriate media.

Institutional pluralism seeks to create a more comprehensive system of complementary extension services that would reach and respond to diverse farmers and farming systems. By involving a variety of stakeholders, such partnership arrangements have the potential to resolve two fundamental generic problems - linking cause and effect, and accountability or incentive to deliver quality service. This approach also recognises that to meet diverse needs and conditions in the farming sector, more investment is needed in the whole agricultural knowledge and information system, rather than in public sector extension services alone. This implies significant role changes for ministries of agriculture as they move away from service delivery toward creating an enabling policy environment, coordinating and facilitating the work of other players. NGOs are a prevalent partner in agricultural extension in developing countries and frequently focus on areas inadequately served by government.

Many NGOs strive to be participatory, democratic, responsive, cost-effective and focused on the needs of hard-to-reach target groups. However, some NGOs push their own agenda and are more accountable to external funding sources than to the clientele they aim to serve (Farrington, 1997).

Another effective way of making extension more accountable to clients has been increasing control by beneficiaries, e.g. through farmer organisations. In many parts of the world, farmer associations, organised on commodity lines have been highly successful in providing extension services to their members. However, their impact depends on how participatory the methods are. Participatory approaches overall have positive effects for most of the generic problems of extension. For example, farmer leaders with appropriate local backgrounds may be able to perform many extension agent roles in a cost effective manner, thereby solving problems of scale and coverage. Participatory approaches also improve cause-effect relationships through farmer-led experimentation, analysis and farmer feedback. Fiscal sustainability is improved through mobilising local resources. Cost-effectiveness and efficiency are achieved by using relevant methods that focus on expressed farmer needs and local people taking over many extension roles (Axinn, 1988). Interaction with knowledge generation is enhanced by combining indigenous knowledge with feedback into the agricultural knowledge system.

Finally, the arrival of new information and communication technologies (ICTs) has naturally led to an interest in its potential to enhance extension delivery and in connecting people with other people (Gakiru *et al.*, 2009; Zijp, 1997). Innovations in this category are most directly associated with overcoming the generic problems of scale and complexity and are most effective when considered in combination with other innovations as a 'force multiplier'. Examples are community communication centers or telecottages for local information access, communication and education in rural areas. However, radical change in perspective in favour of a pluralist, cross-sectoral, systems' perspective to harness their full potential is required. In addition, ICTs cannot replace face-to-face contact between extension agents and farmers and information alone is an insufficient condition for local change.

The analysis by Feder *et al.* (1999) suggests that in designing extension programmes, the approach is less important than its ingredients. Identifying ingredients of success and finding ways to replicate or transfer these characteristics to improve the performance of another approach seem most appropriate. The authors also argue that ingredients of a sustainable approach - instead of focusing on massive, technocratic, and sophisticated efforts as was done in the past - tend to be inherently low cost and to build relationships of mutual trust and reciprocity. From these relationships, commitment, political support, accountability, fiscal sustainability, and effective interaction with knowledge generation develop.

For example, one very popular extension and education program worldwide is the farmer field school (FFS) approach, now in place in at least 78 countries. Such schools use experiential learning and a group approach to facilitate farmers in making decisions, solving problems, and learning new techniques. Despite its popularity, up-scaling in Africa is faced with growing concerns and interest among stakeholders and donors regarding the applicability, targeting, cost-effectiveness and impact of the approach

(Davis *et al.* 2010). Other extension approaches are being tested, such as the community-based worker (CBW) systems in Uganda and Kenya (CBW, 2007). Community-based services offer the potential to reach many more people within the limited financial resources available to African governments. In addition, they allow communities to influence services to meet their own, locally-specific needs, and to monitor the performance of delivery agents. Few statistical data are available, but reported benefits of projects using the CBW approach included adoption of new technologies, replanting of trees, income from sales of seedlings, fruits and honey, improved livestock management, improved soil conservation and greater understanding of land use rights. But, with the exception of the health sector, the scale of CBW systems is small and the policy environment and coordination of these remain undeveloped. The main criticism suggested that CBWs are not always sufficiently knowledgeable and equipped to pass on information to others adequately (CBW, 2007). In their review of community-based agricultural extension approaches, Feder *et al.* (2010) concluded that communities can also fail in extension delivery. Elite capture, for example, was a major constraint, as well as limited availability of competent service providers, deep-seated cultural attitudes that prevent effective empowerment of farmers and difficulties in implementing farmers' control of service providers' contracts.

2.3 Concept of relay organisations and rural resource centres: ICRAF's experience in Cameroon

Three main research areas have been explored by researchers of the World Agroforestry Centre (ICRAF) in Cameroon for the last decade, i.e. tree improvement and integration of trees in agricultural landscapes, soil fertility management with trees and shrubs, and marketing of agroforestry tree products. Consequently, agroforestry innovations ready for dissemination include: vegetative propagation techniques (marcotting, rooting of cuttings and grafting), integration of trees through the development of multistrata agroforests, soil fertility management techniques, and improved marketing strategies for commercialisation of agroforestry tree products mainly through the organisation of group sales. To accelerate the uptake of these new agroforestry techniques by farmers in Cameroon, ICRAF established collaboration with local organisations that were already involved in agricultural extension in different areas of the country. These organisations are called "Relay Organisations".

Relay organisations (ROs) are boundary-spanning actors that link research organisations like ICRAF, and farmer communities. They join with researchers in conducting participatory technology development, implying a two-way interaction of capacity building and institutional support on the one hand and feedback on the technology development on the other hand. The ROs disseminate innovations to farmers using demonstrations, training and technical assistance, after which farmers provide feedback and by so doing, help develop the innovations further. In their respective zones of intervention, ROs identify farmer groups that are interested in working on aspects of production of agroforestry trees and commercialisation of the products. Then, with the assistance of ICRAF, they conduct a diagnosis of organisational and technical constraints to production and commercialisation of target species. Collective action is often a desired intervention, in which case ROs prepare the groups for collective action by organising a series of training sessions on group dynamics, leadership, marketing strategies, financial management, stock management, etc. The ROs also provide technical assistance in such areas as nursery, tree planting and harvest and post-harvest techniques.

At the same time, the development of Rural Resource Centres (RRCs) has been a key element of the scaling-out strategy of the World Agroforestry Centre. Some ROs involved in the dissemination of agroforestry, but not all, use the rural resource centre in their extension approach (Box 1). Rural Resource Centres are places where agroforestry techniques are practised and where farmers can come for information, experimentation and training. A typical rural resource centre consists of the following: a tree nursery, demonstration plots, a small library, a training hall and eventually accommodation facilities. Depending on which innovations are relevant to the area, the rural resource centre may also host a unit for processing of agroforestry products and/or a seed multiplication plots. RRCs are managed by community-based organisations, which can be Non-Governmental Organisations or farmer groups; in this context also called Relay Organisations.

APADER (Association pour la Promotion des Actions de Développement Endogènes Rurales), created in 1993 and located in Bangangte (West Cameroon), is running a RRC, where agroforestry innovations are developed together with farmers and adapted to local conditions. The RRC is equipped with 2 motorbikes, a training hall, offices, computers, a printer, a generator and internet access. The centre also has a tree nursery, seed multiplication units, demonstration plots and a processing unit (dryer and grinder). Through its RRC, APADER has trained about 280 farmers and is technically supporting 28 farmer groups. APADER has also initiated a network of 23 nurseries, called UGICANE (Union des GICs des Agroforestiers du Ndé). Ten of these nurseries have developed into profitable enterprises and each generates about 500,000 FCFA (1,000 USD) a year. APADER is also providing organisational support to COFTRAKOL, a cooperative composed of 25 women, specialised in processing of karité (*Vitellaria paradoxa*) and other oleaginous products such as safou (*Dacryodes edulis*). Through its achievements, APADER has succeeded in developing strong partnerships with a number of research and development partners, such as the Ministry of Agriculture, the Institut de Recherche Agricole pour le Développement (IRAD), the Zenü Network, the University of Dschang, Peace Corps and the Programme National de Développement Participatif.

Box 1. Example of a Relay Organisation using the Rural Resource Centre approach

3. Methodology

3.1 Research framework

The methodology used to assess the performance of relay organisations in the dissemination of agroforestry innovations in Cameroon was inspired by the framework for designing and analysing agricultural advisory services, developed by Birner *et al.* (2006). This analytical framework (fig 1) "disentangles" the major characteristics of agricultural advisory services on which policy decisions have to be made. As shown in figure 1, the performance of agricultural advisory services is explained as a function of: (1) characteristics of the advisory services and the linkages with research and education; (2) frame conditions and the "fit" of the service with those frame conditions; and (3) the ability of clients to exercise voice and hold the service providers accountable. The framework also develops an impact chain approach to analyse the performance and the impact of agricultural advisory services. In this sense, the farm households play a central role in the analytical framework as their interaction with the advisory services is critical to both performance and impact. However, Birner *et al.* (2006) recognise that the framework covers a wide range of issues and that in practice it may often not be feasible to cover all of them in a single study. Hence, in order to increase our understanding of why some ROs perform better than others and to guide reforms in agroforestry dissemination in Cameroon and beyond, the present study only focuses on some of the elements as explained below.

According to Birner *et al.* (2006), frame conditions are those variables that cannot or only indirectly be influenced from a policy perspective, yet still have an impact on the performance of agricultural advisory services. Box F in figure 1 refers to frame conditions related to *farming systems and market access*, while box C entails *community characteristics* (e.g. land size, education levels and social capital) that must be taken into account in designing agricultural advisory services. As far as characteristics of extension services providers are concerned, the present study will look at *capacity and management* (box M) which refers to the number, training levels, skills, attitudes, motivation and aspirations of staff members, as well as to the organisation's incentives, mission, orientation, professionalism, ethics and organisational culture. Management procedures applied in the organisation, such as monitoring and evaluation systems, ways of managing performance and stimulating feedback from farmers, may also determine effectiveness and will therefore be examined. Box A on the other hand, refers to *advisory methods* used by field staff in their interaction with farmers. These methods can be classified according to various aspects: number of clientele involved (individuals or groups), type of decisions on which advice is provided (types of crops or livestock, managerial decisions, group activities, etc.), and media used.

Performance of agricultural advisory services (box P), according to Birner *et al.* (2006), refers to the quality of the "outputs" and can be captured by the following indicators: (1) accuracy and relevance; (2) timeliness and outreach of advice, including the ability to reach women and disadvantaged groups; (3) quality of partnerships established and feed-back effects created; and (4) efficiency of service delivery and other economic performance indicators. The authors also highlight that performance indicators are more useful if they include information provided by clients, an aspect that has been taken into account in our study. Finally, the box H represents the immediate outcomes of the work of the agricultural advisory services, which are *changes in farmers' behaviour*. These changes can be measured by increased capacity of clients, adoption of innovations and change of practices whether in the domain of production, management or marketing. An important element in the framework, as shown by the arrows in figure 1, is the ability for farmer households to exercise voice and formulate demand. This ability is influenced both by characteristics of the farm households and of the advisory service. For example, a favourable advisory staff to farmer ratio and participatory advisory methods improve the possibilities of farm households to exercise voice and hold the service providers accountable.

3.2 Variables of performance

Based on the framework described above (Birner *et al.*, 2006), the performance of relay organisations in the present study has been evaluated in terms of their effectiveness and relevance. *Effectiveness* measures the degree to which an organisation achieves its objectives (Etzioni, 1964; Heffron, 1989), while *relevance* assesses the capacity of an organisation to respond to the needs of its stakeholders and to gain their support in the present and in the future (Centre de Recherches pour le Développement International [CRDI], 2004). The following indicators were used to evaluate the performance of relay organisations: number of groups and number of farmers technically supported, diffusion and adoption rate of innovations disseminated, average nursery production of groups supported, knowledge and mastery of farmers trained, and satisfaction of farmers.

The *rate of diffusion* of agroforestry innovations was calculated by dividing the number of technologies that were received at the level of the farmers by the number recorded at the level of ROs. For example, when 8 sub-themes that are inventoried at the level of a RO are also used by the farmers supported by this RO, than the diffusion rate would be 100 %. On the other hand, the *rate of adoption* is calculated by dividing the number of farmers that use the innovation by the total number of farmers interviewed.

For the nursery production, the idea was to use data for 3 consecutive years, but due to the paucity of nursery records kept by the groups, we were unable to obtain reliable data. *Satisfaction* was assessed by simply asking farmers whether there were not satisfied at all, quite satisfied, satisfied or very satisfied with the way ROs interacted with them.

3.3 Hypotheses

Concerning factors affecting performance, the degree to which relay organisations are able to achieve their objectives and satisfy their clients was hypothesised to depend on both *internal* and *external* factors. At internal level, it was assumed that their capacity to disseminate agroforestry innovations depends on human, financial and material resources at their disposal, as well as the technical capacities of their staff, their experience with agroforestry and type and duration of their collaboration with agroforestry research. On the other hand, external factors that are likely to affect the outcome of the relay organisations' work included the need for agroforestry in the area or existence of problems that can be addressed by agroforestry, road infrastructure, market access, and farmers' experience in collective action.

It was therefore hypothesised that relay organisations in category I (favourable internal and external factors) would have the best performance, while those in category IV (unfavourable internal and external factors) would perform the least. Comparison between category II and III, both presumed to have an average performance, would inform about which set of factors (internal or external) affects the performance of relay organisations more. Because, if organisations in category II perform better than those in category III, we could conclude that internal factors influence the performance of relay organisations more than external factors and vice-versa.

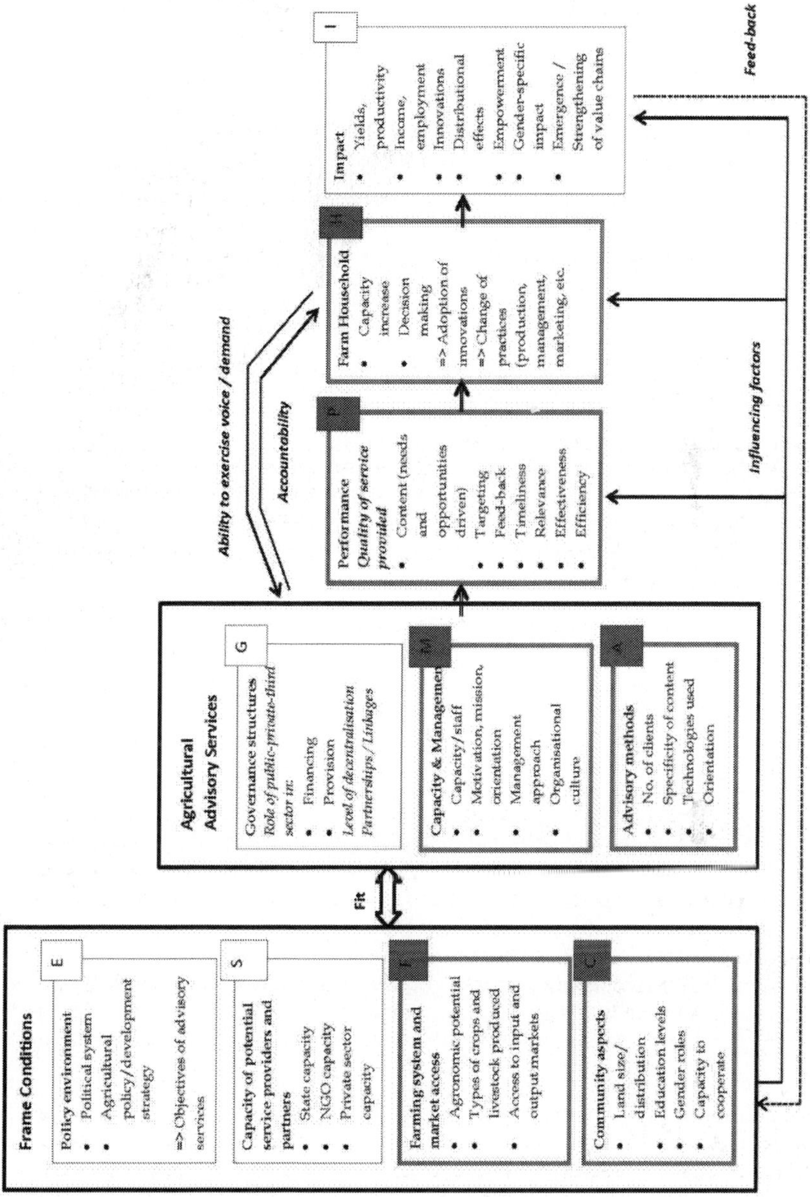

Fig. 1. Framework for designing and analysing agricultural advisory systems
Source: Birner *et al.*, 2006 (p 26)

3.4 Study area and sampling procedure

The study which involved relay organisations working in collaboration with ICRAF on agroforestry dissemination was carried out in 3 agro-ecological zones of Cameroon, i.e. the western Hauts Plateaux, the forest zone with monomodal rainfall and the forest zone with bimodal rainfall. Characteristics of the study sites are summarised in table 1.

In order to test the hypotheses laid out in 3.3 above, the 18 relay organisations were grouped in 4 categories based on whether internal and external factors were favourable or unfavourable (table 2).

Characteristics	Western Hauts Plateaux	Forest monomodal rainfall	Forest bimodal rainfall
Location	From Nde division to North-West region and part of South-West	From Littoral to South-West, and coastal area of South region	Centre, South and East regions
Coordinates	5°00 - 7°00 N ; 9°50 – 11°15 E	4°00 – 6°30 N; 8°30 – 10°00 E	2°00 – 4°00 N; 10°31 – 16°12 E
Relief and vegetation	Mountainous areas characterised by savannah vegetation; plateaux and valleys crossed by gallery forests	Mountains with steep slopes and valleys. In the west, dominated by a volcanic chain (Mt Cameroon, Manengouba, Nlonako and Koupe)	Mid-altitude plateau (300-600 m asl.)
Soils	Young soils on slopes (Incepticols), highly weathered soils (Oxisols), soils with horizon B (Alfisols and Ultisols) and plateaux with rich volcanic soils. Organic material more than 1.5%. Moderate to high N level, high Mg level and very low K	Rich and deep Andosols in the north, supporting big industrial plantations. In the south, lowlands with sandy Ferralitic soils	Mainly Ferralitic, acid, clay soils of red or yellow colour according to the season. Low nutrient retention capacity. Rapid degradation of nutrients after cultivation, explaining the practice of shifting cultivation
Climate	Type Cameroonian of altitude with 2 seasons: dry season (mid-November to mid-March) and rainy season (mid-March – mid-November). Rainfall between 1500 and 2600 mm. Relatively low temperatures (20°C on average)	Type equatorial oceanic; hot and humid with 2 seasons: rainy season (mid-March to mid-November) and a dry season with high humidity. Rainfall of 4000 mm per year, with records of 11,000 mm on the Mt Cameroon. Stable temperatures (25°C on average)	Sub-equatorial Congo-guinea type, with 4 seasons: short rainy season (March-June), short dry spell (July-August), long rainy season (Sept-Nov), long dry season (Dec-Feb). Rainfall between 1500 and 2000 mm over 10 months. Rather constant temperatures (23° - 27°C)

Characteristics	Western Hauts Plateaux	Forest monomodal rainfall	Forest bimodal rainfall
Agro-ecological potential	Fertile soils suitable to agricultural activities, especially food crops, horticulture and arabica coffee, often in association in two cycles per year. Small livestock husbandry.	Northern part has big industrial plantations of banana, rubber, tea and oil palm. Also food crops (tubers, maize, cowpea) and horticulture. Small livestock husbandry and aquaculture	Soils suitable for cultivation of banana, plantain, cocoyam, cassava, sweet potato, yam, maize, groundnut, pineapple, cocoa, oil palm, rubber, vegetables and robusta coffee. Small livestock husbandry and aquaculture.
Socio-economic characteristics	80 % of population is involved in agriculture. 3 main areas can be distinguished with specificities in terms of agriculture: Bamoun land (moderate population density, vast spaces for livestock), Bamilike land (high population density, multistrata agricultural systems), grassfields in NW. Land is mostly inherited and agriculture is rather small-scale (1.3 ha per household)	Considered as the hub of Cameroon in terms of agro-industrial activity. Average population density: 176 inhabitants per km^2. About 40 % are immigrants from other parts of the country and abroad	Low population density, apart from areas around Yaounde and in the Lékié division. Land is mostly inherited and agriculture is small-scale, characterised by high rural exodus. Shifting cultivation is still the main agricultural practice.
ROs operating in these zones	APADER, RIBA, PIPAD	FOEPSUD	FONJAK, ADEAC, GICAL, SAGED

Table 1. Characteristics of the study sites in Cameroon
Source: Kemajou (2008); Moudingo (2007); Njessa (2007)

A stratified sampling strategy was used. First, 8 relay organisations were chosen to represent the 4 categories described above, i.e. 2 per category, represented with an asterisk (*) in table 2. The choice was guided by the duration of collaboration with ICRAF, the diversity of their activities and their geographical location (figure 2). Duration of collaboration with ICRAF has been used as a proxy for their experience in agroforestry because capacity building in agroforestry, more particularly in tree domestication in Cameroon has been mainly done by ICRAF. We deliberately choose ROs with longest experience in each of the categories in order to have a view over several years. The geographical location was closely linked to the nature of the external factors which determined the category of ROs. Second, 27 groups, one third of the total number of 86 farmer groups supported by the ROs were randomly selected and their

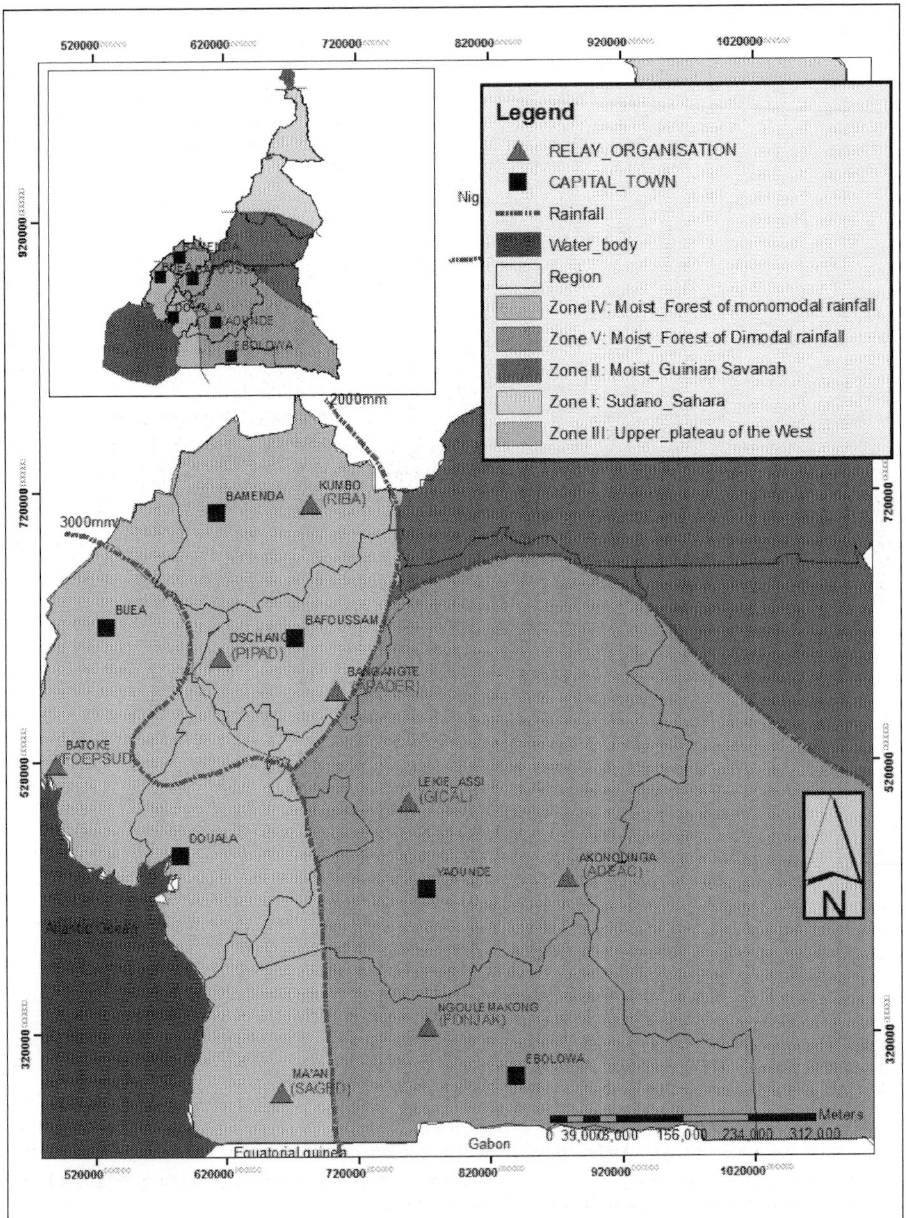

Fig. 2. Location of studied relay organisations in Cameroon
(map drawn by Ngaunkam, 2011)

leaders were interviewed to assess the performance of the ROs. Third, 30 % of individual farmers, members of the farmer groups selected in step 2, were randomly chosen for interview. It must be noted that the choice of farmer groups and group members per relay organisation was not based on duration of collaboration with the RO or on their individual experience with agroforestry. On the other hand, farmers who stopped collaboration with ROs were also interviewed wherever they were available. They were identified by the leaders of the groups interviewed.

3.5 Data collection methods

Information was collected in July-August 2010 at 5 different levels. Four ICRAF staff members were interviewed as resource persons to inventory agroforestry innovations developed with ROs and to identify criteria for selection and evaluation of ROs. The second category of respondents was composed of leaders of the 8 ROs selected for this study. Information collected at this level included general information about the ROs, their human, financial and material resources and their involvement in the participatory development of agroforestry innovations. Semi-structured interviews were then held with the leaders of 27 farmer groups in order to identify innovations received at group level, dissemination approaches used by the ROs and group achievements in terms of agroforestry.

		External factors	
		Favourable	Unfavourable
Internal factors	Favourable	PROAGRO (2000) **RIBA (2002)*** **APADER (2004)*** MIFACIG (1998)	**FONJAK (2000)*** **ADEAC (2003)*** CAMECO (2005)
	Unfavourable	RAGAF (2008) **PIPAD (2008)*** AJPCEDES (2008) **FOEPSUD (2005)*** CIMAR (2009) FEPROFCAO (2009)	**GICAL (2000)*** APED (2008) **SAGED (2008)*** CAFT (2004) CANADEL (2010)

Table 2. Categorisation of relay organisations according to internal and external factors likely to affect performance
[In brackets: year of start of collaboration with ICRAF;
* Relay Organisation selected for the study]

At the level of individual farmers, 76 group members (35 women) and 7 farmers (all male) who stopped collaboration with the ROs were interviewed to record which of the agroforestry innovations they had adopted and whether they were satisfied with the support given by the ROs. The opinion of those who stopped collaboration was sought with a view of identifying strengths and weaknesses of the ROs and reasons for stopping collaboration. We also wanted to find out whether they were still using some of the agroforestry techniques they had learnt from the ROs.

Data were entered and analysed in Excel and SPSS using Multivariate Analysis of Variation and Multiple Component Analysis.

4. Results and discussion

4.1 Presentation of relay organisations and their functioning

It must first be noted that all ROs studied already existed before they started working with ICRAF. Four of the eight ROs (APADER, RIBA, ADEAC, FONJAK) had been collaborating with ICRAF for more than 6 years, suggesting a great experience in the domain of agroforestry. GICAL, as a farmer group, had been collaborating with ICRAF on tree nursery management for about 10 years but was only promoted to relay organisation in 2009, which explains its uncontested expertise in tree propagation but much less so in other domains. PIPAD and SAGED joined ICRAF's network of partners only 2 years ago, and were therefore put in category III and IV respectively. It is worthwhile noting that the ROs in the West and Northwest regions of Cameroon, known as highly hierarchical societies with strong traditions of associations, all had endogenous origin. This is in contrast with ADEAC, FONJAK and SAGED from the Centre and South regions which had been created under impulse from the outside.

Nevertheless, all ROs had more or less the same objectives, i.e. diffusing agroforestry technologies developed in collaboration with ICRAF (100 %) and improving local people's livelihoods in general (62 %). The following activities were mentioned by all relay organisations: tree domestication, tree planting, establishment of demonstration plots and organisation of study and exchange visits for farmers. Seventy-five percent of the ROs were involved in soil fertility management and half of them accompanied their groups in collective action for marketing of agroforestry products. For the achievement of their objectives, relay organisations developed partnerships with international, national and local organisations, governmental bodies and projects. However, less than half of the ROs studied collaborated with governmental institutions or programmes such as the Ministry of Agriculture and Rural Development (MINADER), Ministry of Forests and Fauna (MINFOF), Institute of Agricultural Research for Development (IRAD), National Programme for Participatory Development (PNDP) or CAPLANDE. It has also been noted that the longer ROs had been active in agroforestry, the greater their expertise and the greater the demand for their expertise. In this sense, 7 out of 8 ROs noted that MINADER had solicited their expertise at least once.

All relay organisations in this study got part of their financial resources from ICRAF support, revenues from the nursery and through service provision (e.g. training). Contributions from members constituted a source of income for one third of the ROs, while the sales of livestock and agricultural products were used to finance day-to-day operations of one RO each. This suggests a genuine effort from ROs to become financially autonomous.

In terms of qualified staff, we noticed big differences between the ROs (Table 3). Logically, category I and II (favourable internal factors) disposed of the most experienced staff, while category III and IV were less well endowed with qualified staff. However, the person in charge of agroforestry within the ROs had in three-quarters of the cases appropriate qualifications, such as agroforestry technician or agricultural engineer. Unfortunately, only 2 staff members had received specific training in gender issues. Likewise, category I and II were better equipped with office furniture and transport facilities than category III and IV (Table 4). GICAL and SAGED (category IV) did not dispose of any means of transportation of their own, which seriously constrains the diffusion of innovations, especially because road infrastructure in their zone of intervention is not good.

Category	RO	Total number of staff	Number trained in farmer organisation	Highest qualification of agroforestry staff	Staff trained in gender issues
Cat I	APADER	7	4	MSc agribusiness	No
	RIBA	3	3	Agric technician	No
Cat II	ADEAC	6	6	Agric technician	No
	FONJAK	8	6	Agric engineer	Yes
Cat III	FOEPSUD	5	5	Agric technician	No
	PIPAD	18	2	Agric technician	No
Cat IV	GICAL	1	1	Secondary School	No
	SAGED	6	3	Secondary School	Yes

Table 3. Human resources of ROs

Category	RO	offices	library	meeting room	computer	printer	internet key	motorbike	vehicle
Cat I	APADER	2	1	1	4	2	2	2	0
	RIBA	14	1	1	2	1	1	1	1
Cat II	ADEAC	5	0	1	2	1	1	1	0
	FONJAK	6	0	1	6	1	0	1	3
Cat III	FOEPSUD	1	0	0	0	0	0	0	0
	PIPAD	9	1	2	3	1	1	1	3
Cat IV	GICAL	0	0	0	0	0	0	0	0
	SAGED	1	0	1	1	1	0	0	0

Table 4. Material resources of ROs

4.2 Role of ROs in development and dissemination of agroforestry innovations

Interactions between ROs and ICRAF formally took place during planning and evaluation meetings twice a year. In addition, ICRAF staff carried out regular field visits to assess progress of activities, hand out nursery material and provide technical assistance whenever required. Another means of communication between ROs and ICRAF were the technical reports. In general, 75 % of staff of ROs seemed to be satisfied or very satisfied with the interactions they had with ICRAF. Even though all ROs recognised that their feedback on the agroforestry technologies disseminated was valued by ICRAF and taken into account in the further development of the innovations, only 25 % identified their active involvement in participatory research as a distinctive role, in addition to dissemination of innovations. Participation of the ROs in the development of the innovations seemed to be facilitated by the presence of rural resource centres, where focus is put on interactive learning and farmer experimentation. Ways to enhance the contribution of ROs in technology development suggested by ROs were increasing the number of formal meetings (75 %), providing a framework for technology evaluation (25 %), and organising workshops where specific technologies are reviewed (13 %).

Three main categories of agroforestry innovations have been recorded at the level of ICRAF staff, relay organisations and farmers: (i) tree propagation and integration in farmers' fields, (ii) soil fertility improvement with trees and (iii) marketing strategies for agroforestry tree products. The rate of diffusion and adoption of these innovations have been evaluated by dividing these categories into 14 sub-themes or knowledge domains, as will be demonstrated in the next session on performance of ROs.

All 8 ROs studied used a combination of approaches to disseminate agroforestry, namely theoretical and practical training of farmers, open-door events to sensitise and demonstrate new technologies to a wide public and establishment of demonstration plots showing the benefits of agroforestry innovations. In addition, two of the ROs (APADER and RIBA, belonging to category I) operated a Rural Resource Centre, which is equipped with a nursery, experimental and demonstration plots, a training hall and accommodation amenities. Rural Resource Centres are assumed to facilitate the diffusion of technologies to farmers because they encourage continuous interaction between farmers, relay organisations and research, making the technologies more relevant and acceptable; and increase farmers' access to information, skills and planting material.

4.3 Performance of relay organisations

Performance of relay organisations was assessed in terms of number of groups supported and farmers trained, technical knowledge on and mastery of agroforestry techniques by farmers trained, diffusion and adoption rates of innovations disseminated, and farmers' satisfaction.

Number of groups supported and farmers reached

Figure 3 shows the number of farmer groups and group members who received technical assistance from the relay organisations studied. We noticed that ROs of category I provided assistance to the highest number of groups, though ROs of category II and III reached more farmers overall. This can be explained by the bigger size of farmer groups supported by the latter. In terms of gender, all ROs taken together, 46 % of the farmers reached were women. This proportion is high, relative to many development interventions, and is a combined result of deliberate efforts to bring women to training sessions and the targeting of women's groups for particular agroforestry technologies, such as soil fertility improvement and commercialisation of agroforestry tree products that traditionally belong to the women's domain (e.g. *Irvingia gabonensis* and *Ricinodendron heudelotii* nuts for spices and *Gnetum africanum* leaves for consumption as a vegetable). The proportion of female farmers trained was particularly high for RIBA (67 %), which mainly disseminates soil fertility improving techniques, and ADEAC (67 %) which is predominantly promoting post-harvest and group marketing of *Ricinodendron heudelotii* nuts. On the contrary, the proportion of women in groups supported by GICAL was the lowest (18 %) which can be explained by the strong focus on vegetative propagation. Overall, 36 % of the farmers trained by the ROs studied were younger than 35 years old. There was no clear relationship between the number of youths reached and the category to which a RO belongs. FONJAK however was standing out with 61 % of its farmers being less than 35 years old, followed by RIBA (46 %).

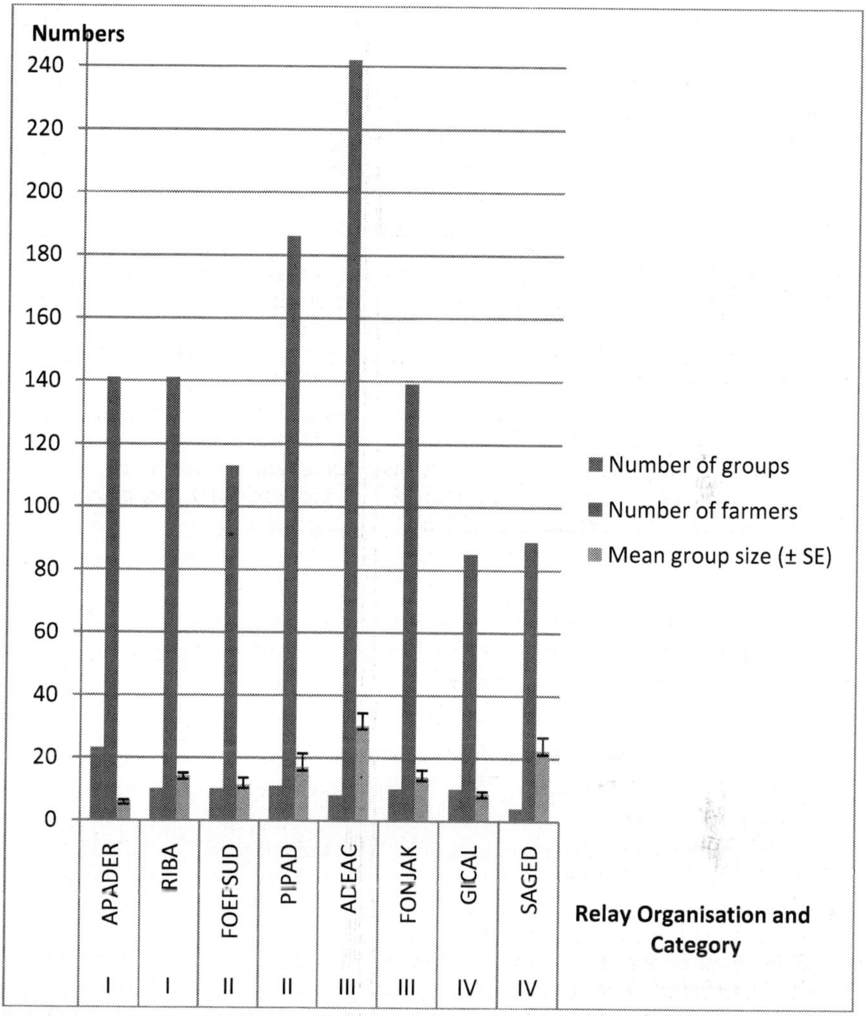

Fig. 3. Number of groups and farmers supported by ROs and mean group size

Knowledge and mastery of agroforestry techniques

Farmers' knowledge on agroforestry technologies was assessed by asking group members whether they had no knowledge, basic knowledge, good mastery or whether they could actually teach other farmers on the different topics taught by ROs. The farmers interviewed could have participated in training sessions or have learned the techniques through their group leaders. In total, 14 knowledge domains were identified in the field (Fig 4). However, the maximum number of topics taught by any one RO was 11 and the minimum 7. Overall, 44 % of the respondents had basic knowledge on all technologies, 14 % said to have mastery of the technology and 6 % could also teach other farmers on the topic, irrespective of knowledge domain or relay organisation considered. Knowledge domains that were best acquired by farmers included rooting of cuttings and tree spacing, while topics less mastered were post-harvest technologies, group sales and conflict management, all related to developing marketing strategies for agroforestry products. This is related to the fact that ROs had been introduced to tree propagation earlier than to marketing-related aspects and were therefore able to gain more expertise on tree propagation issues. Looking at differences per category of ROs, we noticed that the proportion of farmers who had no knowledge on agroforestry innovations was much higher for ROs from category IV (49 %) than from category I (21 %), while the opposite was true for farmers who could teach others (Fig 4).

Diffusion and adoption of innovations

In terms of adoption, farmers interviewed mainly applied the following agroforestry techniques: marcotting, rooting of cuttings, grafting, soil fertility management and use of njansang cracking machine (post-harvest technique). Average rates of adoption varied from 52 % for farmers trained by ROs of category III to 61 % for those backstopped by ROs from category I. However, adoption was very variable according to the techniques, as is demonstrated in figure 5. Nevertheless, highest rate of adoption was recorded for the marcotting technique and the lowest for soil fertility improvement. This can be explained by the fact that marcotting is a dividable technique (can be done on a single tree), applicable to many different species independently of ecological zones and does not need much equipment. On the other hand, soil fertility management is a technology that requires land tenure security and a higher upfront investment in planting a large number of trees or shrubs, and therefore is more difficult to adopt. It was interesting to note that, of the respondents who stopped collaboration and left the farmer groups, 65% continued to practice marcotting, 43% continued rooting of cuttings and 43% continued grafting. On the other hand, only 14 % were still using trees and shrubs for soil fertility management after they left the farmer groups. Reasons for leaving the group were both personal (illness, absence, etc.) as well as related to the way in which the group was managed (problems with use of nursery material and sharing of benefits). Nobody actually mentioned that they left the group because the agroforestry practices offered by the ROs were not useful.

Farmers' perception of performance

Finally, farmers' overall level of satisfaction of ROs was assessed by asking respondents whether they were very satisfied, satisfied, a bit satisfied or not satisfied at all with the way their ROs interacted with them. All ROs taken together, respectively 11 % of the farmers interviewed were very satisfied and 67% satisfied with the performance of the ROs. In fact, 78 % of the respondents mentioned good technical support as one of the strong points of the work by ROs, followed by regular follow-up of group activities (reported by 39 %) and contact with a range of other partners through the ROs (26 %). Most respondents also felt that the language used by ROs was adapted to the target population. Moreover, staff of ROs were said to be patient and tolerant, and the techniques disseminated were relevant to farmers' needs. Only 10 % expressed that they were not satisfied at all with the performance of the ROs. The major points of dissatisfaction among respondents who were not satisfied were failure to find buyers for their products (86 %), delays in implementation of activities (70 %), absence of financial assistance (69 %) and non-respect of appointments (56 %).

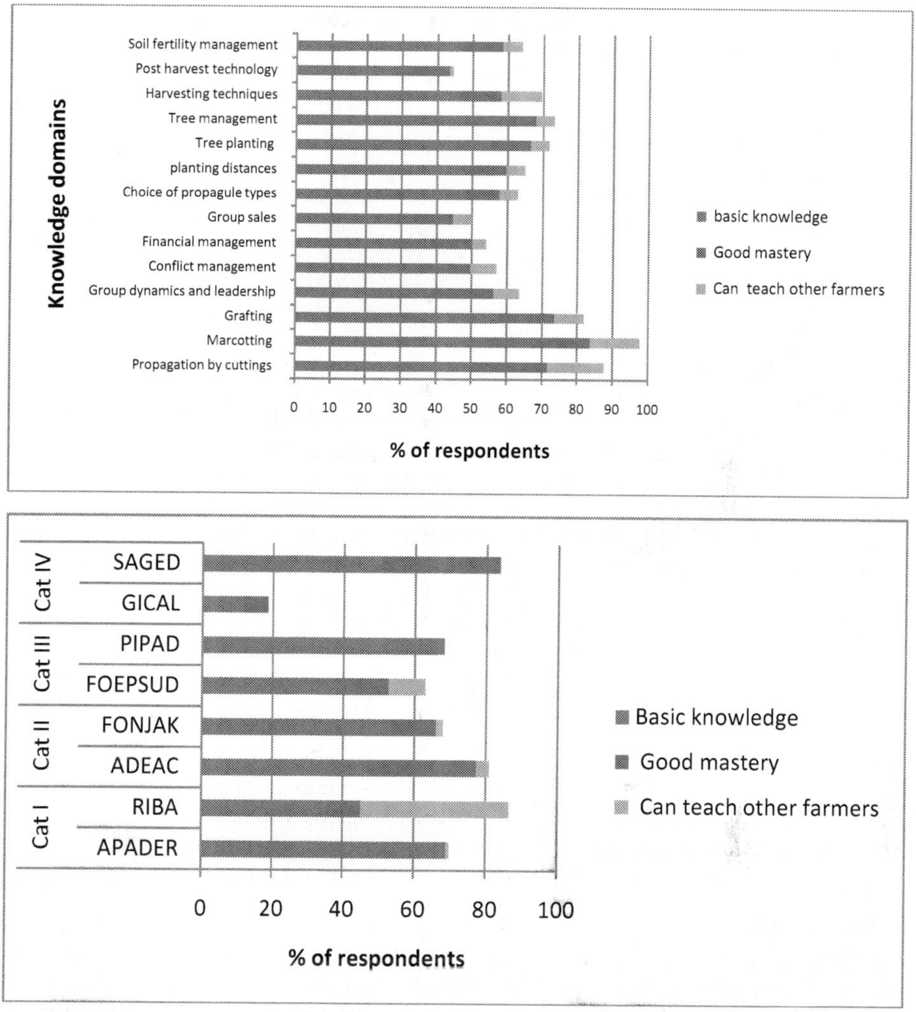

Fig. 4. Knowledge and mastery of agroforestry techniques, by technique (a) and by relay organisation (b)

4.4 Analysis of effect of internal and external factors on performance of relay organisations

As demonstrated above, the relay organisations studied were successfully diffusing agroforestry innovations to farmer groups overall. Nevertheless, differences have been observed between categories of relay organisations for a number of performance indicators, as shown in table 5. Though differences were not statistically significant, results suggest that relay organisations which operate under favourable internal and external factors (Cat I) perform best for most of the performance indicators. Also, the study puts forward that external factors such as existing opportunities for agroforestry, strong farmer associations and good road and communication networks (Cat III), might affect the effectiveness of relay organisations more than their internal capacity, reflected by their human, material and financial resources (Cat II). However, this needs further investigation.

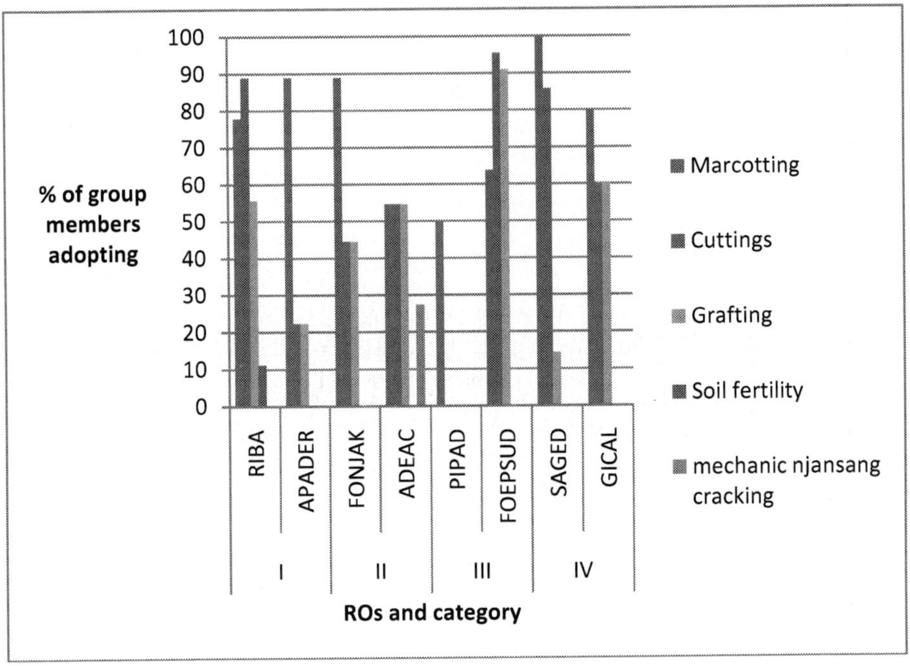

Fig. 5. Adoption rate of agroforestry innovations per RO and category

Since analyses above did not find any significant differences between the performances of different categories of relay organisations, a Multiple Component Analysis was done. Figure 6 shows the distribution of the 8 relay organisations studied, following performance indicators. From this, three groups can be distinguished. First, APADER stands on its own in terms of highest average nursery production and most groups supported. This can be explained by appropriate qualification and experience of its staff and the presence of a resource centre. Second, GICAL, also standing on its own, obtained a high proportion of satisfied farmers and the highest adoption rate but for a limited number of techniques. On the other hand, GICAL also had the highest percentage of farmers with no knowledge at all on several domains, which can be justified by the fact that GICAL only has 1 resource person to do extension. At last, there seems to exist a strong correlation between the following relay organisations: PIPAD, FONJAK, FOEPSUD, ADEAC, RIBA and SAGED, meaning that results obtained by these organisations, in terms of diffusion rate, number of farmers trained, % of farmers with basic knowledge, mastery and who can teach others, varied little.

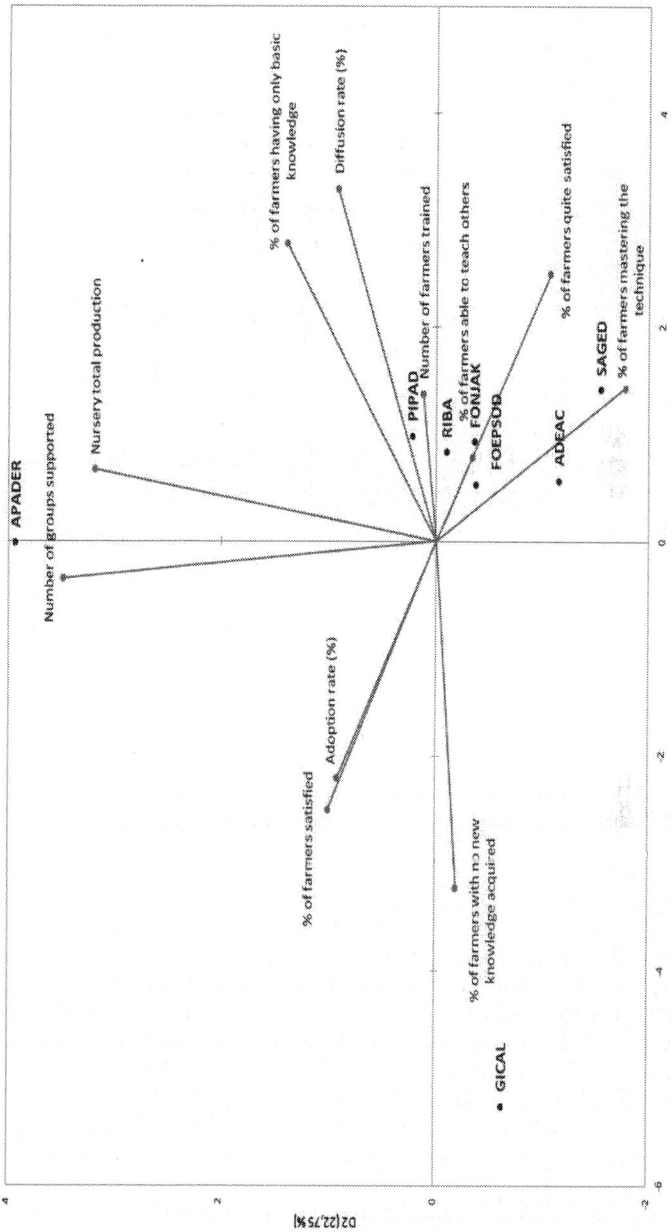

Fig. 6. Categorisation of relay organisations according to performance indicators

Indicators	Cat I	Cat II	Cat III	Cat IV	Std Error	Sign.
1. Number of groups supported	17.00	10.50	9.00	7.00	3.40	**0.319**
2. Number of farmers trained	141.00	149.50	190.50	87.00	31.58	**0.284**
3. Diffusion rate	91.00	83.50	81.00	66.00	11.64	**0.551**
4. % of farmers without knowledge on techniques	21.00	36.00	32.50	49.00	18.77	**0.775**
5. % of farmers having basic knowledge	51.00	45.50	50.00	34.50	15.63	**0.869**
6. % of farmers mastering techniques	6.50	17.00	9.00	16.00	7.00	**0.676**
7. % of farmers able to teach other farmers	21.50	1.50	8.50	0.00	10.50	**0.525**
8. Adoption rate	61.00	53.00	54.50	56.00	7.52	**0.883**
9. % of farmers very satisfied	16.50	41.00	45.50	14.50	10.15	**0.195**
10. % of farmers satisfied	61.00	52.00	53.50	85.50	16.65	0.528

Table 5. Comparison between categories using performance indicators

5. Conclusion

In the light of renewed interest in agricultural extension worldwide, this paper reviewed some of the major challenges and institutional innovations that were introduced to overcome these problems. One of such innovations, under testing for the last 5 years in Cameroon, is involving community-based organisations, called relay organisations, in the dissemination of agroforestry innovations. Their performances in terms of reaching farmers, increasing farmers' knowledge on agroforestry and enhancing adoption of agroforestry innovations were evaluated and factors that affect performances were investigated.

Results show that, overall, the relay organisations studied were successfully diffusing agroforestry innovations to farmer groups. On the other hand, differences in performances of relay organisations could not easily be explained by either external or internal factors. Nevertheless, the fact that relay organisations that operate in areas with relatively good road and communication networks and opportunities for agroforestry, and also have adequate internal human, material and financial capacity seemingly performed better, provides us with some indications of support that might be required to further strengthen these relay organisations and increase their extension capacity. The findings nevertheless call for in-depth studies involving more relay organisations to increase our understanding of what factors affect performance of organisations in disseminating agricultural innovations.

Definitely, the involvement of grassroots organisations in the extension of agroforestry has increased the relevance of the techniques and the quality of services rendered to the beneficiaries, as can be seen from the relatively high level of satisfied farmers. Already, farmer-led experimentation and adaptation is common in the rural resource centres and farmers are encouraged to provide feedback about the new techniques to research via the relay organisations. The approach has also succeeded in reaching a relatively high number of women and youths, often overlooked in 'traditional' extension systems. One challenge though in this approach remains the technical expertise of RO staff. For example, our study has shown that organisations with few people doing all the work are limited in the range of innovations they can deliver to farmer groups. Another aspect related to this is the quality of the messages delivered. This calls for continuous training, coaching and upgrading of extension staff.

One of the criticisms of more 'top-down' and bureaucratic extension systems is the insufficient links with other stakeholders, such as research, input supply, credit and marketing actors. In the case of the rural resource centres, creating linkages and networking should become easier; though so far concrete linkages have been established with research and in some cases with traders. It is expected, however, that more opportunities for linking with other stakeholders will develop with time.

Last but not least, one of the generic problems of agricultural extension, namely the difficulty of cost recovery, has not been addressed in the current study. It is expected that community-based extension would be more cost efficient compared to other approaches. However, our current understanding of the sustainability and financial viability of the approach is not sufficient to draw any conclusions and more research is required in this domain.

6. Acknowledgement

The authors are grateful to the sponsors of the tree domestication programme in Cameroon: the International Fund for Agricultural Development (IFAD), the Belgian Development Cooperation (DGDC) and the US Department of Agriculture. We sincerely thank Prof Tchouamo Isaac for his contributions to theoretical background and survey design and Lazare Kouodiekong for help with data analysis. We also want to acknowledge the assistance of James Roshetko, Evelyn Kiptot and Ben Lukuyu for reviews on earlier drafts of this paper. We pay tribute to the staff of the relay organisations for their relentless efforts to bring tree domestication to scale and their availability to collaborate in this study. Finally, we thank all the farmers who patiently participated in the interviews.

7. References

Anderson, JR. 2007. Agricultural advisory services. Background paper for the World Development Report 2008. World Bank, Washington DC.

Asaah EK, Tchoundjeu Z, Leakey RRB, Takoutsing B, Njong J & Edang I. 2011. Trees, Agroforestry and Multifunctional Agriculture in Cameroon. *International Journal of Agricultural Sustainability* 9 (1): 110-119.

Axinn G. 1988. Guide on Alternative Extension Approaches. FAO, Rome.

Birner R, Davis K, Pender J, Nkonya E, Anandajayasekeram P, Ekboir J, Mbabu A, Spielman D, Horna D, Benin S & Cohen M. 2006. From "Best Practice" to "Best Fit". A Framework for Analyzing Pluralistic Agricultural Advisory Services Worldwide. *International Service for National Agricultural Research Discussion Paper* No. 5. IFPRI, Washington DC, USA.

CBW partners in South Africa, Lesotho, Uganda and Kenya. 2007. Community-based Worker Systems - a possible solution to more services, reaching many communities, and within budget. *ODI Natural Resources Perspectives* nr 110.Overseas Development Institute, London, UK.

Centre de Recherches pour le Développement International [CRDI]. 2004. La performance organisationnelle. Available from : www.slidefinder.net/%C3%89/%C3%89valuer-performance organisationnelle-Niveau-CRDI /accessed on 11-05-2010.

Davis K, Nkonya E, Kato E, Mekonnen DA, Odendo M, Miiro R & Nkuba J. 2010. Impact of Farmer Field Schools on Agricultural Productivity and Poverty in East Africa. *IFPRI Discussion Paper* No. 00992. IFPRI, Washington DC, USA. 43p.

Etzioni A. 1964. *Modern Organizations*, Prentice Hall, Englewood Cliff, CA. 223 p

FAO. 2011. FAO Investment Centre. Increased agricultural investment is critical to fighting hunger. (22/09/11) Available from: www.fao.org/investment/whyinvestinagricultureandru/en/

Farrington J. 1997. The role of Non-Governmental Organisations in extension. In: FAO. 1997. *Improving Agricultural Extension: A Reference Manual*. FAO, Rome.

Feder G, Anderson JR, Birner R & Deininger K. 2010. Promises and Realities of Community-Based Agricultural Extension. IFPRI Discussion Paper No. 00959. IFPRI, Washington DC, USA.23p.

Feder G, Willett A & Zijp W. 1999. Agricultural Extension: Generic Challenges and Ingredients for Solutions. Policy Research Working Paper 2129.The World Bank, Washington DC, USA. 32p.

Franzel S, Coe R, Cooper P, Place F & Scherr SJ. 2001. Assessing the adoption potential of agroforestry practices in sub-Saharan Africa. *Agricultural Systems* 69 (1-2) 37-62.

Gakiru M, Winters K & Stepman F. 2009. Inventory of Innovative Farmer Advisory Services using ICTs. The Forum for Agricultural Research in Africa, Accra, Ghana.

Heffron H. 1989. *Organization theory and public organization: The political connection*. Prentice-hall, USA.

Kemajou E. 2008.Impact de la domestication participative des arbres locaux sur les conditions de vie des populations locales : cas de la province du Centre, Cameroun. Mémoire de fin d'étude. Faculté d'Agronomie et des Sciences Agricoles, université de Dschang, Cameroun, 87P.

Moudingo E. 2007. La situation des forêts au Cameroun. Wildlife Conservation Society. Douala, Cameroun. 24P. (21-05-2010) Available from www.wrm.org.uy/countries/Africaspeaks/Cameroun_Situation_Forets.pdf

Njessa B. 2007. Impact du projet pipeline sur les populations riveraines du Centre Cameroun. Mémoire de fin d'étude, Université de Dschang, Faculté d'Agronomie et des Sciences Agricoles. 58P

Simons AJ & Leakey RRB. 2004. *Tree domestication in tropical agroforestry*. In: Nair PKR, Rao MR & Buck LE. New Vistas in Agroforestry: A Compendium for the 1st World Congress of Agroforestry. Kluwer Academic Publishers, Boston. Pp. 167-182.

Tchoundjeu Z, Asaah EK, Anegbeh P, Degrande A, Mbile P, Facheux C, Tsobeng A, Atangana AR, Ngo Mpeck ML & Simons AJ. 2006. Putting participatory domestication into practice in West and Central Africa. *Forests, Trees and Livelihoods*, Vol 16: 53–69

Zijp W. 1997. Extension: Empowerment through Communication. Paper presented at the symposium "Rural Knowledge Systems for the 21st Century: the Future of Rural Extension in Western, Central and Eastern Europe". Reading, Cambridge and Edinburgh, UK.